World War II
A Concise History
Second Edition

Donald D. Leopard
State University College at Buffalo

D1471019

**WAVELAND
PRESS, INC.**

Prospect Heights, Illinois

For information about this book, write or call:

Waveland Press, Inc.
P.O. Box 400
Prospect Heights, Illinois 60070
(708) 634-0081

Map Credits

Acknowledgment is due to Martin Gilbert and George Weidenfeld & Nicolson Ltd. for permission to reproduce the maps on pages 13, 26, 32, 35, 42, 48, 53, 67, 81, 85, 134, 147, 160, and 175 from the *Recent History Atlas,* © 1966 by Martin Gilbert, cartography by John Flower.

The maps on pages 63, 71, 88, 98, 100, 105, 112, and 115 are used with permission of Cassell PLC, from *Second World War* by Basil Liddell Hart, © 1970 by Cassell & Co. Ltd., cartography by Richard Natkiel.

Copyright © 1992, 1982 by Waveland Press, Inc.

ISBN 0-88133-506-1

All rights reserved. No part of this book may be reproduced, stored in a retrieval system, or transmitted in any form or by any means without permission in writing from the publisher.

Printed in the United States of America

7 6 5 4 3 2 1

Contents

Contents

Maps

Acknowledgment

To all those students who have sat through my classes on World War II over the last two decades I owe a great debt of thanks. The enthusiasm they manifested encouraged me to write this text, and their continued interest led me to revise it to the point of this second edition. Secondly, Barbara Leopard and Ralph Raico aided me in many ways in completing this project. The improvements in this edition should be credited to the publisher and the editorial staff of Waveland Press. In particular, I wish to thank Laurie Prossnitz who edited this edition. Any errors of omission or commission belong to me.

Donald D. Leopard

1

The Diplomatic Background

The Nazi invasion of Poland, September 1, 1939, marked the beginning of a European conflict which eventually spread to involve most of the world and its people. This European *cum* world conflict is known in the history books as World War II. Unlike World War I (1914-1918), World War II has evoked little controversy as to who started it and why. The culprit, as everyone knows, was the leader of Germany, Adolph Hitler. Yet, it can be argued that Hitler had no wish to embark upon a plan of world conquest or intent to start a world war. Judging from his writings and subsequent actions as dictator of Germany, Hitler's basic objective was to reorder the European state system. Such a reordering was designed to place Germany in the dominant position in Europe and, given Europe's hegemony in world affairs, a commanding position on the international scene.

As the principal loser in World War I, Germany was stripped of her colonies, judged guilty of having started the war, and forced to pay reparations for war damage. The Treaty of Versailles which had determined Germany's losses and guilt was seen as a dictated peace by German nationalists. They argued that the treaty had been imposed by the Allies and not negotiated as a proper treaty should be. For many Germans, the 1919 treaty was both a humiliation and a burden. Hitler and his Nazi Party gained national attention through their

1

vehement attacks on the Versailles settlement and their equally bitter attacks on the Weimar Republic. The Republic, the government responsible for accepting the treaty, was typified by the Nazis as a government of traitors. In 1933, Hitler was made Chancellor of Germany. From the time he assumed the Chancellorship of Germany until 1939, Hitler labored successfully to remove all disabilities and restrictions placed upon the German state by the terms of the Versailles Treaty of 1919.

Revisionism

On the international scene, Hitler's policies of *revisionism*, that is, elimination of treaty restrictions, brought a varied response from Germany's former enemies. The French were particularly alarmed by Hitler's diplomatic initiative. France felt threatened when, in 1933, Germany withdrew from the League of Nations. In 1935, Hitler claimed a diplomatic victory when Saarland voters elected to rejoin Germany. The plebiscite had been provided for in the 1919 treaty, but the Nazi propaganda machine hailed it as another of Hitler's diplomatic coups.

In 1936 Hitler took a large gamble and sent German troops into the demilitarized zone of the Rhineland. This action was not welcomed by his General Staff, but the gamble was taken and the French, though shocked by this violation of the Versailles Treaty and the Locarno Agreement of 1925, accepted this remilitarization of the Rhineland. In fact, the French government heeded the advice of its military leadership which advised, perhaps wrongly, that a massive military response would be necessary to remove German troops from the Rhineland and that such a response was beyond the means of the French army at that time.

France's former ally, Great Britain, was less disquieted by Hitler's revisionism. Many of England's politically prominent leaders, Former Prime Minister David Lloyd George for one, saw the Treaty of Versailles as unfair to Germany and favored a degree of change in the treaty. Therefore, the division of opinion between the two former allies proved to be an asset to Hitler's plans of revisionism.

In domestic affairs Hitler was even more audacious. When Hitler came to power in 1933 he called for and received an enabling act from the compliant *Reichstag* (parliament). This gave him the power to take actions without seeking approval of that elected body. As *Fuehrer* (leader), he moved quickly to crush any opposition to his policies. Labor unions, churches, and other institutions which had enjoyed independence from state control were placed under state direction. The 1933 Concordant with the Vatican effectively disarmed those German Catholic prelates who had spoken out against Hitler and the Nazi Party. The Protestant Churches, particularly the Lutheran Church, had a tradition of compliance to the directives of the state. Therefore, the only remaining opposition from religious leaders would be individual and local—and such opposition could easily be dealt with. Labor unions were consolidated and placed under state control.

On June 30, 1934, units of Hitler's elite guard, the *Shutzstaffle* (SS), launched a Blood Purge, also referred to as "the Night of the Long Knives," against "enemies of the Fuehrer" both within and outside the Nazi Party. Principal among these "enemies" were the leaders of the *Sturmabteilung* (SA). This organization had been of great importance in the early, violent days of the Nazi Party, and, in combination with the SS, had a membership of nearly 400,000, far larger than the German *Reichswehr* (army). Among those murdered in the purge was the SA leader, Ernst Roehm. Roehm had long advocated that Germany should have a "national army" with goals and leadership conforming to those of the Nazi Party. This concept, which Hitler consistently had played down, boded ill for the tradition-minded German officer class. The murder of Roehm was to give a clear signal to the military leadership that Hitler had no intention of making revolutionary changes within the German military establishment. After the elimination of Roehm, German officers gave their personal oath of allegiance to Adolph Hilter. In oath and interest the German military was now tied to Adolph Hitler.

When Germany's President, Paul von Hindenburg, died in August 1934, the voice of the last German of national stature not linked or indebted to Hitler was stilled. Hitler was to combine the two offices of Chancellor and President. His dictatorship was now complete.

In March 1935, Hitler ordered the creation of a German Air Force, the *Lufftwaffe*, and called for universal military conscription to bring the total of German forces to 300,000. He tried to assuage the fears of the French by attempting to negotiate a size limitation on rearmament, but, when the French failed to respond, Hitler proceeded to rearm with impunity.

In the economic sector, Hitler and his advisers began to build a corporate state system. State direction rather than state ownership was the goal, and it was attained with relative ease. Soon the economic as well as the social and political aspects of German life were under state direction. Economic controls, deficit financing, and complex barter-trade agreements with a variety of European and Latin American states brought an economic upturn. Production and trade rose, and unemployment dropped dramatically. Though some wealthy Germans complained that import restrictions diminished the comforts of everyday life, most German citizens could but applaud the economic miracles which Hitler and the Nazi Party had accomplished.

It is difficult for today's reader to believe that anyone could have seen any good in the Nazi regime or any virtue in its leader. But historical hindsight should not blind one to the fact that nazism, for all its limitations on thought and freedoms, was looked upon by most Germans as preferable to the bleakness of the Depression under the Weimar government. Though the rest of Europe and the world (with the possible exception of Scandinavia) was in the grips of the Depression, in fascist Europe there was the illusion, at least, of economic recovery. In Germany workers were employed, and young people were seemingly assured a better future. Reports from foreign travelers contrasted the bustle and purpose of Germany to the despair and apathy found in other parts of depressed Europe.

Repression

Beneath the facade of modernity and progress, however, there existed a growing apparatus of repression. Concentration camps burgeoned and so-called "enemies of the state" were constantly being ferreted out by the ubiquitous *Gestapo* (secret police). Though the designation "enemy of the state" was a vague term used to cover a multitude of crimes, real or imagined, Hitler's Germany placed bolshevism, liberalism, and Judaism in the top-most category. The fear of bolshevism, represented by Soviet communism, was cleverly exploited by Nazi propaganda. In a distortion of logic the Jew was identified with both the evil nemesis of communism and democratic liberalism, the latter being the curse which had brought Germany to near ruin during the Weimar years. Whatever the empty theme used, be it exploitative capital-ism, liberalism, or bolshevism, the Jew—cultural parasite in Nazi rhetoric— was designated as either the originator of that "ism" or its most unprincipled, consummate practitioner. Therefore, of the many "enemies" within Hitler's Germany, the Jew was public enemy number one. Beginning in 1933, disabilities were heaped upon this segment of the German population, laws of exclusion were enacted, and slowly, inexorably, the Jews were disenfranchised and transformed into "nonpersons" in Hitler's Germany.

Propaganda, cleverly and constantly presented, can be interpreted in many ways by diverse peoples. Hitler's stress upon sacrifice for the nation, the call for a "New Order," appealed to young, idealistic Germans and stood in seeming contrast to the sleazy, pornographic attacks on ethnic groups. But Hitler's propaganda mill used both idealism and absurdity in a bewildering, effective mixture. If one thumbed through the yellowing pages of the old Nazi newspapers, shock would be the undoubted response to the banality, even grossness, of the constant themes slandering various ethnic and religious minorities. One could legitimately ask, "Was there no one in Germany who saw through the propaganda and recognized the absurdity of the attacks, the ridiculousness of pseudo-scientific racialism?" The answer to such a question is two-fold. Many did, but they were unable or unwilling to speak out. For others, the rhetoric concerning purity of the blood and the condemnation of the Jew were but rabble-rousing designed to stir the inert masses and insure their participation in building a new and better European order.

Racialism, the classification of human races on a sliding scale from highest to lowest, was not merely a ploy to attract the attention of the masses or to create a scapegoat on which the difficulties of the nation could be blamed. Rather, racialism was a basic belief and a major theme of Hitler's writings and speeches. Though it is said one should judge a person more by actions than words, in Adolph Hitler word and deed were closely allied. Long before the development of extermination camps in Poland and elsewhere, within Germany proper so-called undesirables and misfits were being "liquidated" or neutralized via sterilization.

It has become fashionable now to dispute Hitler's personal commitment to racialism. Emphasis has been given to instances where Hitler, and some of his closest advisers, interceded to protect talented people. Such acts by Hitler and Nazi officials do not obscure the fact that racial theories were taken seriously in Germany, and purity of the blood was a deadly earnest doctrine in Nazi ideology. The 1935 Nuremberg Laws defined who was a Jew (anyone of one-quarter Jewish extraction), and took away their citizenship rights. In 1938, using the pretext of the assassination of a German official in Paris by a young Jewish male, the Nazis destroyed synagogues and seized Jewish property.

By these actions authorities made it abundantly clear that the goal of state policy was to drive the Jews from Germany. At the same time, however, the government made it difficult for those who wished to leave to depart with at least sufficient property to assure a new life elsewhere. Moreover, in a world suffering economic depression there were few open arms to receive the penniless refugees, and governments of the West were not quick to revise their immigration restrictions for those fleeing persecution.

From 1933 onward the coercive apparatus of the Nazi state operated to purge Germany of those seen by the Nazis as racial inferiors. When war broke out in 1939, immigration for those who wished to leave Germany was blocked as more and more countries fell to the victorious Germans. It was this factor which prompted the decision which led to the establishment of extermination camps. The philosophy of the Nazi leadership was, simply put, if they cannot be forced out, kill them, kill them all.

Reactions

Just as it was possible for many Germans to believe in the fundamental "good" of the New Order and ignore the malevolency manifested against the non-Aryan, it was equally possible for those on the European political scene to misinterpret the scope of Hitler's political aspirations. Political leaders of the day tended to see Hitler as a typical German nationalist politico. What Hitler apparently desired was revisionism, and such had been the theme of German politicians since the Treaty of Versailles was signed in 1919.

One such national aspiration was *Anschluss*, or the unification of Germany and Austria. Such a union was blocked by treaty restrictions, but, in 1934,

Nazi plotters in Austria attempted to carry out the union by assassination and a coup d'etat. Italy blocked this attempt, and, for a time, Mussolini's Italy was linked with France and Great Britain in a front (Stresa Front) to block German expansionism. This front broke down when Great Britain signed a naval agreement with Germany, and disappeared entirely when Italy attacked Ethiopia. Italian aggression was publicly denounced in the League of Nations, but Germany stayed aloof from the public cry against Mussolini. By 1936, Germany and Italy were tied together in an agreement—The Rome-Berlin Axis, also known as The Pact of Steel—and were cooperating by giving aid to Franco's forces in Spain.

Now that Mussolini and Hitler were in agreement, Hitler had little to fear from France and Great Britain. In March 1938, Anschluss was accomplished without either Britain or France moving to block unification. After Anschluss, Hitler concentrated on securing the Sudetenland. This territory, peopled primarily by Germans, was part of Czechoslovakia. For years the Germans had argued that Czechoslovakia discriminated against its German-speaking citizens. Hitler was to advance the argument that both the people and land rightly belonged to Germany.

Hitler's demands for the Sudetenland prompted a flurry of diplomatic activity culminating in a full-scale international conference convened in September 1938, in Munich, Germany. Neville Chamberlain of Great Britain, Edouard Daladier of France, Benito Mussolini of Italy, and, of course, Adolph Hitler were the principals in the "negotiations" which followed—though negotiations is hardly the term to use in describing the Munich Conference. Hitler demanded the Sudetenland, Chamberlain and Daladier agreed, and the Czechs were forced to give up their territory. Chamberlain gained some peace of mind by securing Hitler's agreement to guarantee the integrity of the remaining territory of Czechoslovakia. Hitler had no intention of keeping that pledge, but it was a sop to Chamberlain who seemed convinced that his statecraft had kept the peace.

Almost before the ink was dry critics condemned the Munich Agreement. It was denounced as an act of appeasement and is often so described in assorted history texts. What is ignored by critics of the agreement is that neither Chamberlain nor Daladier wished confrontation with Hitler. Their constituents were hardly in favor of risking war over Czechoslovakia, and Chamberlain, for one, seemed convinced that appeasement on the Sudetenland issue meant "peace in our time." Later, when Hitler took over what remained of Czechoslovakia, Chamberlain was outraged. Obviously, the British leader had misjudged Hitler, but in underestimating Hitler's expansionist goals Chamberlain was far from being alone.

The abandonment of Czechoslovakia at Munich has prompted many scholarly studies. The "lesson of Munich" is a phrase often used for those instances when an aggressive foreign policy is demanded. This Munich lesson notes that appeasement surely leads to war. Few who despise appeasement note the unique circumstances which prevailed at Munich in 1938, nor appreciate that the democratic leaders who participated in that conference had no mandate to act in a more aggressive manner.

In early 1939 Hitler abrogated the Munich Agreement by dividing Czechoslovakia, directly annexing part and creating the puppet state of Slovakia from the remainder. This unilateral action brought an abrupt change in British policy. Chamberlain hastened to sign an agreement tying Great Britain into a defense alliance with Poland and France. This action, condemned by many writers as hasty and ill-conceived, seemingly aided Poland, but neither Britain nor France had any meaningful plans to aid Poland effectively if she were attacked by Germany. France was committed to a defensive strategy. With most of her troops locked up in the supposedly impregnable Maginot Line, France was in no position to carry out an attack on German soil and the British, with their much smaller land forces, were tied to the French lead.

The Western Allies realized that their defense agreement with Poland was inadequate, and they attempted to involve the Soviets in their plan for the defense of Poland. The Poles would hardly have welcomed Soviet help, especially if it involved the deployment of Soviet troops within Poland, but the Allies were hopeful that the Soviet Union might stand with them against Germany. The anti-fascist policy of the Soviets had been manifest in Europe for sometime. How effective and sincere this policy had been was subject to interpretation. Yet, in rhetoric and action, aid to the Spanish Republic, for example, the U.S.S.R. stood in opposition to Hitler's expansionism. It was with this in mind that the French and British dispatched a mission to the Soviet Union. This mission had little to offer the Soviets and no real power to negotiate an agreement.

However, as early as February 1939, the Soviets had begun tentative diplomatic communications with the Germans which were to culminate in the Nazi-Soviet Pact of August 1939. The official history of the U.S.S.R. in World War II denounces Stalin for being duped by Hitler. However, this is not a denunciation of the pact itself, but of Stalin's reportedly naive belief in Hitler's continued good will up to June 1941. These histories, published in the 1960s, were anti-Stalinist in their bias, and represented the continuation of the de-Stalinization process begun in the late 1950s. In fact, the Nazi-Soviet pact is an example of the paramountcy of national interest over ideology. Both the Nazis and the Soviets were ideologically at opposites, but both Stalin and Hitler recognized the value such an agreement offered. For Stalin the pact offered, in its secret articles, a free hand to the Soviets in dealing with Estonia, Latvia, and Lithuania and an opportunity to regain part of Poland, which had gained its independence after World War I. These were tangible gains which would strengthen the Soviet state. Likewise, the pact offered the Soviets time to prepare for war. Stalin realized that in entering into an agreement with Hitler's Germany the U.S.S.R. would be safe while Hitler's armies were involved in the West. What critics contend is that Stalin failed to realize that eventually the Soviet Union would be a target for German expansionism. More recent scholarship tends to indicate that Stalin was not beguiled by German protestations of friendship and saw the pact as a way to buy time to prepare the Soviet state for the war that was to come some time in the future.

Germany, too, needed time. Plans were drawn and preparations made for the invasion of Poland. This invasion would bring a declaration of war from Poland's allies in the West. If the Soviets were added to this list of enemies Germany would find herself fighting a two-front war. This Eastern-Western Front warfare had brought disaster to Germany in World War I. Therefore, an agreement with the Soviets was crucial to Hitler's plans for war. Both Hitler and Stalin were to gain from the pact which, for a time, united Soviet communism and German fascism in a cynical marriage of convenience.

By late August 1939, the stage was set for the invasion of Poland. This attack was to unleash a conflict which grew to engulf the world.

Summary

From 1933 to 1939, Hitler transformed Germany into the most dynamic and disruptive state in Europe. Hitler's aggressive foreign policy stripped away the restrictions imposed upon Germany by the Treaty of Versailles (1919). Germany broke all ties with the League of Nations, remilitarized the Rhineland (1936), consummated the long sought union with Austria (1938), and secured the Sudetenland (1938).

In domestic affairs Hitler seemed to have accomplished the impossible by transforming the German state from a depression-ridden nation to one of full-employment, relative prosperity, and serious purpose. This "German miracle" attracted world attention, and Hitler's talk of a "New Order" gained him supporters and admirers outside Germany. Beneath the surface order and promise, the darkness of repression was evident. Concentration camps housed a multitude of criminals whose crime was that of being an "enemy of the state." The secret police were efficient and brutal. German citizens of Jewish origin were systematically humiliated, attacked, and finally, stripped of property and citizenship rights. Few voices were raised against such policies outside Germany and none within.

By 1939 both England and France were aware of the dangers Hitler's expansionist policies posed for European peace. As the threat of war grew, the Western democracies hurried to forge an alliance system to block Germany's expansion. An attempt was made to enlist the Soviets in an alliance, but Stalin realized that, for the short run at least, the U.S.S.R. would be better served by an alliance of convenience. German overtures for a non-aggression pact, and her secret negotiations for division of territories and spheres of influence in Eastern Europe were accepted by Stalin. Since the Nazi-Soviet

Pact protected Germany from any immediate threat from the East, Hitler was free to lead Germany into a war which would, he thought, bring about the reordering of the European state system.

Suggested Reading

Abel, Theodore. *Why Hitler Came to Power*. Cambridge, 1970. This sociological study was the result of a questionnaire sent to Nazi Party members who joined the Party before 1933. It gives a sampling of those who supported Hitler before he attained power.

Bullock, Alan. *Hitler, A Study in Tyranny*. London, 1952. This is something of the old standby of biographies of Hitler.

Churchill, Winston. *The Second World War*. Vol. I., *The Gathering Storm*. London, 1948. An Englishman's view of the diplomacy and politics of Europe before the war written in Churchill's own particular style.

Drucker, Peter F. *The End of Economic Man*. New York, 1939. Although Knolte's, *The Three Faces of Fascism* (New York, 1967), is the most recommended historical analysis of the rise of the Fascist/Nazi phenomenon, Drucker's work is far more intriguing and imaginative.

Shirer, William. *20th Century Journal*. Vol. 2., *The Nightmare Years, 1930-1940*. Boston, 1984. More famous for *The Rise and Fall of the Third Reich* (1960), Shirer recounts his own experiences in Berlin during these crucial years when Europe was in economic depression, but Shirer seemed not to notice. It is an interesting chronicle nonetheless.

Taylor, A. J. P. *The Origins of the Second World War*. New York, 1963. Once controversial, it is now something of a standard survey.

Taylor, Telford, Ed., *Hitler's Secret Book*. New York, 1961. A short book, it is often dull and sometimes chilling, but it is worth browsing through for those who attempt to fathom Hitler's thought processes.

2

The Future of Warfare
1919 to 1939

Hitler's plan to reorder the European state system was to lead Europe into war. In his *Secret Book* Hitler noted that politics and war are but two sides of the same coin: the struggle for national survival. War was but an instrument of national policy, and in 1939 this instrument was put to use.

Hitler's reasoning was hardly the prevailing point of view in Europe. If World War I had demonstrated anything to thinking people, it was that war was not an instrument of national policy but proof of such policy's failure. Many harkened to the words of Carl von Clausewitz, nineteenth century author of the classic study, *On War*, who wrote that modern nationalism had added a new element to warfare. This element was the will of the nation to resist. Wars which invoked the nationalistic spirit and called for the total cooperation of all citizens of the state would be absolute in nature. To win such a war the victor would not only be obliged to destroy the enemy's army in the field but to crush the national will to resist. World War I appeared to have been just such a war. To most thinking people any future European war would follow that self-same path toward even greater destruction. One did not have

11

to be an intellectual or a student of Clausewitz to know that World War I had been a total war. It took no great intellect to know that such a war had brought only destruction for victor and vanquished alike. For the generation which had survived the war and that which came of age afterward, the thought of another war was too horrible to contemplate. To maintain the peace became the preoccupation of national leadership in the democratic states of Europe.

Anglo-French Military Planning

Speculation as to the course of future wars was hardly a popular topic, but military theorists charged with the responsibility of defending the nation in war addressed themselves to this unpopular topic. The results of their planning and theories were conflicting. Military leaders in France and Great Britain were convinced that the successful termination of the 1914-1918 conflict had vindicated their strategy of attrition. World War I had been fought by massed armies which sought to exhaust the enemy through attack, defense, and counterattack. The goal of this strategy was to weaken the enemy to such an extent that a counterattack could "breakthrough" his defenses and end the war. This strategy had proved costly, but, in the end, successful: Germany had signed the Armistice of 1918. Therefore, such planners reasoned, future wars would follow the same pattern with victory awarded to he who husbanded his resources and looked to the defense.

In reality, World War I was, at least after 1914, a conflict where maneuver and movement were hardly possible. The battle lines on the Western Front stretched from the borders of Switzerland to the English Channel. There was no opportunity for flanking operations, though an attempt was made by the Allies to launch an amphibious operation to flank the German line in Belgium. This was a costly failure. Other attempts were tried to break the deadlock of trench warfare. The Germans trained small, skilled groups of infiltrators to move into enemy lines to prepare for the major attack. The use of artillery was studied and adaptations were made in its coordination with an infantry attack. New weapons were introduced. The tank, for example, showed promise, but mechanical difficulties, the inhospitable nature of the battlefield terrain (tanks were often stuck in the cratered, muddy landscape of "no-man's-land"), and the lack of understanding as to how best to use this weapon in an infantry assault rendered it ineffective until late in the war. Air power was used as an assault weapon and attempts were made to employ such power to destroy supply lines and disrupt communications. Again these attempts came late in the war. In the end, attrition seemed to have worked. The German offensive of the summer of 1918 faltered and failed, not because they failed to use innovative battle tactics, but because the German army had neither the forces nor the materials to match that of the Allied Powers.

Many younger officers who reflected on the innovations used in 1917 and

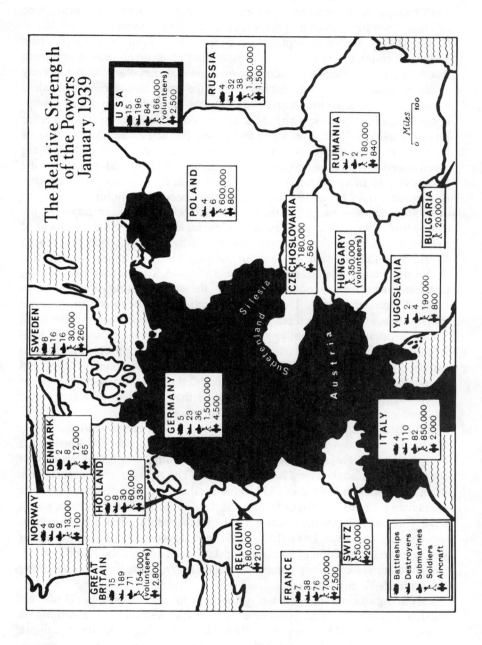

The Relative Strength of the Powers January 1939

1918 brought their interpretations and analysis to the unpopular profession of arms. Two British military writers, Captain Basil Liddell Hart and Major General J.F.C. Fuller, formulated a concept of what future wars might bring which ran counter to the accepted doctrine. Both men advanced the argument that developing technology tended to make massed armies obsolete. A relatively small, professional army of elite troops using the power and mobility of modern technology would decide the course of future wars. Such an attack group, using massed armor to spearhead the attack, could penetrate a static defense line on a narrow front. The speed and power of such an attack on a narrow front would lead to a breach which could be instantly exploited by these mechanized forces to penetrate enemy territory in depth. Mobility was the key to victory in any future war, they argued, and, with mobility, the issue of combat would be settled with maximum speed and minimal loss.

No doctrine was sacred to these writers. The whole organization of the armed forces was called into question. General Fuller particularly bemoaned the impersonalization of the command structure as it had developed during World War I. Both men, students of military history, emphasized the role of the individual commander on the course of battle. They argued that existing command structure was too unresponsive to the shifting course of events which typified a modern battle. Therefore, generals should be closer to the front and free to adapt preordered plans to fit the changing developments on the field.

Both Liddell Hart and Fuller gained some converts to their views in Great Britain. A small tank corp was incorporated into the army. This tank force proved effective in field exercises, but, in general, most ranking officers held to tradition. To conservative military minds, the tank was seen as support for an infantry attack; massed armies, rather than elite, mobile forces, were the true guarantors of victory in any future war.

If the British Imperial General Staff seemed less than receptive to new ideas, the French were downright hostile. Charles de Gaulle, then a colonel in the French army and a partisan of the theories of Fuller and Liddell Hart, put his views into a book, *Vers l'armie de métier* (The Army of the Future). This book, published in France in 1934, advocated the creation of what de Gaulle termed an army of maneuver and attack. De Gaulle's call for an elite, shock troop force of 100,000 men mirrored the thinking of the advocates of mobile, mechanized armies in Great Britain. France, however, had committed her resources to the creation of an elaborate static defense line, the Maginot Line. This fortress system, when completed, stretched from the Swiss border along the German-French frontier.

Part and parcel of this defense system was its impenetrability. However, the line did not cover all possible attack routes. Belgium, once committed to a comparable defense system, delayed in completing its planned network of forts, and in 1936 decided its best line of defense was reliance on neutrality. This meant that France was again vulnerable to an attack through Belgian territory. Supposedly, this gap would be plugged by moving French troops into Belgian territory when and if the nation was attacked. Committed to a policy of defense, French military thinking grew more and more complacent to the point of hostility to any ideas which seemed to cast doubts on their ability to defend the French nation.

Air Power

While much of the debate concerning the possible course of future wars failed to excite great public attention, popularizers and specialists alike gained public attention in the advocacy of a new and deadly type of warfare, air warfare. During World War I, public interest had been aroused by the exploits of a small group of airmen who carried the war into the skies over no-man's-land. Airplanes fascinated the public, and pilots became popular heroes. Aerial combat was, in the public mind at least, a one-on-one encounter, and it was easier for journalists to romanticize aerial exploits than to report the facts of slaughter on the battlefields below.

After the war, interest in the airplane continued to grow. Stunt fliers, called "barn stormers," thrilled audiences at county fairs and air shows. Endurance and speed records became popular fare, and the pilots who accomplished such feats were the heroes of the hour. Behind the headlines and crowd pleasing exploits, serious work was being done to convert this seeming toy into a useful tool of modern civilization. Among the many uses of this new tool was the one which had first brought it into full, public view; its potential as an important weapon of war.

As early as 1921, General Guilliamo Douhet, often credited with originating the concept of strategic bombing, wrote a book in Italy which graphically sketched the role that aircraft would play in future wars. Douhet reasoned that such conflicts would rely heavily on new technology, and the most important technological development of the century was the heavier-than-air craft. Aircraft could bring the war to the enemy, and he envisioned gigantic armadas blackening the sky over enemy cities. These armadas could rain down such destruction from above as to reduce the great cities of the world to rubble. Urban populations would be terrorized by such attacks, and the nation's will to resist would falter and collapse under the wrathful pressure of aerial bombardment. Douhet discounted the role of land armies and surface fleets. Victory in future wars would come in a matter of hours or days and would be accomplished through air power alone. The fact that air armadas were far beyond the technology of the day did not seem to dissuade him, nor did he doubt that aerial bombardment would terrorize and cow urban populations quickly and completely. His futuristic views of air warfare were comprehensive, but his work did not gain full public attention until the 1940s. This late general dissemination of Douhet's work has led to a dispute over his influence on air power advocates outside Italy. Long before Douhet's work came to public attention, Marshal Trenchard and others in Great Britain were becoming known for their outspoken support of the air power thesis.

In World War I the warring powers experimented with the concept of strategic bombing. The first such attempt was the German bombing raids on London using lighter-than-air craft (Zeppelins). Though damage was light and the Zeppelin vulnerable to anti-aircraft and fighter attack, these raids made an impression on those who suffered through the bombings. More resources were allocated to defense of cities and this, by necessity, diverted resources from the battlefront. Later, both sides used aircraft to bomb cities and disrupt lines of communication and supply. Given the limited range and capabilities of the aircraft of that time no great damage was done. However, the effect on civilian populations, which might be overstated, and the fact that scarce resources had to be diverted to defend cities cannot be dismissed in a time when all resources were being stretched by the demands of the front. Strategic bombing continued to draw supporters, though its ability to reduce cities to ashes and civilian populations to terrified masses was more fantasy than fact at that time.

In America, General Billy Mitchell argued the air power thesis so vehemently and publicly as to wreck his military career. His court martial and disgrace made Mitchell something of a martyr to the unproven thesis that air power was the ultimate strategic weapon. In looking at the story of General Mitchell, air power advocates fail to point out that at least some of the objections to his doctrine was its utter disregard for what was referred to in military circles as the ''rules of war.'' The concept of a ruthless attack upon unarmed civilians violated those rules which military leaders felt were necessary to curb the unbridled use of force in modern warfare.

In spite of such publicized debates, air power advocates were to receive support for research and development of aircraft, and the evolution of air power doctrine was given serious consideration during the inter-war period. In America the emphasis was on the offensive use of aircraft in war, and military planners devised a strategy of using air power to destroy the enemy's means of production. Therefore, the American position was that bombers would fly deep into enemy territory and destroy their production facilities. This led to the development of precision flying—bombers flying, in daylight, in tight formation to protect themselves from enemy fighter attacks. Once in enemy territory, precision bombing would be used to destroy specific targets. It is interesting to note the faith American airmen placed in the Norden bombsight which was supposed to assure hits on precise targets. The Americans considered it to be one of their most important secret weapons. However, plans for the sight were in German hands well before the outbreak of World War II, but the Germans saw little use for this type of device as it did not fit their air power doctrine. Neither did the British subscribe to the theory of precision bombing and, instead, were to utilize streams of night-flying bombers against general targets such as enemy cities.

In the inter-war period, particularly after 1936, Sunday supplement writers wrote futuristic horror tales of vast air armadas, massive bombardments, and deadly gas attacks raining destruction upon a hapless and helpless European city. In overselling the case for strategic bombing the partisans of air power created a counter-clamor for some manner of air defense to protect civilians from the horrors of a strategic bombing raid. Much to the chagrin of those who saw air power as an offensive weapon, public concern and political pressure forced governments to push for defensive plans, i.e. bomb shelters, air raid alerts, and gas masks for the civilian population. Research to develop an early detection/warning system (radar) was stepped up. Such efforts, minimal as they might have been, were to prove crucial in the war to come.

The preoccupation with strategic bombing tended to overshadow the tactical application of air power. Yet, the Spanish Civil War (1936-1939) was to demonstrate that air transport furnished both mobility and flexibility to military commanders, and further demonstrated the value of aircraft in disrupting communications and transportation as well as playing an important role in deciding the outcome of a conventional land battle. The experience gained by the Germans in the Spanish Civil War was to make the Luftwaffe an integral part of *Blitzkrieg* (Lightning War), but the lessons of tactical air power seemed to have been lost on those charged with war planning in England, France, and Poland. This failure to see the value of close air support in a battle situation was to plague the Allies during the coming war, and the lack of coordination between ground and air was problematic, particularly for the Western Allies, throughout the course of World War II.

Naval Power

During the inter-war period a variety of naval conferences were convened and agreements signed. Air power advocates had demonstrated that aircraft could sink a warship, but surface fleet advocates argued that maneuverability of a ship at sea would minimize the risks of a successful air attack. Most naval officers of the world's navies were surface fleet sailors. Aircraft carriers were developed and placed in service, yet the training of most fleets stressed the surface battle as the only way to secure a decisive victory at sea. The Germans, who had little success with its surface fleet during the "Great War," were of a like mind. When rearmament was ordered German naval commanders moved to develop fast surface raiders, sometimes referred to as "pocket battleships," which could harry the sea lanes of the world. Though submarines (U-boats) had played an important role in the last war, the submarine was not given first priority in production and mission. It was not until 1943 when Admiral Dönitz succeeded to the command of the German navy that the U-boat was given first priority in German naval strategy.

The Japanese doctrine was similar to that of other nations, and Japanese naval maneuvers stressed the idea that, in any future war, the decisive battle would be fought by the surface fleet. It is interesting to note that the Japanese plan for massive battle to be waged against the American fleet in the western

Pacific was in line with American naval doctrine which called for, in the event of war, a surface fleet battle in these same waters against the fleet of Imperial Japan.

In summing up the military planning of the Anglo-French General Staffs, it has been fashionable to condemn their shortsightedness and to typify their thinking as past-oriented. There is truth in such a generalization but not the whole truth. Theories of mobile warfare and the ability of air power to dominate in modern warfare were yet unproven in battle or, at least, not sufficiently demonstrated as to impel staff planners to change time-proven strategic thinking. However, evidence was mounting giving credibility to these new theories. To a small degree the Spanish Civil War (1936-1939) was a proving ground for mobile warfare and the tactical and logistical use of air power. Rather than adjusting plans to take this new element into account, the commitment to a static defense was even more pronounced as Allied planners prepared for the outbreak of war. As late as 1939 British military leaders announced to an increasingly anxious public that the land armies of her allies, France and Poland, were the best in Europe. From a statistical point of view such an announcement seemed valid. That numbers alone are but poor indices of the fitness of an army was a point only a few, unheeded prophets raised to counter the optimism of such public statements.

German Strategy

As World War I had helped shape the military thinking of the Allied, winning side, what of Germany? Much has been written of the debt the Germans owed to the teachings of General Fuller and Captain Liddell Hart. In interviews conducted after the war and in the memoirs of surviving German officers these two British military intellectuals have been given credit for helping shape German military planning and strategy. General Heinz Guderian, *Panzer* (armored) leader and the man credited with much of the German success during the Polish campaign, was a partisan of the concept of mobile warfare. He read and disseminated the writings of Fuller and Liddell Hart and labored to perfect the German army as a model attack force. His own writings give full credit to the influence of both Fuller and Liddell Hart.

Actually, German General Staff thinking was steeped in the tradition of the past. Frederick the Great of Prussia had stressed rapidity of movement and had demonstrated the value of mobility in innumerable battles. The hero of the Franco-German War, Helmuth von Moltke, had emphasized mobility and velocity of attack against the defense minded French in 1870. Count Alfred von Schlieffen, one of Germany's greatest military strategists, had devised a plan for Germany to fight on two fronts. This plan which bears his name was first developed in the 1890s and called for an offensive thrust against France through Belgium. This attack, using railways (the most rapid transport then available), was postulated on the belief that speed and force would lead to a quick victory. The second phase of the plan called for an equally rapid movement of forces to counter France's ally, the Soviet Union, from invading Germany from the East.

The application of this plan in 1914 led not to victory but to defeat. The German offensive was stopped at the Marne, and the war in the West changed from a war of mobility to one of attrition. The preoccupation of the German General Staff after the 1914 reversal was that of "breakthrough." In attempting to renew the offensive, casualties grew, and with each German failed offensive came an Allied counteroffensive.

Breakthrough then became the Allied goal, and in 1918 a weakened Germany succumbed to defeat. For the German army this defeat was a bitter blow and extremists were to argue that the defeat was less the result of failed strategy than the failure on the home front to support the war to a just conclusion. All this is by way of saying that German military thinking was channeled into a belief that, due to her geographic position in Europe, static defense would be insufficient to protect the homeland from her enemies in the West and those on her eastern frontiers.

After World War I, the Allies attempted to curb Germany's expansionist tendencies by disarmament. The German army was reduced in number to 100,000 officers and men. Both in manpower and in the type of armament prescribed by the Versailles Treaty, the German army was reduced to the role of a domestic peace-keeping force. Throughout the 1920s successive German governments sought to revise such restrictions even to the point of secretly agreeing to cooperate with the Soviets in developing and testing modern weapons and in the training of troops. The effects of such cooperation are difficult to assess, but it does indicate that Germany was prepared to go to any lengths to prepare herself for the day when treaty restrictions would be lifted.

When Hitler came to power in 1933, the promise of revisionism was within sight. Yet, it was not until 1936 that Germany moved toward full rearmament. To build a modern army takes time, and rearmament moved even slower than the General Staff had planned. As late as 1939, Germany had, in reality, two armies. One, a relatively small, elite force of approximately 14 divisions trained in mechanized, mobile war; the other, a hodgepodge of 70 odd divisions manned by half-trained recruits or by overage veterans of World War I. It would be the elite force which would bear the burden of war in 1939, yet it was this elite force which the General Staff counted upon to serve as the cadre upon which the new German army was to be built. The German *Wehrmacht* (armed forces) seemed but a small organization when compared with the active divisions and reserves which her neighbors, France and Poland, could muster. Such an unfavorable balance of military strength prompted Hitler's generals to urge caution upon their leader. In 1936 they counselled Hitler that if the French challenged Germany's remilitarization of the

Rhineland, German forces would be unable to meet the challenge and would be obliged to withdraw. No challenge was given, other than diplomatic notes of protest, and the Rhineland was remilitarized. Caution was the watchword of the German General Staff during the move toward Anschluss with Austria and the debate over the Sudetenland. In each case, Hitler's audacity brought success, but many of his generals were uneasy. The source of this unease centered around their opinion that the Wehrmacht was not ready to fight and win a war. Their concern did not stop Hitler from ordering the attack on Poland. The General Staff was obliged to make a virtue of necessity and employed their best forces in the September 1939 attack. In many ways the success of Blitzkrieg was as much a surprise to Hitler's generals as it was to their counterparts who watched and waited on the Western Front.

It has been argued that Hitler's decision to go to war was prompted by his belief that the new methods of warfare would bring a swift and complete victory for Germany. Such a supposition is rather unlikely. It is true that Hitler was supportive of General Guderian who was a partisan of the new theories of mechanization and mobility. Hitler, however, tended to favor those who promised swift and easy solutions. Rather than seeing Hitler as a serious student of mobile warfare, it would be closer to the mark to interpret his decision for war as a logical consequence of his experiences and prejudices. Hitler's tremendous success in dealing with the leaders of Europe had convinced him that the democratic nations of Europe were decadent; any evidence reinforced his prejudiced views. Thus, he could dismiss the fears of his General Staff since he believed that Germany's enemies lacked the resolve to fight an all-out war. Hitler then concluded that the reordering of the European state system could be accomplished with relative speed and minimal loss.

Summary

The experiences of World War I left an indelible impression on those who had lived through the war years. The necessity of avoiding future wars was a theme both in political rhetoric and public opinion. Unconvinced that peace was a perpetual condition, military thinkers looked to the defense of their respective countries. General Staff planning among the democratic states of Europe centered around improving the strategy of defense and counterattack which had proved effective in World War I. This view was not shared by theorists who argued that tanks, motorized transport, and airplanes had changed the nature of modern warfare. Their thesis was that massed armor supported by air and artillery could smash a static defense line. The narrow breach would allow tanks and mechanized infantry to pour through and to penetrate enemy territory in depth. Such a deep penetration would force the enemy nation to sue for peace. Though the theory of mobile warfare gained some audience and influence, the general consensus of opinion among English, French, and

Polish military leaders supported the concept of massed armies and static defense.

Though discussion of the new techniques of mobile warfare was largely conducted among professional soldiers and military specialists, the possible military uses of air power excited a larger, public debate. Air power advocates postulated that strategic bombing of enemy cities could quickly end any future war. The most practical result of this sometimes fanciful debate was that of forcing nation states, particularly Great Britain, to take measures to bolster air defenses. The debate stressed the strategic uses of air power and tended to neglect the tactical value of aircraft in a conventional land war.

Naval doctrine emphasized that surface fleets would play the crucial role in any future war. Though air power and the value of submarines were not completely neglected, doctrine and training emphasized the primary role of the surface fleet in naval warfare.

German strategy followed a somewhat different line than that taken by England and France. German military thinking was shaped, in large part, by that nation's geographic location in Europe and historical circumstance. With only a small force with which to work, German planners were forced to rely upon a professional, elite army which would serve as a cadre when and if the restrictions of Versailles were lifted to allow the creation of a new, enlarged Wehrmacht. The German General Staff hoped to have time to build an army comparable in size to those Germany would face in a war. Time was not given to them, and when the army was ordered on the offensive, the German generals were forced to rely on their small elite force to carry out the offensive.

Hitler's opting for war seemed less the result of his belief in the effectiveness of Blitzkrieg than his belief that Germany's enemies lacked the resolve and will to maintain the European status quo. He gambled that his plan to reorder the European state system could be realized without unbearable cost to the Third Reich.

Suggested Reading

Clausewitz, Carl von. *On War*. Princeton, New Jersey, 1976. Clausewitz's observations on total war may be found in Book Eight, Chapter Three. For those who would find Clausewitz's style a bit overwhelming, read Howard, Michael, *Clausewitz* (New York, 1983).

Cleary, Thomas, (Trans.). *The Art of War, Sun Tzu*. Boston, 1988. Originally written more than two thousand years ago, this work is well worth reading for those who wish to understand the practice of warfare.

Irving, David. *Churchill's War*. Vol. I. *The Struggle for Power*. Western Australia, 1987. A revisionist view of the diplomacy leading up to the war. It was a very controversial book and not well received, but it is, at least, a different view.

Keegan, John. *The Second World War*. New York, 1989. A very popular book, it is excellent on the move toward war and, of course, a very interesting study of World War II. The reader might also wish to read other works by Keegan, which include, *The Face of Battle* (New York, 1974) and *The Price of Admiralty, The Evolution of Naval Warfare* (New York, 1989). Parts Three and Four of the latter work are of special interest to the student of World War II.

Paschall, Rod. *The Defeat of Imperial Germany, 1917-1918*. Chapel Hill, North Carolina, 1989. An excellent study of tactics and strategies developed during the closing year of the war.

Wilmott, H. P. *The Great Crusade, A New and Complete History of the Second World War*. New York, 1989. An excellent general study, but of particular interest to those who wish a concise account of developments in Asia during the inter-war period.

3

The European War
September 1939 to May 1940

From the vantage point of the present, writers and historians are able to underscore and pinpoint the illusions and delusions of the past. Certainly, it is obvious to us now that the superior mobility of the elite, German strike force which attacked Poland on September 1, 1939, would be a crucial factor in determining the outcome of the invasion. What is obvious to us now might well have been seen as visionary, even absurd, to those charged with the defense of Poland. Poland, after all, had acquired something of a reputation for her military prowess during the inter-war period. Her cavalry regiments had been instrumental in fending off attacks from the east in the 1920s. Her armies had secured her frontiers from attack during the tumultuous years after World War I, and as late as the summer of 1939, her forces were being touted in the West as among the finest in Europe. The cream of the Polish army was its horse cavalry. The infantry was well trained but was far from being a mechanized, mobile force. The artillery enjoyed a reputation for excellence, but it, too, relied more on horses than on horsepower. Finally, Poland's air force was small and its tank forces practically nonexistent.

Such limitations, obvious to those of us who enjoy the luxury of historical perspective, were not alarming to those who prepared for the war which would come on September 1, 1939. Hitler's dismemberment of Czechoslovakia had led Chamberlain to bring Great Britain into an alliance with Poland. Now England and France were allied in a pledge to aid the Polish nation in the event of war. European geography and the limitations of the technology of that day made such a pledge less than a guarantee of security; however, neither Poland nor her allies thought such a pledge empty and meaningless. Their military thinking centered on the proposition that the war to come would be fought in much the same way as the last war. Poland, with her small army and her huge reserves, would meet and hold the attack until such time as her allies in the West could mobilize their forces and press the attack against Germany's western frontiers. Sea and air power would isolate Germany and the war of attrition, in the mode of World War I, would begin. Defense, not mobility, was the watchword of the Allies, and time, they conjectured, was on their side. The possibility that Polish defenses would be cut to pieces, outflanked, and outmaneuvered before the West could bring real military pressure upon Germany was not a subject for consideration let alone anxiety.

Accordingly, Marshal Edward Smigly-Rydz distributed his forces to guard Poland's long frontier with Germany. This frontier was extended in March 1939 to include the border Poland shared with Czechoslovakia which was now occupied and/or dominated by Germany. Therefore, Poland was forced to defend her borders to the north, south, and west and was blissfully unaware that her eastern border with the U.S.S.R. was, as noted in the secret articles of the 1939 Nazi-Soviet Pact, under threat of attack.

Criticism of the Polish plan is obvious. Marshal Smigly-Rydz had scattered his armies too widely for effective control. One-third of the Polish forces were kept in reserve in the Warsaw area, but this reserve was not a mechanized, mobile force able to respond rapidly to relieve a threatened defense sector. Again, we must remember that such a disposition was quite orthodox and conformed to the grand strategy which was to be endorsed by the leaders of the armies of Poland's allies. Other factors were considered in the disposition of forces. The areas of Polish territory vulnerable to attack included the most productive industrial and raw material producing areas in Poland. Therefore, economic necessity and national pride were important factors which helped shape Marshal Smigly-Rydz's plan of defense. Historians have dealt extensively with the inadequacies of this plan and have emphasized the fact that the Polish leadership relied too heavily on the counterattack. Other writers have noted that the Polish preparations were yet to be completed by September 1, and her full reserve contingent was not yet mobilized. Yet, there is no doubt that war was imminent. From August 25-31, Hitler attempted to negotiate with the Polish government, demanding cession of certain Polish territory as an alternative to war, but such demands were, of course, dismissed. German-Polish negotiations strike something of an insincere note, for the fact remains that Hitler had spoken to his generals on August 23 ordering them to destroy Poland as rapidly as possible.

Invasion of Poland

The September 1 attack began with the almost complete destruction of the Polish air force. The Luftwaffe hit the Polish bases at first light destroying most of Poland's airplanes on the ground. Immediately after the dawn attack German ground forces invaded Polish territory. A total of five armies, divided into two Army Groups—the Northern Group under Field Marshal Fedor von Bock and the Southern Group under General (later Field Marshal) Gerd von Rundstedt—thrust across the Polish frontier initiating a form of attack which became known as Blitzkrieg, i.e. lightning war. Theoretically, this type of mobile warfare is designed to punch a hole in the enemy's line, reinforce the breach with mechanized infantry to keep the hole open, and then pour troops through the breach. In the Polish campaign field commanders wrote their own textbook. Using their superior mobility, German Panzer commanders out-flanked the slower moving Polish forces. Tactical air support was used to hit pockets of resistance on the battlefield and to disrupt communications. In league with the attack force, Germans residing in Poland constituted a fifth column which served to disrupt communication, spread false reports, and to create as much panic as possible. The disruption of communication between field commanders and their headquarters brought confusion to the whole command structure. Conflicting orders, some of which were transmitted by fifth columnists, undermined confidence, and the surprising mobility of German forces frustrated efforts to maintain any semblance of a front. Units which effectively turned a German tank attack would find that within a few hours the position had been flanked and rendered untenable. Withdrawal became a nightmare as refugees clogged the roadways and tied up all transport. Therefore, the orderly retreat of Polish units often deteriorated into an attack to the rear. The enemy appeared to be everywhere at once and relief nowhere in sight.

On the morning of September 3, Great Britain's ambassador to Germany presented Hitler with a formal declaration of war, the French declaration was delivered that afternoon. In actuality, this had little effect on the conduct of the war in Poland. By September 4, units of the German army had penetrated fifty miles into Polish territory. The speed of the attack was surprising to the German Army Group commanders who worried that such a deep thrust might be vulnerable to a severe counterattack. However, reports from the front indicated the confusion of the Polish forces, and within a week elements of the Northern Group were 140 miles within Polish territory. On September 9, the Polish government left Warsaw as German forces were too near the city to make it a secure seat of government. On September 10, Marshal Smigly-

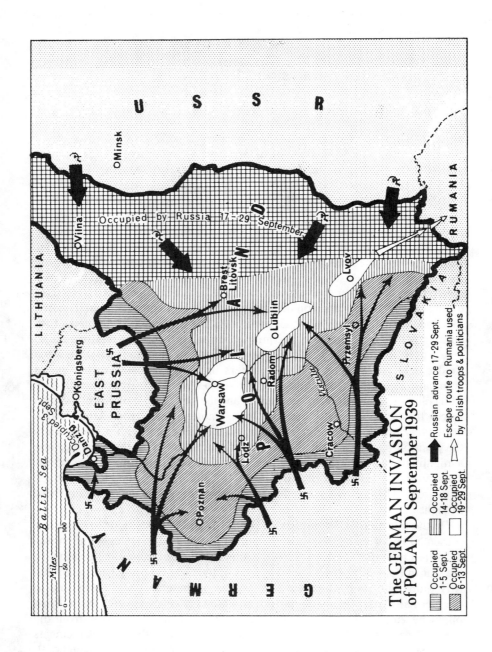

The GERMAN INVASION
of POLAND September 1939

Russian advance 17-29 Sept.

Escape route to Rumania used
by Polish troops & politicians

Occupied
1-5 Sept.
Occupied
6-13 Sept.
Occupied
14-18 Sept.
Occupied
19-29 Sept.

Rydz issued orders for a general withdrawal to the southeast. It was his hope that a defense position could be established; however, such a move was blocked by the rapid movement of the German forces which had penetrated east of the Vistula River. Any hope of a defense in the East was completely shattered on September 17 when Soviet forces invaded Poland. On September 18, 1939, the Polish government crossed over the Rumanian border into exile. On September 28, the Warsaw garrison surrendered, and on October 6, all organized Polish military resistance ended.

Many Poles continued to resist through underground activities. Others managed to escape occupied Poland and to fight the Germans on other fronts. The Soviets, though guilty of a known massacre of Polish officers at Katyn Forest (1941), were eventually to allow the formation of a Polish unit recruited from prisoner-of-war camps in the Soviet Union. Such Polish units were to distinguish themselves in North Africa and Italy. Poland, however, ceased to be. In London a government in exile was established, but both the Germans and the Soviets regarded Poland as occupied territory which was to become part of the Greater Reich or the Soviet Union. In German-occupied territory the SS reign of terror followed the advance of the German army. So persistent were these groups in fulfilling racist policies that local field commanders protested that these *Einsatzgruppen* (flying squads of assassins) interfered with military operations. Such criticism was brushed aside, and the death squads were given free reign. It was not until later that the SS began to organize racial murder on a methodical basis with the establishment of extermination camps in Poland and elsewhere. Millions of European Jews were to die in these camps, exterminated in gas chambers and incinerated in ovens. Millions of other peoples, Poles, Soviets, and the myriad of European "races" classified by Nazi doctrine as sub-human also were to fall victim to Hitler's policies of genocide.

In spite of the Polish defeat, the contribution of the Poles to the Allied war effort was to be profound in the area of intelligence. In the 1970s it was finally revealed that the German encoding device, Enigma, which was one of the most closely guarded secrets of the war, had in fact been penetrated. The Poles had been able to penetrate German code from the Enigma machine in the 1930s, but, in the early spring of 1939, the Germans had changed the code machine from a three-roll to a four-roll electronic encoding machine. This machine, resembling an electric typewriter, relied on the concept of a random sequence in the transmission of letters and numbers. By increasing the number of rolls used in the encoding/decoding process, the difficulty of breaking the code was increased geometrically. The Poles managed to bring to the West one of their three-roll machines which was passed on to the British. Eventually, this led to the establishment of the complex at Bletchley Hall. There, Allied scientists, intelligence experts, and linguists developed the technology and expertise to break the German Enigma code, which led to the famous Ultra Secret project that was to provide the Allies with access to German war plans throughout the war. This contribution by Poland to Ultra Secret, so important to the Allies, is one which has not received the attention it deserves in many of the books written on Allied intelligence breakthroughs during World War II.

The "Phony War"

The rapid attack and quick victory of Hitler's armies in Poland was the subject of worldwide consternation and a seeming lack of initiative among the Allies. In most history books the September 1939 to May 1940 phase is called the period of "Phony War," or, as some call it, "Sitzkrieg." In reality, there was activity in the West. Much of this activity consisted of developing elaborate, often fantastic plans, to strike at Germany's eastern army flank through Greece or her northern flank through Scandinavia. The planners even considered launching an attack through neutral Belgium against the German industrial heartland, the Ruhr.

Hitler, too, had his plans. He demanded a rapid offensive against France, through Belgium. He argued that it was necessary to attack soon before British aid to France tipped the balance against Germany. Hitler's generals were less than enthusiastic. Though they might well agree that a protracted war in the West was not to Germany's advantage, still the numerical superiority of the French army gave them reason to pause. Hitler was convinced that German technical superiority would more than counter French numerical superiority. Also, he argued that the German soldiers' will to fight and win would be the edge which would give Germany victory over the decadent French.

The German General Staff had good reason to be uneasy about an early offensive against France. General Maurice Gamelin, the French commander, had devised a plan which anticipated a German attack through central Belgium. This plan, called Plan D, was postulated on the apparent reality that the German attack would follow the plan used in World War I. That is, Gamelin anticipated a "modified Schlieffen Plan" of attack. Gamelin reasoned that the German attack plan could be countered by moving French and British forces into Belgium to establish a line of defense. Belgium, though cooperative with French defense plans, had, in 1936, returned to her reliance on neutrality as a shield against aggression. Therefore, Gamelin's plan for establishing a defense line could not be implemented until Belgium had been attacked. This, however, did not seem an impediment to Plan D, and both the French and British military leaders were confident they could meet and hold a German thrust through Belgium. In short, the Allies continued to be enamored of the strategy of defense and relied on the Maginot Line to the south and Plan D in the north to check the German attack. In this sense the Allied Powers were ready to re-fight World War I.

The German plan, Case Yellow, was the work of the army high command,

Oberkommando des Herres (OKH) commanded by Field Marshal Walther von Brauchitsch and his chief of staff General Franz Halder. The plan called for a push into central Belgium to split the Allied force, and, eventually, to build up forces there for a decisive attack on France in 1942. This plan was one which Plan D obviously envisioned, but it did not suit Hitler. Neither did it suit the leader of the Southern Army Group Field Marshal Rundstedt or his chief of staff General (later Field Marshal) Erich von Manstein. The plan they propounded was to draw Allied forces into central Belgium then launch an attack through the Ardennes to flank the Allies, cutting their forces off and opening France to attack. This plan for a quick victory appealed to Hitler, but he was, seemingly, willing to acquiesce to Case Yellow. However, an incident occurred which changed all that. Two Luftwaffe officers carrying information regarding Case Yellow crash landed in Belgium. It was decided that because of the survival of these documents the plan must be changed. Case Yellow, planned for January 17, 1940, was scrapped and the Ardennes offensive, the Manstein Plan, adopted.

The coincidence of this event has led some writers to argue that Admiral Canaris, chief of German Military Intelligence (the *Abwehr*), had engineered this breach of security to forewarn the Allies of German plans. Certainly, the loss of the complete war plans was to cause consternation at *Oberkommando der Wehrmacht* (OKW) headquarters. Convinced that security had been breached, a new plan had to be devised. Such an alternative was already being readied by General Manstein. Manstein's plan called for a secondary attack through central Belgium to draw in the Allied forces. This would be followed by a main Panzer thrust through the Ardennes, across the Meuse River to Sedan. From there the German Panzer forces would wheel north toward Abbeville, secure the channel ports, and effectively bottle up and destroy the Allied forces in Belgium.

Manstein's concept had secured little support from his superiors, but thanks to the aid of General Guderian, Marshal Rundstedt, and others, OKW's rejection was ignored, and Hitler received the Manstein plan. His enthusiasm was such that he came to think of Manstein's idea as his own. Therefore, he impatiently brushed aside the obvious criticisms of an Ardennes attack. The fundamental criticism was that the plan was too daring. The Ardennes, with its narrow valleys and inadequate system of roadways, seemed hardly a suitable area for the launching of a major attack. The movement of troops and vehicles through this labyrinth of roadways could only result in delay, confusion, and disaster, or so the plan's detractors argued. Certainly, these dangers did exist, but Hitler, who had an admiration for the audacious, sponsored its adoption, and preparations were made to implement the new attack plan by the spring of 1940.

The "accident" of January 1940 was to result in disaster for the Allies. It is ironic that Hitler's fear that security had been breached was unfounded. The errant Luftwaffe officers had indeed been picked up by the Belgians, searched, and interned. However, the secret plans in their possession were viewed by the Belgian, British, and French officers who ultimately studied them as tools of deception devised by cunning German intelligence officers to mislead the Allies. Such were the misfortunes of the Western Allies during this period of the "Phony War."

While the Western Front remained relatively quiet (French sentries scanned the German lines from the comparative safety of the fortresses of the Maginot Line), a shooting war was being fought at sea. In September 1939, the German South Atlantic raider, the *Graf Spee*, was detected by a squadron of British cruisers, damaged, and later scuttled at sea by her crew after being ordered out of her sanctuary in Montevideo Harbor. This successful action did not offset the losses the British navy suffered in the growing battle for the Atlantic. One of the more humiliating losses occurred in October 1939, when the battleship *Royal Oak* was torpedoed and sunk by U-boat #47 while it rested at anchor in the supposed safety of the British base at Scapa Flow. In the North Atlantic German U-boats and surface raiders caused serious damage to British shipping, and the danger increased as the German U-boat fleet grew in size during the fall and winter months. The Battle of the North Atlantic had begun, and during this period of time, the British were to bear heavy losses to its merchant fleet. Convoys were organized and escort vessels outfitted, but at this stage of the war, the U-boat enjoyed an edge over the overaged ships and inferior detection systems of the British navy. It seemed that the Royal Navy would have to relearn the lessons of World War I. The neglect in the training of officers and men in the intricacies of convoy protection and antisubmarine warfare during the inter-war period was to cost Great Britain and her subsequent ally, America, dearly until the spring of 1943.

As with the war on the ground, the air war was seemingly in limbo. Royal Air Force (RAF) bombers made occasional propaganda raids on Germany dropping leaflets rather than bombs. Such forays accomplished little except, as one wit remarked, to furnish toilet paper to the population of Germany. Leaflet raids were obviously designed to keep up morale at home by demonstrating some form of action against the enemy. It is doubtful that anyone really believed that propaganda raids alone would turn the Third Reich from the path of aggression. Yet, such actions typified the attitude of the Allies during the period of Phony War when it was not yet apparent to western democracies how desperate their situation really was.

Soviet Expansionism

In the East, Stalin had not rested on his laurels. In October he moved to secure an agreement with Latvia, Lithuania, and Estonia to garrison Soviet troops in those countries. This was the death knell of independence for these states. Once territories of the old Russian Empire, they had been designated by the Versailles Treaty as independent states. With Soviet occupation their independence came to an end. In August 1940, these three states became "republics" within the Union of Soviet Socialist Republics. Stalin also secured additional territories, Bessarabia and northern Bukovina, from Rumania in 1940. These annexations were accomplished through negotiations and intimidations. However, Stalin's expansionist ambitions were not accomplished solely by the threat of force. In fact, in his urge to readjust Soviet boundaries, the Soviet leader began negotiations in October 1939 to establish new frontiers between Finland and the U.S.S.R.

On the surface, at least, Stalin's bid for territorial readjustment was logical and generous. What the Soviet leader hoped to accomplish was to secure Leningrad from attack. To do this, it would be necessary to move the Soviet-Finnish frontier on the Karelian Peninsula north by a few kilometers. Likewise, access to the Gulf of Finland would have been assured by the ceding of certain Finnish-held islands and leasing the port of Hango to the Soviets. In the North, the security of Murmansk was to be assured by the readjustments of the frontier in the Petsamo region. In exchange for these adjustments the Soviets offered territories in compensation. Superficially the offer seemed generous, and the Finns would have secured a net gain of over 1,000 miles of territory; however, the Finnish government found the offer unacceptable. Negotiations were broken off in late November 1939, and on November 30, 1939, Soviet forces attacked Finland.

In anticipation of trouble from her neighbor, the Finnish government had constructed a defense line girding the narrow waist of the Karelian Peninsula. The Mannerheim Line was to block effectively the Soviet advance. On the Eastern frontier, the Finns used their small army to foil Soviet attacks. Frustrated in their attempts at a quick victory, the Soviets tried to bomb Helsinki into submission, but this too failed. Eventually, the war in Finland became an embarrassment to the Soviets and a source of encouragement to the West. The tiny Finnish army proved more mobile, more versatile, and more imaginative than the Red Army. The gallant Finnish defense attracted world attention, and unrealizable schemes were hatched among Allied military planners to aid the doughty Finns. However, the beginning of the end came in February 1940. The Red Army massed over fourteen divisions against a ten-mile sector of the Mannerheim and began to chip away at the fortification by using massed artillery barrages and aerial bombardment. A breach was made in the line, and the Soviets then wheeled their forces in a flanking attack across the frozen Gulf of Finland isolating Viipuri. On March 6, a Finnish peace delegation was dispatched to the U.S.S.R., and on March 13, at the insistence of Field Marshal Mannerheim who had masterminded the Finnish defense, the Soviet terms were accepted.

The blame for the poor showing of the Red Army in this brief, fierce conflict has been charged to Joseph Stalin by post-World War II Soviet writers and officials. According to his Soviet detractors, Stalin's purge of the army in

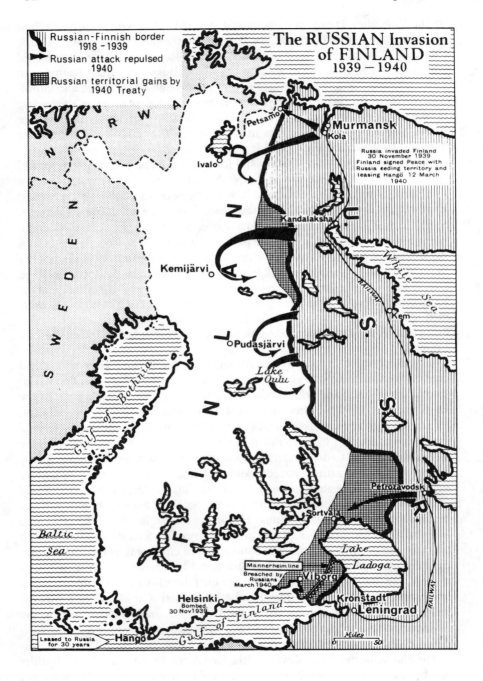

Russian-Finnish border
1918 - 1939
Russian attack repulsed
1940
Russian territorial gains by
1940 Treaty

The RUSSIAN Invasion
of FINLAND
1939 - 1940

Russia invaded Finland
30 November 1939
Finland signed Peace with
Russia ceding territory and
leasing Hangö 12 March
1940

Petsamo

Murmansk

Kola

Ivalo

Kandalaksha

Kemijärvi

Kem

White Sea

RAILWAY

Pudasjärvi

Lake
Oulu

Sortvala

Petrozavodsk

Baltic
Sea

Mannerheim line
Breached by
Russians
March 1940

Viborg

Lake
Ladoga

Helsinki
Bombed.
30 Nov 1939

Kronstadt

Leningrad

RAILWAY

Leased to Russia
for 30 years

Hangö

Gulf of Finland

Miles
0   50

Gulf of Bothnia

SWEDEN

NORWAY

FINLAND

U.S.S.R.

the late 1930s was a major factor in diminishing the fighting effectiveness of the Red Army. However, it would be unwise to overemphasize this aspect. The Soviet army, following the doctrine of most armies of the day, was dependent on rail, roads, and vehicles. Their movements were slow and predictable, their supply lines, particularly those on Finland's eastern border, were difficult to maintain. Most importantly, they fought as a conventional force against a small, rather unconventional army that knew how to utilize terrain and adapt to it. Small units could easily avoid and harass the ponderously slow moving Soviet forces. After months of fighting the Soviet commanders began to learn their lessons. They concentrated their forces and breached the Finnish defenses. After that victory was assured.

The exact losses suffered by the Red Army during this conflict are conjectural. Some Soviet sources note as high as 40,000 plus killed in this short war. The fact that such heavy losses could be inflicted by a small force on the overwhelming power of the Red Army was a source of astonishment to many observers who saw overwhelming force as the dominating factor in warfare, and some writers have argued that the poor showing of the Soviet army against the Finns deluded both Winston Churchill and Adolph Hitler in their evaluation of the fighting qualities of the Red Army. Certainly, for Hitler, the denigration of the effectiveness of the Red Army was to have dire consequences in the future.

Invasion of Norway

During the Soviet-Finnish War, Allied planners had debated a plan to aid Finland by advancing through Norway, seizing the Gellivare iron mines in Sweden, thereby cutting off Hitler's supply of iron, and thence to the aid of Finland. This plan was, of course, not implemented, but serious thought had been given in Allied circles regarding the invasion of Norway. As early as February 1940, while the Soviets were making gains against the Mannerheim Line, British vessels violated Norwegian territorial waters by seizing the German freighter, *Altmarck*. The *Altmarck*, a supply ship for German raiders and U-boats, carried a cargo of captured British seamen enroute to German internment camps. This action was, however, a violation of Norwegian neutrality and had the dual effect of irritating the Norwegians and convincing the Germans that the Allies had serious designs on Norway. As early as December 1939, Vidkun Quisling, leader of a Nazi-type Norwegian party, tried to convince the Germans that his party had strong support in Norway. He asked for, and ultimately received, German aid to finance his plan to deliver Norway into the Axis camp. Quisling overestimated his influence, and German intelligence indicated that his support in Norway was minimal. Still, Hitler was concerned that the Allies might intervene in Norway.

After the defeat of Finland in March 1940, the Allied impetus for the invasion plan was, seemingly, lost. However, as Finland went down to defeat, the plan to seize Narvik and the Gellivare fields gained greater support in Allied councils. Churchill pushed the scheme for intervention and ultimately secured the support of Prime Minister Chamberlain and Premier Daladier of France. Plans were formulated to mine Norway's coastal waters on April 5 and then to send an Allied invasion fleet to take Norwegian ports, particularly Narvik. Unfortunately, for the Allies, the invasion armada was delayed and did not sail for Norway until the 7th of April. Meanwhile, Hitler had authorized General Falkenhurst to prepare a plan for the invasion of Norway. On April 1, 1940, Hitler set the date for the attack on Norway to begin in the early morning of April 9. With speed and boldness the Germans launched the attack. Narvik and Trondheim were seized quickly. German paratroopers captured Norway's air fields, and the Luftwaffe dominated Norway's air space. Oslo alone caused the Germans some pause. Norway's coastal batteries sank the German cruiser *Blücher* and held off the invading fleet. However, German paratroops, who had captured Forneau airdrome near Oslo, marched toward the capital. This small force pulled off their bluff, the King and Queen fled the city, and Oslo was occupied by German forces. Denmark, too, fell on April 9. A small German force marched into Copenhagen and, after a short skirmish with the Palace Guards, took over the city. A second force landed in Jutland, brushed aside resistance, and by the end of the day, Denmark was under German control.

The rapid German attack was a surprise to the Norwegians and the Allies alike. Though the Allied invasion fleet was readied for the operation against Norway on the 7th of April, it was not until the 14th that Allied forces landed around Narvik. The delay was caused, in part, because the Royal Navy hoped to engage and destroy the German surface fleet. Though the British fleet had some success against German vessels, the transport of troops to Norway was delayed. When Allied forces landed near Narvik on April 14, it was in German hands. On the 16th and 17th Trondheim was attacked, and on the 18th Allied forces struck at Andalsnes. However, success on the ground escaped the Allied invading forces. Troop movements were hampered by heavy, wet snow, and the domination of the air by the Luftwaffe caused havoc among the poorly supported Allied forces. By April 30, 1940, the British and French forces were being evacuated from Andalsnes, and on May 1, the evacuation of Namsos began. The British were successful in taking Narvik from the Germans on May 28, but were forced to evacuate that port on June 8.

Thus, in spite of British surface fleet superiority, the Germans were able to invade and to hold Norway. The rapid capitulation of the Norwegian forces has sometimes been attributed to Quisling's pro-Nazi collaborators. However, such fifth columnists played a minimal role when compared with the force and rapidity of the German attack against an unprepared and small Norwegian army. German success against the Allied forces was gained through greater mobility of their forces, air control, and better leadership. The debacle in

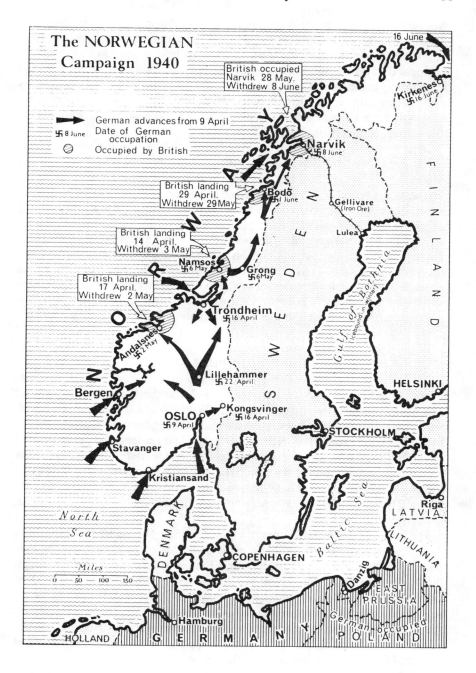

The NORWEGIAN
Campaign 1940

British occupied
Narvik 28 May.
Withdrew 8 June

➤ German advances from 9 April
⚹ 8 June   Date of German occupation
⊘   Occupied by British

16 June

Kirkenes
⚹16 June

Narvik
⚹8 June

FINLAND

British landing
29 April.
Withdrew 29 May

Bodö
⚹1 June

Gellivare
(Iron Ore)

British landing
14 April.
Withdrew 3 May

Lulea

Namsos
⚹6 May

Grong
⚹6 May

British landing
17 April.
Withdrew 2 May

SWEDEN

Gulf of Bothnia
(icebound in winter)

Trondheim
⚹16 April

Andalsnes
⚹2 May

Lillehammer
⚹22 April

HELSINKI

NORWAY

Bergen

OSLO
⚹9 April

Kongsvinger
⚹16 April

STOCKHOLM

Stavanger

Kristiansand

Riga

LATVIA

North
Sea

DENMARK

Baltic Sea

LITHUANIA

Miles
0   50   100   150

COPENHAGEN

Danzig

EAST
PRUSSIA

Hamburg

German occupied

HOLLAND   G E R M A N Y   P O L A N D

Norway prompted a bitter debate in the British Parliament which ultimately led to a vote of "no confidence" in the Chamberlain government. On May 10, 1940, Winston Churchill was selected to lead a coalition government comprised of both Conservative and Labour Party ministers. It is ironic that the Norway campaign, a project championed by Winston Churchill, was, by virtue of its failure, to springboard him to power. Yet, Winston Churchill was to bring to the war effort an energy that had been sorely lacking during this period of the Phony War.

Defeat seemed the order of the day for the Allies and the small nations of Eastern Europe and Scandinavia. Poland, Norway, and Denmark had been defeated, and Finland had lost her fight with the Soviets. Though the peace that was negotiated was hardly a vengeful one, the Finns smarted under the terms and were to be receptive to later German promises for a return of her lost lands. Quisling, who hoped to become the all-powerful Norwegian leader, had little support among his own people and was ultimately shunted aside. Though defeated, the Norwegians and Danes were to resist in various and several ways their Nazi overlords. Both nations did their best to subvert the racist decrees of their German masters, and both Norwegians and Danes were to develop a highly effective underground resistance apparatus which was to create difficulties for the German occupation force.

Summary

The Allied plan for the defense of Poland and the West against German expansionism was based on the lessons of World War I. However, the Polish army, outmaneuvered and outgunned, could not hold back the German attack. Mobility on the ground, superiority in the air, and leaders who demonstrated the ability to handle these new techniques of war were to give the Germans a vital edge in overcoming the traditional military organization of the Polish forces. With Poland's defeat, the Western Allies deluded themselves into thinking that their defensive plans would be sufficient to hold back any German attack.

The Maginot Line and Gamelin's Plan D seemed to assure the Allies that their defenses would hold. Hitler's plans, however, were to change. The new plan called for a "feint" through central Belgium and a major attack through the Ardennes. Thus, for the West, this period of Phony War was one of preparing fanciful plans for attacks on Germany's flanks. For Hitler's generals, it was a time for preparation and rethinking of their offensive plans. At sea, the British had a few successes against the German surface fleet, but, on the whole, the U-boats held sway over the shipping lanes of the North Sea and prepared to increase their zone of operation.

The Soviets, profiting from their agreement with Germany, now moved to dominate Latvia, Lithuania, and Estonia and sought to readjust boundaries with Finland. This attempt led to a short war wherein the Soviets suffered military defeat at the hands of a more skillful and mobile Finnish army. The initial success of this tiny army could not be sustained against the mass of the Red Army, and by March 1940, Finland had to sue for peace.

The Soviet-Finnish War prompted Allied leaders to contemplate an invasion of Scandinavia to aid Finland and, perhaps more importantly, to seize the Gellivare iron fields in the hope of crippling Germany's war production industry. By hints and direct action the Allies made clear their designs on Norway. Hitler, who had initially hoped to see Norway remain neutral, was prompted to order an invasion plan. This plan coincided in date with that of the Allied plan. The essential difference was that the German attack was carried out on schedule and followed the new pattern of Blitzkrieg. The Allied attempts to stem the German tide in Norway led to defeat. The Norway debacle spelled the end of the Chamberlain government and the formation of a new, coalition "War Cabinet" in Great Britain. This heralded the end of the Phony War in more ways than one. Winston Churchill took over the reins of power on May 10, and on that very day, Hitler's tanks thrust across the borders of Belgium and the Netherlands. The war in the West had begun in earnest.

Suggested Reading

Andrew, Christopher. *Her Majesty's Secret Service: The Making of the British Intelligence Community*. New York, 1986. Chronicles the development of Great Britain's intelligence service up to and including the Ultra Secret program.

Erfurth, Waldmar. *The Last Finnish War*. Washington, D.C., 1979. Details the Finnish campaign and wartime activities in Finland from 1939 to 1945.

Gilbert, Martin. *The Second World War*. New York, 1989. A solid one-volume history of the war. Chapters one through four cover the 1939-40 period.

Gjelsvik, Tore, (Trans. Thomas K. Derry). *Norwegian Resistance*. Montreal, 1979. Covers the war and resistance movements in Norway.

Khrushchev, Nikita Sergeyevich, (Trans. Strobe Talbot). *Khrushchev Remembers*. Boston, 1970. Beginning on page 150, Khrushchev chronicles the disasters of the Red Army campaign which he blames on the excesses of Stalin.

Polish Ministry of Information. *The German Invasion of Poland*. London, 1940. The first part of a collection of documents including authentic reports of the September 1939 campaign.

Stevenson, William. *A Man Called Intrepid*. New York, 1976. One of the first books which revealed the Ultra Secret to the general public.

Reference Material

Those interested in World War II would profit by adding to their library the following:

Keegan, John. *The Times Atlas of the Second World War*. New York, 1989. An oversized book, but the color maps are excellent.

Parrish, Thomas. *The Simon and Schuster Encyclopedia of World War II*. New York, 1978. A reference guide which is not too voluminous.

4

The Triumphs and Defeats of the Axis Powers
May 1940 to June 1941

On May 10, 1940, German parachute troops landed near Rotterdam; German armored divisions burst through the Belgian frontier barricades; and the Allies responded by implementing Plan D, the left shoulder push into Belgium to meet the German attack. To the south, German Panzers were wending their way through the 70 miles of the Ardennes in their approach to the Meuse River near Sedan. Within five days the Dutch army surrendered; in 17 days the Belgian King arranged for an armistice; within 24 days 224,000 men of the British Expeditionary Force (BEF) and some 114,000 other Allied troops had been evacuated from Dunkirk, and on June 22, 1940, in an historic railway car in the forest of Compiègne, the Franco-German armistice was signed. On June 25, 1940, the armistice went into effect. France had fallen, and Great Britain stood alone against the triumphant forces of Hitler's Third Reich.

This recitation of dates and events evokes a sense of inevitability about the course of events. Yet, it should be remembered that the German edge for victory was slight indeed. In fact, prior to the attack, the German General Staff was not at all convinced that its army could defeat the Allies let alone accomplish this victory in such a short period of time. The generals knew full well that France possessed more and superior armor, and that the Allies also enjoyed superiority in artillery and infantry. It was in the course of events, during the fog of battle, that the German edge emerged. It was General Heinz Guderian, despite obstacles and delays laid in his path by his superiors and by Hitler himself, who engineered the brilliant sweep across the Meuse and, thence, north to Abbeville and the English Channel—thereby bottling up the cream of the Allied forces at Dunkirk. Guderian accomplished this feat by following the precepts of mobile warfare against a superior, but conventionally led, defensive force.

As noted in the previous chapter, the Allied Plan D called for a left shoulder push into central Belgium to meet and stop a German offensive. Belgian forces, when attacked, would fall back to link up with the French army and the BEF, and a defense line would be formed to stop the German offensive. The anticipation of a modified Schlieffen plan of attack was both rational and accurate. Gamelin's strategy, however, did not envision that the German main thrust was to come through the Ardennes.

Invasion of Belgium

On the eve of the attack the Germans had established two Army Groups. Group B, under Bock, was charged with the attack on The Netherlands and the thrust into Belgium. Army Group A, under command of Rundstedt, was to attack through the Ardennes. Bock's Army Group had the difficult task of thrusting as deeply and swiftly as possible into The Netherlands and Belgium and, thus, keeping the Allied defenders off balance. However, this area was intersected with canals and rivers which hampered rapid movement. Both Dutch and Belgian military planners appreciated that fact, and, consequently, all strategic bridges had been mined with explosive charges which could be detonated easily by the bridge sentries in the event of an attack. To forestall this destruction, the German paratroop division, under command of General Kurt Student, had been charged with securing the bridges. The bulk of Student's paratroop force was dispatched to The Netherlands to secure the bridges. These paratroopers, augmented by an air-transport regiment (i.e., a light infantry regiment transported by aircraft), secured and held the strategic bridges over the Rhine until German ground troops arrived. A smaller detachment of parachute and air transport troops was dispatched to the Hague. Its attempt to seize the heads of the Dutch government was foiled, but the attack did spread confusion and panic. Luftwaffe raids on Rotterdam pummelled the city and spread additional panic among the Dutch. Only one Panzer division could be spared for the ground attack on The Netherlands, but this force was ample for the task, and, in spite of the dispatch of a French division to aid The Netherlands, the Dutch army was forced to capitulate after five days of fighting.

The proximity of the Dutch border to Belgium made it imperative that the Belgian bridges be taken before sentries, forewarned by the invasion of their neighbor, could blow the bridges. Again, German paratroops were employed to foil the defender's plans. In all cases where paratroops were engaged the Germans secured the bridges before they could be destroyed. In some instances these attacks looked like scenes in an adventure film. In one case German paratroops pulled the sputtering fuse from a charge just before it reached the detonator. In another, using a trenchcoat disguise, a German paratrooper passing himself off as a civilian killed the unsuspecting sentry with a pistol shot at close range. Perhaps the most audacious action was against the Belgian fort of Eben Emael. This fort, which guarded the Albert Canal, was of great strategic importance. Therefore, a small contingent of German paratroops were landed by glider on the roof of the fort. They subdued the anti-aircraft personnel on the roof, blew up the casements with a new type of plastic explosive, and pinned down the fort's garrison until the main German forces arrived.

The bold use of parachute troops and air transport troops facilitated the rapid movement of German forces into Belgium, and the use of such troops led to the proliferation of alarmist reports. Parachutists were reported sighted everywhere, and many civilians panicked. Railroad stations were crowded with hysterical refugees, and the road systems were filled by fleeing civilians. Clogged roads meant intolerable delays, and it proved difficult to keep the lines of transportation clear for the rapid movement of military personnel and equipment to the rapidly changing front. Belgian refugees spilled over into France, and French civilians, alarmed by the exodus from Belgium, joined the growing flood of refugees rushing to find a safe spot far from the sounds of war.

German forces were less encumbered by refugees. With ruthless efficiency they cleared the roadway of stragglers by strafing the roads with aircraft. Tank commanders, when faced with clogged roadways, would open up with machine-gun fire causing the refugees to leap for the ditches. Despite civilian panic and the growing tide of refugees, the Allied Command was certain that Plan D would prove successful.

This certainty was not unduly shaken when Guderian's XIX Panzer Army reached the Meuse River near Sedan on May 13. Using air support to neutralize the efforts of the French defenders, a division of Panzer infantry was ferried across the river in rubber rafts. The Panzer infantry secured and expanded a bridgehead on the west bank while engineers rushed to finish a bridge across the river. By the 14th only one division was across the river, and a single bridge linked them to the main German forces. The Germans were successful in defending the bridge against air attack, and by late afternoon all three Panzer

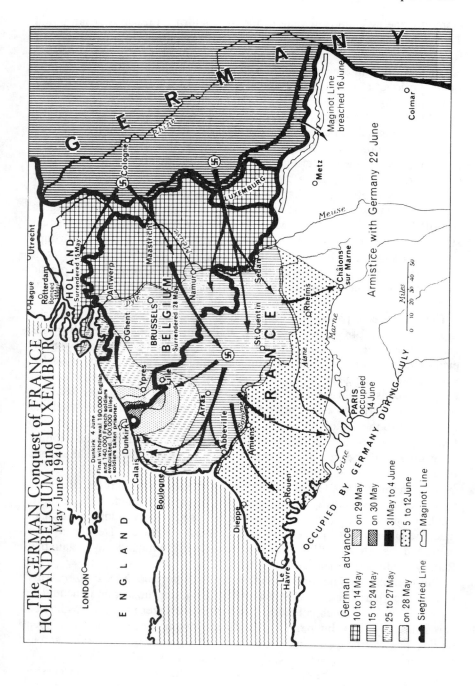

The GERMAN Conquest of FRANCE
HOLLAND, BELGIUM and LUXEMBURG
May - June 1940

German advance
10 to 14 May
15 to 24 May
25 to 27 May
on 28 May
on 29 May
on 30 May
31 May to 4 June
5 to 12 June
Maginot Line
Siegfried Line

OCCUPIED BY GERMANY DURING JULY

Final withdrawal 190,000 English
and 140,000 French soldiers
evacuated. 100,000 Allied
soldiers taken prisoner.

Dunkirk 4 June

PARIS
occupied
14 June

Armistice with Germany 22 June

Maginot Line
breached 16 June

Miles
0 10 20 30 40 50

divisions had crossed the Meuse. Permission was secured for further advance, a 24-hour reconnaissance in force, and, by the 16th, Guderian's three divisions were augmented by four other Panzer divisions which had crossed the Meuse at Montherme and Dinant. As the seven Panzer divisions reached the Oise River, a halt was called. Hitler and his General Staff did not share Guderian's view that a tank force could operate independently and were overly concerned that the Allies would launch a flank attack and destroy the Panzer force. Therefore, the advance was delayed for two days while an infantry force was marched into position to guard the southern flank of the German thrust.

On the Allied side, the rapid German advance came as a great surprise. However, most of the Allied decision makers calculated that the Germans would be forced to pause and regroup. Therefore, there was no sense of urgency in their planning. That Premier Paul Reynaud of France was concerned at the pace of events was evidenced when, on May 16, he replaced General Gamelin with General Maxime Weygand. General Weygand did not take command until the 19th, but by that time the line in Belgium was already cracking, and Guderian's force was only one day from the English Channel. In short, conservatism in military thinking existed on both sides, however, Guderian's successes pulled the rest of the German army with him. In the Allied camp, the replacement of Gamelin with Weygand meant only that a new commander would execute the old orders.

By the 20th of May the best of the Allied fighting forces were trapped in Belgium, and the German forces were moving northward to take Boulogne and Calais. A counterattack by regiments of the Royal Tank Corp at Arras gave the Germans some pause, but this weak thrust did little to ease the Allied plight.

On the 25th of May orders were given for an Allied withdrawal to the remaining escape port on the Channel, Dunkirk. The next day, the King of the Belgians, Leopold III, arranged for an armistice. The Belgian surrender on May 27 should have come as no surprise to the French and British. Leopold's small army was trapped and outnumbered, and, in Leopold's eyes, continued bloodshed was pointless. The surrender of the Belgian army certainly made clear to even the most confirmed optimist that the French and British forces were faced with only one alternative, evacuation; therefore, the Belgian surrender has given rise to many controversies. King Leopold was made something of a scapegoat in Allied circles. His unpopularity with the Allies was assured when he refused to leave his country and remained, under German custody, in Belgium until the end of the war. Recent evidence indicates that Leopold followed the dictates of his conscience and what appeared to him to be sound military thinking. Unfortunately for the King, his actions were reproachful to the Allies, and he was never again to occupy the Belgian throne.

The controversy over the Belgian surrender is nothing compared to the debate over Dunkirk. The successful evacuation of more than 300,000 Allied soldiers became a symbol of resistance and perseverance in Allied circles. What was, obviously, an Allied defeat prompted by their inability to meet the demands of modern mobile warfare was translated into a victory by retreat in the annals of history written by the ultimate victor. Operation Dynamo, the Dunkirk evacuation, was a marvel of planning and cooperation. Though German aircraft wrecked the docking facilities of the port, an efficient ferry service was developed. This service continued from May 26, the date of its authorization, until June 4. In all, 338,000 Allied soldiers were evacuated from Dunkirk. This successful evacuation left behind more than 100,000 soldiers, mostly French, of the rear guard who fought a very difficult holding action. However, those left behind were seen by many of the French as symbols of the treachery of their supposed ally. In total, nearly 500,000 Allied soldiers, mostly British, were evacuated from French ports during those last few days in May. These dramatic rescue operations were well-planned, brilliantly executed, and generally viewed as true heroic achievements. But the fact remains that Hitler's forces could have stopped them.

Why they did not has given rise to countless theories and speculations. The conventional view of the Dunkirk operation is that Hitler, fearful of a French counterattack on the German southern flank, wished to deploy his Panzers in that sector and left the destruction of the Allied forces at Dunkirk to the Luftwaffe. Air Marshal Hermann Göring's hand is seen in this decision; however, after the war, Luftwaffe sources revealed that Göring's air forces were not employed with full efficiency over Dunkirk. Again, it is argued that Hitler made the decision not to use the Luftwaffe's full capability in that sector. Still, others argue that even if the Panzers had been employed, they would have proved less than effective in the Dunkirk area because of the unsuitability of the terrain for armored attack. Such controversies lead to the ultimate debate. Did Hitler, for political reasons, allow the Allied forces to evacuate Dunkirk? Hitler had, in his Mein Kampf, expressed admiration for the British Empire. His remarks to his generals and, later, to the Reichstag evidenced an interest in coming to some kind of terms with Great Britain. Terms which would allow him a free hand on the continent, while preserving intact Britain's empire and worldwide interests. Since Hitler was such a complex man—a political man—many of his generals, in statements made after the war, concluded that Hitler held off at Dunkirk in the hopes of gaining some sort of peaceful settlement with Great Britain. Whatever the truth of such speculations (which are resented by more recent British works on the subject) the fact remained that Great Britain was in dire straits. Though she had rescued a large part of her expeditionary forces and a goodly number of Allied troops, her arsenal of materials had been sadly depleted. By the end of June 1940, England would be faced with the bleak prospect of continuing the war alone with only the Royal Navy and Royal Air Force to protect her against possible German invasion.

Invasion of France

In the south, the French defense preparations were in a shambles. With most of her armor having been lost in Belgium, France had to prepare a defense in depth with too few experienced troops and woefully inadequate equipment. The Maginot Line remained intact but was relatively useless. Reynaud urged his generals to prepare for a hard fight, even contemplating the evacuation of French forces to North Africa to continue the war there, but other political leaders were less than enthusiastic.

The German attack began on June 5, but it was not until June 9 that the breach on the Marne occurred. General Weygand immediately urged that France capitulate. This consideration was rejected by the Reynaud government, but the order was given to evacuate Paris. Reynaud chose Tours as his new capital but not for long. In spite of Churchill's urging for continued resistance, political opposition to Reynaud's demand to continue the war grew. On June 16, 1940, the Reynaud government was voted down and a new government formed under the leadership of Field Marshal Henri Phillipe Pétain, the hero of the famous World War I battle at Verdun. Shortly afterward, negotiations were begun between the two warring powers for an armistice. On June 25, 1940, the terms went into effect. Germany received three-fifths of France's territory to be occupied and administered by Germany. The remaining territory was under the control of the Pétain-Laval government at Vichy. The Vichy government was to continue to control France's overseas territories and retained control of the French fleet at Toulon and Oran.

France was to be subjected to other indignities as well. Mussolini belatedly declared war on France on June 10. Though the Italian attack on the Maginot Line was unsuccessful, Mussolini did secure Corsica, Savoy, and parts of Provence. The defeat was a great shock to the world, and, for a time, the French people heeded the words of Pétain who indicated that this defeat was a retribution against a decadent society. It is difficult to believe that, in those days, only a few people saw that the Vichy government could only be a puppet dancing to the strings pulled in Berlin. Yet, for a time, the French people swallowed the bitter pill of defeat and few paid heed to the voice of Charles de Gaulle who proclaimed a new, Free France. His June 30 broadcast from London was to have an important long-term effect, but in those dark days it seemed a lone voice in the wilderness.

For the Germans the victory had been almost miraculous. With minimal losses, Germany had gained what she had only dreamed of in 1914. A new European Order was now possible. Non-German peoples within this sphere of the new order were soon to learn that Germany and Germans were to be the chief beneficiaries of any new order that might come. Yet, in those early days, there were those who believed that conformity to the new order would eventually lead to a better life for all. The process of disillusionment with nazism was not to take a very long time. Still, it must be said that for most defeated nations, it appeared that the "Thousand Year Reich" was, indeed, a reality with which they must learn to live.

The victory which Hitler had predicted had come to pass with a rapidity that amazed the world. To attribute it all to the new techniques of Blitzkrieg is a simplification. What the German forces had, and the Allied forces did not, was a coherent plan and a coordination of effort. The organization of OKH was efficient and the German leaders were well aware of the role of the various elements in the attack plan. Luftwaffe officers understood the needs of the mechanized and infantry units and acted accordingly. Unlike the Allied forces, German officer training was postulated on the concept that the leadership should not only understand how the various elements of a battle force function but be able to command any of these elements. For example, Field Marshal Albert Kesselring, whose fame stems from the brilliant German defensive operations of the Italian campaign, was the commander of Luftflotte 2 (a German air fleet) during the Battle of Britain. Such versatility was not to be dreamed of in the Allied command structure. Coordination was also a German attribute. For example, Panzer groups maintained contact and coordinated attacks with their artillery support, something the Allies seemed not to learn until the very end of the war and only then on occasion.

Another factor that facilitated the German victory was the inherent difficulty of coalition warfare. Certainly, the Allies were fighting a common enemy, but neither their objectives nor their interests were the same. For example, General Robert van Overstraeten, King Leopold III's military adviser, realized that the French and British had no interest in defending all Belgian territory. Though Belgian forces fought well (German official after-action accounts noted that the Belgian army gave a better account for itself during the campaign than either the British or French armies), when French and British forces began to withdraw, without forewarning the Belgians, their leadership followed the rational course of surrender.

Coordination between the French and British commands was faulty at best. Clear lines of command were not established between the Allies and even coordination within the separate commands of the two armies was poor. Therefore, events on the battlefield were not the only important factor in the German victory. The problems of coalition warfare became evident during the campaign of 1940, but they were not to end with that campaign.

Battle of Britain

Hitler's generals had planned for the defeat of France, but neither they nor Adolph Hitler imagined that England would continue to hold out in the face of her utterly helpless military position. Hitler anticipated some sort of a compromise settlement and was ill-prepared for the intransigent attitude of his cross-Channel foe. The British decision to shunt aside German offers of a settlement were not merely bluff and bravado. The Royal Navy was a battle-ready fleet, and, since 1939, Air Marshal Hugh Dowding of the RAF had developed a fairly effective air defense system. This system incorporated modern fighter aircraft, primarily the *Hurricane* and the *Spitfire*, and a system of early detection known as radar. This technological innovation was made practical by the work of Sir Robert Watson-Watt and consisted of a device which could detect approaching aircraft at considerable distances. In the pre-transistor days of 1940, radar equipment was too heavy and bulky for use in aircraft. However, with considerable forethought, the British government had erected a network of radar sites which could cover the air approaches to the homeland. Information from such sites would be funneled to a central control system which would then alert fighter bases of an impending attack and direct their aircraft to intercept the attackers. To augment and supplement the radar sites an elaborate network of visual sighting stations was established to verify and support the electronic warning system. Further enhancements were made in 1940, such as the installation of air to ground radio communication sets in fighter aircraft. Other improvements were made during the course of the conflict, but initial preparations were to serve RAF Fighter Command well.

Great Britain's decision not to commit greater numbers of her fighter squadrons to the French campaign also proved prudent. The decision was made by the General Staff under recommendation of Air Chief Marshal Sir Cecil Newell. Simply put, RAF fighter forces in France were suffering tremendous losses without much effect on enemy movement. The drain on home defenses was not warranted by the results so the recommendation was accepted. Partisans of Air Marshal Dowding have dramatized this decision to the point of saying that Dowding threatened to resign if more planes were sent, but there seems to be more myth than fact in that story.

In July 1940, the Germans began making preparations for a cross-Channel attack on Great Britain. Such an amphibious operation would require an enormous number of transport ships and landing craft, neither of which were in abundance. Troops would have to be trained in landing operations. Additionally, all manner of supplies and materials had to be gathered to make such an undertaking feasible. It is evident from the preparations made that "Operation Sealion," the name given to the cross-Channel attack plan, did not inspire enthusiasm among Germany's military leaders. To accomplish such an operation it would be necessary to clear the Channel of the Royal Navy and effectively control the air space over Great Britain. If this could be done, then the attack might be successful. Therefore, it fell upon the Luftwaffe to accomplish the task of destroying British defenses through air power.

From July to the first of August, the Luftwaffe concentrated on attacking shipping in the Channel. Losses of merchant ships were enormous, but the Luftwaffe failed to lure out and destroy the RAF. On August 1, Hitler issued

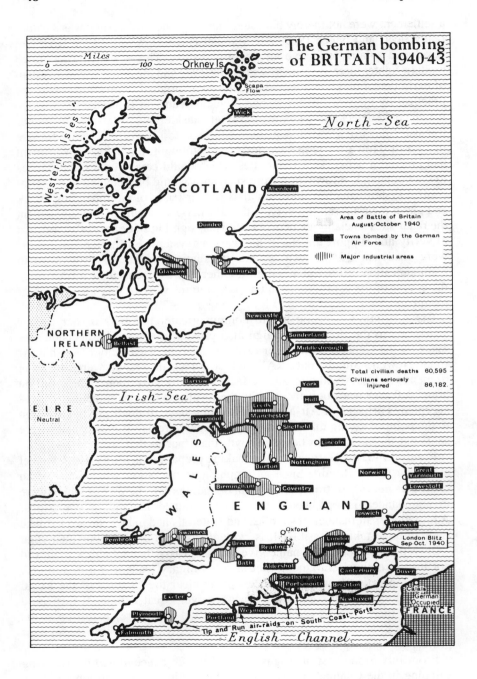

The German bombing
of BRITAIN 1940-43

Orkney Is

Scapa
Flow

Wick

North Sea

Western Isles

SCOTLAND

Aberdeen

Area of Battle of Britain
August-October 1940

Dundee

Towns bombed by the German
Air Force

Major industrial areas

Glasgow

Edinburgh

NORTHERN
IRELAND

Belfast

Newcastle

Sunderland

Middlesbrough

Barrow

Total civilian deaths   60,595
Civilians seriously
injured   86,182

EIRE
Neutral

Irish Sea

York

Hull

Leeds

Liverpool

Manchester

Sheffield

Lincoln

WALES

Burton

Nottingham

Norwich

Great
Yarmouth

Birmingham

Coventry

Lowestoft

ENGLAND

Ipswich

Pembroke

Swansea

Oxford

Harwich

London Blitz
Sep-Oct. 1940

Cardiff

Bristol

Reading

London

Chatham

Bath

Aldershot

Canterbury

Dover

Exeter

Southampton

Portsmouth

Brighton

Newhaven

Calais
German
Occupied
FRANCE

Plymouth

Weymouth

Portland

Tip and Run air-raids on South Coast Ports

Falmouth

English Channel

Miles
0   100

an order to destroy British air defenses as quickly as possible. On August 13, "Eagle Day," the Luftwaffe launched its first major attack on British airfields. The Battle of Britain had begun. From August 13 to September 7, the Luftwaffe attempted to gain air superiority. That they almost succeeded is amazing in the light of the difficulties the Luftwaffe faced. Bad weather and poor intelligence led the German command to overestimate the damage inflicted on British air bases and aircraft. Likewise, the Luftwaffe underestimated the importance of the British radar net. German scientists had pronounced the British radar crude; therefore, the important, yet vulnerable, radar stations were not considered prime targets of the bomber attacks. In fact, radar towers with their lattice construction were hard to destroy; however, other facilities were often hard hit. Radar stations and support facilities were vulnerable to collateral damage and their destruction could effectively shut down radar operations. Visual spotters helped fill the gap as radar stations were put out of action. Repeatedly, the Luftwaffe flew sorties against British defenses suffering heavy losses with each attack. By September the German flight crews were exhausted. The fighter pilots, largely confined to escort duty, were likewise exhausted and demoralized. Göring, a fighter pilot himself during World War I, tended to blame fighter pilots for the heavy losses sustained by Luftwaffe bombing fleets. In fact, due to limited fuel capabilities, fighter pilots had little time over the target to protect the bombers. The theoretical assumption that bombers, flying in tight formation, could protect themselves against fighters proved incorrect.

The RAF also sustained heavy losses. More important than lost aircraft, which could be replaced by highly efficient industrial production, was the loss of trained pilots. British pilots were highly trained with hundreds of hours of flying time and they were not easily replaced. Experienced pilots from Poland, Czechoslovakia, Commonwealth countries, and elsewhere augmented the RAF. Still, the losses were heavy, and by September 7 Air Marshal Dowding feared that if the German attacks continued for another 24 to 48 hours Fighter Command would lose its effectiveness, and the Luftwaffe would dominate British air space.

This did not occur, however. After a lull from September 8 to 14, 1940, the Luftwaffe switched the focus of its attacks from fighter bases to population centers. During September and October London and other cities were subject to repeated air attacks. "The Blitz," as the British called it, did great damage to British cities, particularly London and Coventry, and resulted in heavy loss of life for urban dwellers. In both daylight and night raids English cities were pummelled, yet fighter protection and anti-aircraft fire exacted a heavy toll on the Luftwaffe.

The idea that this shift of focus reflected a choice of strategic bombing over the tactical consideration of gaining air superiority over the British Isles was not, according to more recent scholarship, the German plan. Their hope was that by concentrating on civilian targets they would bring out the British fighters and destroy them. This, of course, did not happen, and the German plan had the effect of channeling the attack to fixed points which could be ascertained by radar, by visual sightings, and to some degree by Ultra intercepts. The latter played a minimal role as the Bletchley Park installation had yet to achieve the efficiency of decoding and analysis that was to come later in the war.

The raids on the cities had the positive effect of relieving Fighter Command from the constant scramble of intercepting German attacks. In fact, Fighter Command had little capacity to confront the Germans in night raids and German aircraft losses resulted more from massive anti-aircraft fire than from Fighter Command. However, the civilian population paid heavily. By the end of October 1940 the British had suffered 13,000 killed and 20,000 wounded in these raids. Night bombing was to continue until May 1941, but the challenge for control of air superiority had been met by the RAF.

The Battle of Britain had been won. The losses to the RAF had been heavy; 915 (the Germans claimed 3058) aircraft were lost, but heavier still were the German losses. Over 1,733 (the British claimed 2,698) German aircraft had been destroyed during the July to October offensive against Great Britain.

Without control of the air space over Great Britain, Operation Sealion could not move forward. In postponing Sealion, Britain was given a reprieve. At the same time, Hitler, who had already ordered planning for the attack on the Soviet Union, had shifted his center of attention to the East. It was this shift which has been judged by military historians to have been Hitler's greatest strategic error of the entire war. For in focusing attention to the East, he left a most implacable foe on his flank. Britain was to survive the defeats of 1940 and to become a principal in the war to destroy Germany's control over Europe.

War in Africa

Outside of Europe war raged in North Africa. Italian control of Libya and Ethiopia posed a danger to British lines of supply and communications in the Mediterranean and on the Red Sea approaches to the Suez Canal. Italy had half a million troops stationed in Libya; in East Africa, the British had no more than 50,000. Still, it was the British who began attacking and harassing Italian positions in Libya in June 1940. By September 1940, Marshal Rodolfo Graziani's army crossed over the Egyptian frontier and established a chain of defenses fifty miles inside Egyptian territory. There the Italian army camped until December 1940. British General (later Field Marshal) Sir Archibald Wavell decided that if the Italians were not going to attack, it was time to attack them. General O'Connor, commander of the Western Desert Force, led his troops on the offensive. Using Matilda tanks, the British penetrated the Italian defenses and began a series of mobile, flanking operations which, by February 1941, threatened to drive the Italian forces from North Africa. O'Connor's forces were called to a halt before they could carry their offensive to Tripoli. In March 1941, his Western Desert Force was stripped of troops who were then dispatched to Greece.

The weakening of British forces in North Africa was to have a disastrous effect there, while Churchill's dispatching of troops to Greece did little to protect that country from the German attack which came in April 1941. During that month, a new aspect was added to the desert war when General (later Field Marshal) Erwin Rommel and his "Afrika Korps" launched an attack which drove the British from Libya.

In July 1940, Italian forces moved across the Eritrean border to occupy a few miles of Sudanese territory then stopped and began developing defensive positions. In August, Italian forces invaded British Somaliland and drove the small British defense force from the port city of Berbera where they were evacuated by sea to Kenya.

British forces pushed the Italians from the Sudanese border town of Ballabat but were checked at Metemma by a strong Italian force. In January, Emperor Haille Salassie of Ethiopia, was flown into that country to help raise forces in the Gondar area to overthrow Italian rule there. In February, British forces attacking from Kenya entered Italian Somaliland and took Mogadishu on the 25th. In March, a force landed at Berbera from Aden and drove Italian forces from British Somaliland, and marched toward Jijiga in Ethiopia. On April 6, British forces took the capital city of Addis Ababa. In May 1941, the Lion of Judea, Emperor Haille Salassie, made a triumphal return to his capital.

Fighting was more fierce in the north, but British and Allied forces took Assmara, Eritrea, on April 1. Massawa fell on April 8, 1941. On May 19, the Duke of Aosta surrendered his forces at Amba Alagi. Curiously enough the Duke's forces were in a defensible position and could have, in fact, been more than a match for the British, but he chose to surrender. It is true that the Italian army became the object of ridicule during the later part of the war, but they demonstrated fighting ability when they were well led by Rommel in the North African campaign. Left to their own, the leadership of the Italian army seemed uninspired and uninspiring. Inferior equipment and poor support facilities added to the problems of the Italian army.

The Duke's surrender did not mark the end of the Ethiopian campaign, and it was not until late November 1941, that General Nasi surrendered his forces at Gondar ending this phase of the war. Thus, British, Commonwealth, and Free French forces had cleared East Africa of Italian troops. The East African campaign is often ignored as but a small interlude in a greater war, however, it did clear the important approaches to the Suez Canal from the South and East, but the largest threat to this supply line was to come from the West.

Hitler Prepares for "Operation Barbarossa"

Though the war in Africa was yet to begin in earnest, in Europe Hitler began making serious preparations for the attack on the U.S.S.R. This plan, designated "Case 21" or "Operation Barbarossa," was to begin in March of 1941 but was postponed until May and, in fact, actually began June 22, 1941. This delay has been explained by some writers as the result of the dispatch of British troops to Greece. Their argument is that the sending of British troops into Greece, while it weakened her North African forces, prompted Hitler to dispatch troops to Greece and thus delay the attack on the U.S.S.R. This delay, it is argued, meant that the German forces would be stopped by the cruel winter of 1941 before they could gain Moscow.

In large part, this theory is a justification for Churchill's act of reinforcing Greek forces at the expense of the North African campaign. The results were so disastrous as to cast doubts on Churchill's strategic ability. While there are those who think of Churchill as something of a strategic genius—Sir Winston, himself, was counted as one of these—there is grave reason to doubt the wisdom of his decision in this and other instances.

Hitler, in preparing for the Barbarossa operation, had worked hard to protect his Balkan flanks. By threat and diplomacy he had secured the support of Bulgaria, Rumania, and Yugoslavia. He had likewise prepared for an operation in Greece to secure Thrace and Salonika. This area, he reasoned, was vulnerable to attack by British forces and should be secured. This limited attack on Greece was not to be; events intervened to make it impossible. The plan of limited advance was to become an all-out offensive.

On March 27, 1941, as operations against Southern Thrace were about to begin, a *coup d'etat* occurred in Belgrade. General Dusan Simovich repudiated the German-Yugoslav agreement, demanded and received the abdication of Prince Paul, and appeared ready to secure an agreement with the Western Powers. This Hitler could not allow, and Panzer forces were sent to take over Yugoslavia. On April 6, 1941, Hitler's Panzers attacked Yugoslavia and Greece. The armored attack proved irresistible, and by April 27, Athens fell. The British forces sent to Greece had been unable to stem the tide of armor and had to be evacuated to Crete and Egypt. On May 20, 1941, German air transports dropped paratroops on the island of Crete. In the battle which followed, Britain met another defeat. After six days of heavy fighting, General Freyberg, the commander of British forces on Crete, reported that his situation was hopeless. On May 31, 1941, the last British troops were evacuated from Crete.

The swift victory in the Balkans secured Hitler's flank from attack, but it was not accomplished without cost. In all, 5,000 Germans were killed or wounded in securing Yugoslavia and Greece. The losses to the Allied cause amounted to hundreds of thousands of captured soldiers and thousands more in casualties. The German losses seem small in comparison to the territory

The GERMAN CONQUEST of
YUGOSLAVIA and GREECE
6-30 April 1941

gained. Also, Hitler's successful Greek campaign embarrassed his ally, Mussolini, whose forces had been bogged down in Albania and sorely pressed by the Greeks.

The campaign in Crete, though viewed as the greatest airborne invasion in history, proved more costly. Four thousand of Student's paratroopers were killed in the invasion and more than 5,000 wounded. Though British losses were three times that number, the sacrifice of so many of his elite forces gave Hitler pause. Never again was he to use these forces in such a dramatic way. He seemed to feel that the day of the airborne invasion was over and turned a deaf ear to Student's plans to seize Malta. This reluctance to use his elite forces is seen by some historians as the greatest Allied gain to emerge from the Balkan campaign. For had Malta been taken, as Student planned, the war in the Mediterranean and North Africa might have taken a more dangerous turn for the Western Allies.

Finally, another footnote of the Balkan campaign was the creation of a partisan movement in Yugoslavia. This resistance movement, beset by inter-necine conflicts between rival groups, was powerful enough to harass the German occupation authorities. Through the years of occupation, six separate offensives were launched by the Germans in an attempt to destroy the Yugoslav partisan bonds of Tito (Josip Broz) and the Chetniks led by Draža Mihajlović. The resistance movement was to continue until the eventual withdrawal of German forces from Yugoslavia.

Summary

In May 1940, the Phony War ended with a vengeance. The Netherlands was overrun and forced to surrender in five days. German forces foiled the Belgian defense and pushed into central Belgium. In conformity with Plan D, the Allies rushed their best troops into Belgium to stop the German attack. In so doing, they moved into a trap for the attack through the Ardennes occurred so quickly that in six days the Allied forces were in great danger of being cut off. The Allied leaders, unprepared for the rapid attack of the Nazi Blitzkrieg, were unable to respond rapidly enough to avert disaster. However, it is also true that the German General Staff was fearful that the deep armored penetration behind Allied lines might bring defeat and delayed rather than pressed the attack. The two-day delay was not sufficient to allow the Allied commanders to counterattack successfully, and Guderian's forces succeeded in reaching the Channel by the 19th of May. The Allied forces in Belgium were cut off. By June, the Allies had managed a successful evacuation from Dunkirk and other French ports. The German forces then turned to cut through the French defenses, and by June 25, 1940, France had fallen. The Vichy government took over what remained of France. Few French people, at that time, heeded the call to continued resistance advocated by de Gaulle's shadow "Free France" in exile in Great Britain.

In July, Hitler's forces, frustrated by Britain's continued intransigence, began the preliminaries of what was to be an invasion of the British Isles—Operation Sealion. The preliminaries consisted of an attempt to neutralize British air and sea power to allow for a cross-Channel invasion. The air battle which developed saw the RAF defenses sorely tested. Superior planning and technology gave the RAF defenders something of an edge, but continued attacks wore down the defense to a dangerous degree. However, the Germans, still seeking to destroy the RAF, began attacking London and other urban areas in the hopes that aerial bombardment would bring out the RAF in concentration and facilitate its destruction. Instead, the Blitz brought relief to the RAF defense forces and ultimately led to an abandonment of Sealion.

Frustrated by the defeat in the Battle of Britain, Hitler turned his attention to what he saw as a primary German objective, the invasion of the U.S.S.R. Preparation for operation "Barbarossa" had been carefully made, but success was, in part, dependent on a secure position in the Balkans. Through intimidation, promises of territory, and diplomacy, Hitler had seemingly secured his position in the Balkans. This was upset by a surprise coup in Yugoslavia, and the new government's attempt to move Yugoslavia into the Allied camp. Hitler responded by ordering an all-out offensive into the Balkans, brushing aside with ease the armies of Yugoslavia, Greece, and the British forces sent to aid the Greeks. German paratroops took over Crete in a costly operation, and German forces now had full control of the Balkan area. The British venture into Greece had cost them heavily, but has been justified, rather speciously, because it served to delay the invasion of the Soviet Union. This contention is doubtful for a variety of reasons, but there is little doubt that the losses of the Crete campaign caused Hitler to be cautious in the use of paratroops. This cautiousness was to have an adverse effect on German operations in North Africa. Likewise, the Yugoslav invasion was to lead to the creation of a partisan movement there which was a source of irritation to Germany throughout the war.

In North Africa, the Italian move against the British in Egypt brought only disaster for Graziani's forces. Wavell, Middle East commander, was well served by General O'Connor whose Western Desert Force drove back the Italians and, by February 1941, threatened Tripoli. O'Connor's forces were stripped to furnish the abortive expeditionary group to Greece. By April, with the arrival of Rommel and the Afrika Korps, British forces in North Africa faced a skilled and relentless foe, and their gains were wiped out; their armies sent reeling back to the Egyptian border. In East Africa, Allied forces, largely British and Commonwealth troops with some Free French forces, battled for Somaliland, Eritrea, and Ethiopia. After some initial reverses, the Allied forces secured the Horn of Africa, and all Italian resistance in East Africa came to an end by November 1941.

Suggested Reading

Beaufre, Andre (Trans. Desmond Flower). *The Fall of France*. New York, 1967.
    A personal narrative of the defeat and the war years in France.
Colville, John. *The Fringes of Power, 10 Downing Street Diaries, 1939-1955*. New
    York, 1985. An account by Chamberlain's and Churchill's private secretary and
    a close friend of Sir Winston. His observations on those dark days of 1939-40
    are particularly interesting, especially so for those who like the "mouse in the
    corner" view of great events.
de Gaulle, Charles. *Call to Honor*. New York, 1955. A vivid account of how France
    was not prepared to fight in 1940.
Ellis, John. *Brute Force: Allied Strategy and Tactics in the Second World War*. New
    York, 1990. Ellis covers both the Allied and Axis Powers during World War
    II and is informative, critical and a bit heavy on his thesis. It is a different approach
    and a valuable critique of the conduct of the war from beginning to end.
Hough, Richard and Denis Richards. *The Battle of Britain, The Greatest Air Battle
    of World War II*. New York, 1989. This recent publication has a great deal of
    information and addresses many of the controversies of the battle with an authority
    found lacking in most of the earlier accounts.
Liddell Hart, B. H. *History of the Second World War*. New York, 1970. This is a
    standard. The first four parts cover the early phases of the war.

5

The Pacific War
December 1941 to April 1942

T he Pacific War had its beginnings long before 1941. In 1931, Japanese forces had moved into Manchuria. In 1932, they attacked China, and by 1937, Japanese armies were bogged down in a land war in China. In large part, Japanese aggression in Asia was designed to secure the economic resources needed to make that nation a viable industrial state. Japan's aggressive acts had been denounced by the League of Nations but that had not kept her from engaging in continued expansionism. To the mind of the *militarists*, a group which was to gain more and more power during the 1930s, the answer to Japan's economic vulnerability was to secure by force of arms those lands and resources she needed. Japan was, after all, devoid of most of the energy resources and raw materials necessary to an industrial power, therefore, expansion into China seemed crucial for Japan's survival.

The United States deplored Japanese actions in China and had tried, in a limited way, to support the Nationalist government of China. Chiang Kai Shek, China's beleaguered leader, was faced with two implacable foes, the Japanese invaders and the Chinese Communists led by Mao Tse-tung. He was able to destroy neither, yet managed to hold out. The failure to secure China frustrated the Japanese military. It became increasingly apparent that in order to secure China, Japan must also control Southeast Asia. Opportunity to do just that came in 1940 with the fall of France and the establishment of the Vichy government. By September of 1940, Japan signed an agreement with Germany and Italy, the Tripartite Pact, which assured Japan a free hand in Asia. In April 1941 she signed a five-year nonaggression pact with the Soviet Union. Thus assured against attack from the North, Japan was free to follow an expansionist policy in Asia. By March 1941 further agreements were signed which gave Japan a favorable strategic position to move into Southeast Asia. In July 1941 she occupied Indochina. This action made the British position in Malaya, Singapore, and Burma very vulnerable to attack. So, too, were the Dutch East Indies and the Philippine Islands threatened by the Japanese occupation of Indochina.

Japanese aggression in Asia was cause for alarm in the United States. As early as March 1940 the United States began advancing loans to China. Later, the export of war materials, airplane gasoline, scrap iron, and the like were embargoed or licensed. These actions were not specifically directed against the Japanese, though they had the effect of cutting off an important source of supply to the Japanese. In response to the Japanese occupation of French Indochina, in July 1941 the United States, Great Britain, and The Netherlands froze Japanese assets in their respective countries. In August 1941 the United States dispatched a lend-lease mission to China. Thereafter, the Chinese received American war materials, and trained pilots were allowed to "volunteer" to help the Chinese fend off Japanese air attacks. These pilots, recruited largely from the military, were, in the legal sense of the term, mercenaries who were to be paid a bonus for any Japanese planes they shot down. This force, popularly known as the "Flying Tigers," was under the command of Claire Chenault and was officially designated as the American Volunteer Group. The group's exploits attracted popular attention in the United States where they were looked upon as defenders of the hapless Chinese people who had been subjected to vicious air attacks by the Japanese. The United States also furnished to the Chinese the best fighter aircraft in the American arsenal, the P-40. The "P" meant pursuit plane and was the alphabet designation used by the U.S. Army Air Corps during World War II to identify fighter aircraft.

In light of these developments it was obvious that the United States had stepped over the boundary of neutrality. From the Japanese point of view, war became a necessity for survival. The American demands, transmitted through diplomatic channels, were seen by the Japanese as devices to block the Japanese dream of hegemony in Asia. In fact, the Roosevelt Administration was well aware that the Japanese were playing a game of negotiation while preparing for war. The Japanese diplomatic code, "Purple," had, in large part, been broken by American cryptographers. In the late 1920s a burglary of the code room of the Japanese Embassy in Washington had given U.S.

intelligence an understanding of the Japanese encoding machines. When war clouds loomed this information was put to use in monitoring Japanese diplomatic radio traffic between Tokyo and Washington. An intelligence operation, known as "Magic," was set up to keep the Administration apprised of Japanese diplomatic strategy. But "Magic" was to be less important in monitoring the military strategy which accompanied Japanese diplomatic endeavors because such information was not forwarded to Japanese diplomats in Washington.

For Americans, the period between May 1940 to December 1941 was one of anxiety. The Roosevelt Administration was fearful that German successes in Europe would undermine the security of the United States. When France fell, anxiety gave way to alarm. Sympathy for the plight of Great Britain was expressed in various ways. Broadcasts from London emphasized the spirit of resistance evidenced by Londoners under the "Blitz," and America's private citizens responded by sending food and clothing as "Bundles to Britain." The Churchill government knew full well that continued British resistance was dependent upon securing a strong ally. The United States was a most likely ally, but certain obstacles had first to be overcome. Throughout the 1930s the United States had followed a policy of neutrality. In 1939 a neutrality act was passed which forbade American ships from entering a war zone. However, the reliance on neutrality was seen as a poor substitute for security. From the summer of 1940 through November 1941, the neutrality act was stretched beyond the breaking point. During this period, the United States opened its arsenals to the British—furnishing arms, vessels, and war materials in exchange for bases in the North Atlantic and the Caribbean. A lend-lease agreement, announced in December 1940, was ultimately to mean that the United States pledged unlimited support to Great Britain. In August 1941, a joint statement termed the *Atlantic Charter* was released. This so-called charter was not a binding treaty, but it did spell out the philosophy and objectives of the two governments and was to constitute an "understanding" which was to be formalized in treaties and documents drawn up during the war. Discussions were held and tentative agreements were also reached as to the war strategy which the Americans and British would abide by if and when the United States entered the war. This understanding called for setting priorities in the grand strategy of a world conflict. The first priority would be victory in Europe; the Asian-Pacific area was to be given secondary priority. This agreement was not made public, yet the dispute over priorities and objectives would have a dramatic impact on the strategic Allied planning of the war to come.

By the spring of 1941 the likelihood of war with Germany was a topic of general conversation. In June of that year German and Italian assets in the United States were frozen, and the Axis Powers reciprocated. This action was partially in response to the sinking of the American ship, *Robin Moor*, by a German U-boat. By this time the United States had begun placing deck guns on American merchant ships. This was the practice Woodrow Wilson had established before the United States entry in World War I, yet, such action was in violation of the rules of neutrality. Therefore, from the standpoint of international law, armed American merchant vessels were in violation and were subject to attack. The subtleties of international law may have escaped the average American, yet, in spite of hostile actions at sea, many Americans were reluctant to become involved in war. The "America First" movement urged noninvolvement and argued that America's best hope for security lay in making the hemisphere a fortress to fend off aggressors. Many prominent Americans feared that entanglement in a European war would not be beneficial to the United States. The memory of the failure of the Versailles Treaty, the disillusionment which came after the euphoria of Wilsonian idealism, were lessons not to be ignored. Others argued that in siding with Great Britain we were supporting a nation which had little or no hope of survival against the forces of the Axis Powers. Arguments and counter-arguments proliferated. It is now known that the British worked assiduously trying to convince the American people to side with their cause; however, America prepared for war with reluctance. In spite of the collapse of neutrality, the philosophy that we would help Britain in every way "short of war" appeared to dominate the thinking of both ordinary citizens and their representatives in Congress. All such blandishments and debates ended on December 7, 1941 with the Japanese attack on Pearl Harbor.

Attack on Pearl Harbor

The Japanese attack on Pearl Harbor brought a solidarity of purpose to America that she had long lacked. Even today, the attitudes concerning the attack follow closely the words of President Roosevelt who noted that the attack of December 7 was a day which "would live in infamy." Yet, the military and political leaders of the United States were fully aware that war was coming. Nor should they have been surprised that it came out of the blue on a bright Sunday morning against an installation that was most vulnerable. However, historical hindsight must not be overused or abused. We now know the Japanese plan which called for a paralyzing stroke against the American fleet was a necessary preliminary for that nation's grand strategy of expansionism.

In order to understand the Japanese attack it is necessary to delve into the complexities of Japanese strategic thinking. The thirst for expansionism has often been laid at the feet of the Japanese army. Certainly, the ascendance of General Hideki Tojo to the position of Minister of War in mid-1940 set the stage for war. Though the Japanese army leadership had thought of expansionism relative to China and Siberia, the events of 1940 made it apparent to them that Japan needed the resources to be found in Southeast Asia. To obtain these they needed the support of the navy.

For many years the Japanese navy had realized that hegemony in Asia would require a confrontation with the United States. Japanese naval doctrine was based on the concept of a "decisive battle." In the case of Japan such a battle would be a surface fleet battle taking place in the Western Pacific against the American fleet, and exercises were held each year to practice such a battle scenario. The Japanese concept of naval warfare was in keeping with the thinking of the British and American navies. In fact, the Japanese emulated British doctrine to the point that English was used to give commands aboard vessels at sea. This practice was abandoned as war loomed and nationalist fervor swept Japan in the late 1930s. Therefore, as had other modern navies, the Japanese concentrated on capital ships. In fact, by the mid-1930s they had planned for the development of a new line of super-battleships which would be crucial in the decisive battle envisioned by Japanese naval leaders. The first of these, the battleship *Yamato*, was commissioned shortly after the Pearl Harbor attack.

Carriers had not been entirely neglected; one critic has noted that Japan built aircraft carriers because the United States built aircraft carriers. Air power was the eyes of the fleet in the minds of surface fleet sailors, yet it had a greater use. One naval officer, Admiral Yamamoto, himself a surface fleet sailor, had vision enough to see the value of the carrier in modern warfare. When the Japanese navy, in what was termed the "eleventh hour," agreed to the war strategy of its army, Yamamoto was designated to devise a plan to neutralize the American fleet in harbor. To deliver such an attack, and to accomplish the broader mission of expansion, air power was a necessity. In January 1941, Yamamoto recruited the talents of brilliant young naval aviator Minoru Genda. Together they began devising a plan which would not only neutralize the enemies of Japan but secure her the resources she needed. By September 1941 the plan was complete. Therefore, when General Tojo assumed the position of Prime Minister in October of 1941 Japan was ready for war.

On the surface, the Japanese plan was both logical and reasonable. Her planners realized that the United States had great industrial power and even greater potential. However, the plan was postulated on the assumption that the United States would not endure a long and costly war in the Pacific. If, with one stroke, Japan could destroy America's seapower in the Pacific, she could then turn her attention to overrunning the crucial resource-ladened Southeast Asian territories. With British and American seapower neutralized, she could then overrun the island chains which dot the Pacific and develop a defense in depth to protect her control over Indochina, Malaya, the East Indies, and the Philippines. From Thailand she could secure Burma and thus threaten India; in the Pacific, the securing of New Guinea and the Solomons would cut off and neutralize Australia.

With all this accomplished the vast Pacific would be Japan's defense against attack. Though it was obvious that the United States would respond with force, it was reasoned that for the United States to reconquer these territories would consume much time and would necessitate huge sacrifices in personnel and material. The war would become one of attrition. Eventually, the United States would be forced to negotiate a settlement which would leave Japan in control of those areas necessary for her survival and growth. In short, China and Southeast Asia would be part of a new order, the "Greater Southeast Asia Co-Prosperity Sphere." In military terms one could say that the surprise attack on Pearl Harbor was but the mobile phase of a strategy of exhaustion which would lead to a negotiated settlement of a war which had a limited objective. Rather than hoping to secure all of Asia and the Pacific, the Japanese aim was to assure her island peoples of hegemony over the most populous, richest part of that vast geographical area. Like so many plans, logic failed to take account of all elements, and the response provoked was not the one anticipated. In short, if the leaders of the United States were misled by arrogance and carelessness in expecting the Japanese to bow to economic and diplomatic pressures, the Japanese were much more dangerously misguided in denigrating the willingness of the United States to respond with a total commitment of resources and a dogged determination to avenge what was popularly considered an unprovoked, infamous attack on her territory.

The attack on Pearl Harbor had been carefully planned. On November 27, 1941, the Japanese armada, composed of six fast carriers and numerous escort vessels, sailed from its base in Japan. The strike force traveled under radio silence and followed a northerly route toward Hawaii. By so doing, they avoided normal shipping lanes and sailed through empty seas toward their destination. Further security came with the advent of the cover of a storm system which masked the movement of Admiral Nagumo's attack force. The disappearance of the Japanese carriers puzzled and worried American naval intelligence, but it was generally believed that the Japanese were planning an attack on Southeast Asia, and the carrier fleet was thought to be in those southern waters. In the early morning hours of December 7, 1941, American destroyers discovered that Japanese submarines were operating near the entrance of Pearl Harbor. Two of these craft were sunk, but such submarine activity did not fully alert authorities to the possibility of an attack. At 7:00 A.M., one of the six radar stations recently erected by the United States Army on Oahu reported a large flight of aircraft approaching the island. Since the operators were inexperienced, it was supposed that the approaching flight was a contingent of B-17 bombers which were being flown in from the mainland.

Thus, circumstances conspired to allow the Japanese attack force to approach its target virtually undetected. This attack force consisted of torpedo planes, high-level bombers, and dive bombers accompanied by a protective fighter screen. The raid began at 7:55 A.M. and ended at 8:40 A.M. when a second wave of high-level and dive bombers struck Pearl Harbor. But it was the first

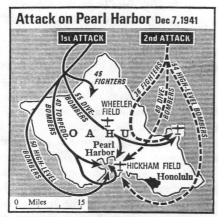

Attack on Pearl Harbor Dec 7.1941

1st ATTACK

2nd ATTACK

45 FIGHTERS

36 FIGHTERS

55 FIGHTERS

55 DIVE-BOMBERS

40 TORPEDO-BOMBERS

80 DIVE-BOMBERS

50 HIGH-LEVEL BOMBERS

54 HIGH-LEVEL BOMBERS

WHEELER FIELD

O A H U

Pearl Harbor

HICKHAM FIELD

Honolulu

0   Miles   15

Invasion of Hong Kong Dec 8/26.1941

JAPANESE OCCUPIED CHINA

(NEW TERRITORIES)

GINDRINKERS LINE

Kowloon

Lantao

Victoria

Hong Kong

0   Miles   10

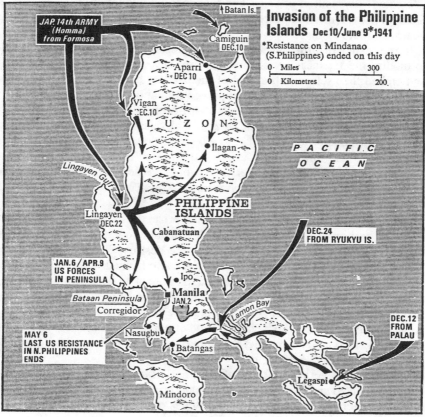

Batan Is.

Invasion of the Philippine Islands Dec 10/June 9*,1941

*Resistance on Mindanao (S.Philippines) ended on this day

0   Miles   300

0   Kilometres   200

JAP. 14th ARMY (Homma) from Formosa

Camiguin DEC.10

Aparri DEC 10

Vigan DEC.10

L U Z O N

Ilagan

Lingayen Gulf

P A C I F I C
O C E A N

PHILIPPINE ISLANDS

Lingayen DEC.22

Cabanatuan

DEC.24 FROM RYUKYU IS.

JAN.6/APR.9 US FORCES IN PENINSULA

Ipo

Bataan Peninsula

Manila JAN.2

Corregidor

Lamon Bay

DEC.12 FROM PALAU

MAY 6 LAST US RESISTANCE IN N.PHILIPPINES ENDS

Nasugbu

Batangas

Legaspi

Mindoro

wave, the torpedo attack, which did most to destroy American vessels in the harbor. By 1:30 in the afternoon the Japanese aircraft had returned to their carriers, and the fleet steamed unharried toward Japan.

The strike had been disastrous for the American fleet; four battleships were sunk, four more heavily damaged. Numerous other smaller craft were sunk or damaged. Aircraft losses were equally heavy — 188 planes destroyed, over 60 planes damaged — and more than 3,400 Americans were killed or wounded. The Japanese losses were light; 23 planes destroyed and approximately 70 damaged. Fewer than 100 Japanese were killed in the attack.

The success of the Japanese attack owes much to careful preparation. Admiral Yamamoto and his staff had evaluated intelligence reports as to the disposition of the American land and sea forces on Oahu and had planned the attack accordingly. The sea pattern of the American defense forces was well established, and the Japanese were not amiss in expecting the traditional "Sunday" disposition of ships and planes to be unaltered on December 7. Sunday, in the American peacetime military environment was a day of minimal watch and late rising.

In the matter of ordinance to be used careful preparation had been made to modify the Japanese aerial torpedoes so they would not plunge too deep and embed themselves in the mud of the shallow harbor. This was a lesson learned from the British who had employed similar tactics in destroying Italian ships in Taranto harbor in November 1940. Admiral Kimmel was well aware of the particulars of the Taranto attack, and was aware that Pearl Harbor, like Taranto, could be vulnerable to a torpedo bomber attack. However, he opted not to use torpedo nets arguing that speed of movement was more important than the use of cumbersome protective devices. This decision, as did so many others, helped to compound the American tragedy that was Pearl Harbor.

Fortuitously for the United States its chief prize, the carrier fleet, was absent from the harbor at the time of the attack. Yamamoto had hoped that at least three of the six American carriers would be destroyed in the raid but was to be disappointed. The American forces were also lucky that Admiral Nagumo resisted the urging of his staff to launch a third attack to destroy the oil storage tanks which serviced the American Pacific fleet. Yet, the Japanese had accomplished a major part of their objective in eliminating a large part of America's Pacific fleet. So began a period of unremitting Japanese successes, and for the next several months the Imperial High Command would ride on the crest of the wave of victory.

In evaluating the after effects of the Pearl Harbor attack one result was both unexpected and curious, but, above all, crucial. On December 11, 1941, Germany declared war on the United States of America. Foreign Minister Ribbentrop delivered and read this declaration to the American Charge in Berlin. According to eyewitness accounts Hitler, who had previously sought not to antagonize the Americans, was happy to declare war upon the United

States. Supposedly, this declaration of war was to show Germany's commitment to the Tripartite Pact, yet the Pact bound Germany to go to war only if Japan was attacked. Certainly, in his book *Mein Kampf*, Hitler had noted that involving the United States in World War I was an unfortunate mistake of the Imperial German Government. Yet, in December 1941, he seemed to welcome war with the United States. Some writers have noted that the publication of the so-called "Plan Victory" was a casual factor in this decision. The "Plan" was a U.S. War Department master plan delineating the strategy of the war to come. Among the actions projected by this plan was a timetable which called for an invasion of Germany in 1943. The plan, published in the *Chicago Tribune*, angered Hitler, according to some writers, and prompted him to support his Japanese allies after the Americans declared war upon them. It is difficult to know what motivated Hitler to declare war. Yet his decision was a dramatic departure from his previous policy of trying not to overly irritate the Americans. For the Roosevelt Administration, however, Hitler's seemingly enthusiastic move to war eliminated the problem of initiating a move to ask Congress for a declaration of war against Germany. Whether Congress would have acquiesced, given the state of relations with Germany, without being forced into a European war is conjectural. Speculation aside, the United States was now involved in a World War.

Japanese Aggression in Asia

In keeping with the Yamamoto Plan the Japanese launched a series of coordinated attacks on American and British held possessions in Asia. The American garrison in the Philippines received news of attack on Pearl Harbor at 2:30 in the morning of December 8, Manila time. Preparations were made, and aircraft were launched in the early morning hours. However, these same aircraft were to be caught on the ground by Japanese bombers at 11:30 A.M. while in the process of refueling. In one swift attack the defenders of the Philippines were to lose most of their air support. On December 17, the few remaining B-17's were sent to Australia, and the navy deemed it wise to withdraw her few surface ships from Philippine waters. Thus the islands were bereft of both air and surface fleet support. It was the expectation of American planners that the Philippines could hold out until the garrison there could be resupplied and reinforced. Unfortunately, the Philippines were to fall long before the United States was prepared to do either.

With a compliment of 35,000 regular troops plus an ill-trained Philippine army of 110,000, General Douglas MacArthur was faced with a dilemma. His plan called for a total defense of the Philippines. Yet he had neither the troops nor the equipment to accomplish such an all-encompassing defense.

By December 10, 1941, General Homma, commander of the 14th Japanese Army, had landed troops on the northern coast of Luzon. With a total force of 57,000 men, Homma moved quickly to establish air bases and secure air superiority. On December 22, Homma landed his main body of troops, 47,000 men, at Lingayen Gulf only 120 miles from Manila. A smaller force landed at Lamon Bay on the 24th. As the Japanese forces marched toward Manila, they encountered only light resistance. On December 26, 1941, Manila was proclaimed an "open city," and American forces began their withdrawal to defensive positions on the Bataan Peninsula. On January 6, 1942, the withdrawal was complete. The battle for the Bataan Peninsula had begun.

Homma's forces had encountered some difficulties in their attack on the Philippines. Though battle casualties were light, malaria decimated the ranks of the 14th Army. Fortunately for Homma, American military intelligence wildly overestimated the number of Homma's forces and tended to discount the strength of their own defenses. Once on Bataan it was found that the American planners had underestimated the number of personnel (augmented by a large refugee population) that they needed to supply. More than 100,000 people were crowded onto this malarious peninsula. Soon hunger, malaria, and dysentery would greatly reduce the fighting effectiveness of the defenders of Bataan. From January 6 to February 8, 1942, Homma's forces attempted to breach the American defenses. Malaria, however, took its toll, and Homma's forces gave up the attack. Illness was not the only cause for the weakening of Homma's army, for the 48th Division was removed from his command and sent to augment the forces invading the Dutch East Indies. By March, Homma had only a few thousand troops on the line to bottle up American forces on Bataan. The Americans were unaware of Homma's weakness and were themselves limited in effective strength by disease and hunger. American morale hit a low point on March 10, 1942 when MacArthur was called to take command of Allied forces in Australia. General MacArthur turned over the Philippine command to General Wainwright. Roosevelt's decision to call MacArthur to Australia was a wise one, for he proved a most able strategist. Yet to those left behind on Bataan and Corregidor it was proof enough that the Philippines had been abandoned.

In late March Homma received reinforcements of over 20,000 fresh troops. On April 3, 1942, he launched an offensive which swept aside the American defenders. On April 9 General King, in command of the Bataan forces, surrendered. What followed has been termed the "Bataan Death March." Though General Homma was to deny later that his men had treated American prisoners savagely, it is evident from survivor accounts that in many instances noncoms in charge of prisoners allowed many to be beaten and murdered by soldiers under their charge. In part this has been attributed to the Japanese military code of conduct which saw surrender as more than dishonorable; it was unthinkable. Therefore, the prisoners were treated as sub-humans. However, this does not take into account the fair and equitable treatment often meted out to downed fliers and other prisoners by the Japanese. The pattern which emerges from the statements of survivors is one of indiscriminate

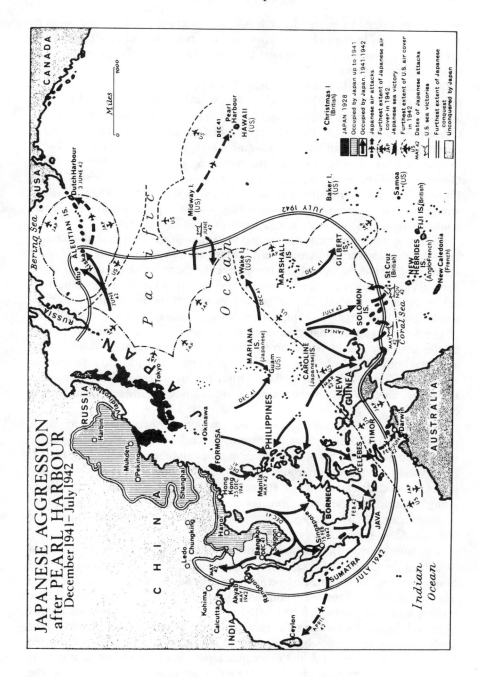

JAPANESE AGGRESSION
after PEARL HARBOUR
December 1941 – July 1942

brutality practiced by particular individuals and groups of Japanese soldiers on the prisoners in their charge. There is little evidence, however, that such brutality was curtailed or punished by either Japanese officers in the field or by higher headquarters.

General Wainwright's direct command was now reduced to the 15,000 man garrison on Corregidor. The island fortress was subjected to massive artillery and air bombardment which crumbled the island's defenses and made life unbearable in the tunnels which honeycombed the island. On May 5 attackers crossed the two miles of water separating Corregidor from the mainland and, in spite of heavy losses, breached the American defenses. On May 6, 1942, General Wainwright announced the surrender of all American forces in the Philippines. The campaign had cost the Americans over 95,000 killed, wounded, and captured. The Japanese losses were approximately 12,000 not counting those lost or incapacitated by disease.

For six months American forces had held against the Japanese attackers—considerably longer than would have other garrisons faced with a full-scale Japanese invasion. In fact, not all troops obeyed the surrender order and many guerrilla groups were to harass Japanese occupation forces throughout the war.

For the Imperial High Command, the victory in the Philippines had been too long and too costly. General Homma was blamed and he was relieved of combat command. (Later Homma would be found guilty of war crimes by the post-war Allied War Crimes Tribunal and sentenced to death for the atrocities committed by his forces during the Bataan Death March). Wainwright also was severely criticized by MacArthur for his surrender of Corregidor. However, General MacArthur came to realize that Wainwright had had no choice.

Hong Kong, the British Crown Colony, which planners believed might be able to hold for 90 days, was overrun by a reinforced division of Japanese infantry supported by air power and artillery in eighteen days. Nearly 12,000 British and Commonwealth troops were captured. The Japanese loss was 3,000 killed, wounded, and missing. The attack began on December 8, and Hong Kong's major defenses, the *Gindrinker's Line*, was penetrated on the 19th of December. On December 25 and 26, the entire garrison of Hong Kong was forced to surrender.

A greater blow to British power and prestige occurred when the so-called "Pearl of the Orient," Singapore, fell to the Japanese on February 15, 1942. Singapore was well protected on its seaward sides, but the Japanese force attacked across the causeway, and Singapore fell from the Malaya side. Many writers note that the British had failed to take account of the possibility that Singapore might indeed be vulnerable from the peninsula side. In actuality, studies had been made which pointed to that port's vulnerability from the landward side. Therefore, the news that Japan was given leave to transport troops through Thailand and were preparing an invasion force to cross the Gulf of Siam for an attack on the Malaya Peninsula was cause for an immediate

British response. A naval force, Force Z, was assembled to meet the threat. The naval attack group was to be spearheaded by the battleship *Prince of Wales* and the battle cruiser *Repulse* which had been dispatched to the Far East in August 1941. Though ships of the line were in short supply, Churchill had thought it important to present a show of strength at a time when war in Asia seemed imminent. However, the defense of Malaya and Singapore was given a lower priority than Egypt, and though some naval vessels could be sent to the Orient, Britain had no air power to spare to support Force Z. From the British point of view her Middle East interests were more crucial to the war effort, and her Asian possessions would have to make do.

General Yamashita was given charge of the attack on Malaya and was allocated three divisions plus support troops and bearers to carry out the task. Yamashita's 70,000 combat troops faced a British force of 88,000. Yet, numbers alone would not determine the issue. The British forces were ill-equipped and ill-trained for the type of warfare which was to come.

Yamashita prepared his campaign with care. Approximately one-quarter of his force was to cross the Gulf of Siam and engage the British forces on the eastern coast, while the remainder of his army was allowed to pass through Thai territory and attacked the British forces along the western coast of Malaya.

The Japanese amphibious assault began early in the morning of December 8, local time. Since Malaya is on the eastern side of the international date line, the Japanese attack was to occur approximately one hour before her naval attack planes struck Pearl Harbor.

The British had sighted a Japanese flotilla in the Gulf of Siam on December 6 but had lost track of the Japanese vessels due to bad weather. The *Repulse* and *Prince of Wales* were sent into the Gulf of Siam to attack the Japanese force which had landed at Kota Bharu. The British were spotted from the air on the 9th, and Admiral Phillips, commander of Z Force, turned his ships toward Singapore. However, news of a Japanese landing at Kuantan caused him to turn to the attack. Phillips calculated that by changing directions yet again he would confuse enemy reconnaissance and have surprise on his side. But Z Force was again spotted by Japanese torpedo planes which attacked Phillips' ships at 11:00 A.M. By 12:30 the *Repulse* was sunk, and the *Prince of Wales* went to the bottom one hour later. The British destroyer escorts were able to save over two-thirds of the crews of the two lost ships, but the Japanese air action had destroyed Z Force. Bereft of naval support and woefully lacking in air support, the British were forced to give ground.

As with all Western armies, the British forces relied heavily on wheeled transport. But the Japanese traveled light. Some 30,000 porters had been engaged to carry supplies, and Japanese troops were accustomed to carrying a bit of rice and living off the food the jungle provided. The British and Indian contingents were no match for an enemy who could live and move through the jungle with comparative ease. The jungle-acclimatized Japanese demonstrated the value of the rigorous training which select Japanese land forces had been undergoing in the jungles of Formosa since 1939. General Percival's army, out-fought and out-maneuvered was forced to retreat down the peninsula. By January 30, 1942, the defeated British forces crossed the straits and planned to make their last stand at Singapore. Malaya had fallen.

Obviously, the sinking of two British war ships had been a bitter blow to General Percival's defense plan. Worse still was the shock the sinkings caused among surface fleet admirals. Naval strategists, though well aware of the disastrous effects of aerial attacks on ships in port, had long contended that it was impossible to launch a successful air attack upon a ship at sea. The belief that evasive maneuvers by a skilled sailor could foil an air attack was disproved by the events of December 9, 1941. It is true that Japanese torpedo planes made a faster attack approach than did Western planes which confused British gunners. But the rapidity and ease with which the Japanese dispatched Force Z was a shock to surface fleet advocates. In spite of this Japanese success, it was not until the later battles of Coral Sea and, in particular, Midway that surface sailors began to see that air power could dominate sea power.

On February 8, 1942, the Japanese launched an assault across the one mile straits which separated Singapore from Malaya; eventually, 30,000 Japanese troops were to cut through British defenses. On February 15, General Percival surrendered his forces to General Yamashita. More than 80,000 British and Commonwealth troops were thus doomed to hard years of captivity in Japanese labor camps in Southeast Asia. Many would not survive the short rations, hard labor, and disease which were the lot of the captive soldiers who had once held sway over Malaysia and Burma.

The initial attack on Burma began on December 10, 1941. Though the British had planned to hold Rangoon, they were unable to do so, and, on March 6, 1942, Rangoon was ordered evacuated. The British then moved to establish defensive positions in the Mandalay area. Their plan to hold in the Mandalay area was frustrated by the rapid advance of the Japanese. Forced from this defensive position the British army in Burma began the long retreat which would force them back to the Indian frontier.

Chinese forces under American General Joseph "Vinegar Joe" Stilwell, Chiang Kai Shek's American adviser, attempted to stop the Japanese from securing control of the Burma Road, the important overland supply link to China. The defenders were forced to retreat, and the Burma Road was closed. Loss of this supply route was to hamper combat operations in the China theater and, ultimately, make it impossible for China to become a staging area for the attack on the main islands of Japan.

By May 1942, Burma was in Japanese hands, and the British faced a possible invasion of the Indian sub-continent which, because of national unrest, was none too favorable to the rule of the British Raj.

The Dutch East Indies was another of Japan's objectives. On February 13, 1942, a small contingent of Japanese troops seized the airfield of Palembang on the island of Sumatra. Five days later a Japanese fleet sailed from Indochina

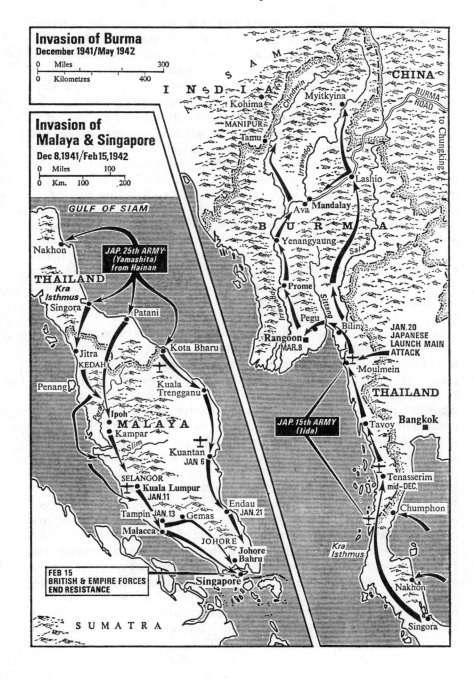

Invasion of Burma
December 1941/May 1942

| 0 | Miles | | 300 |
| 0 | Kilometres | | 400 |

Invasion of Malaya & Singapore
Dec 8,1941/Feb 15,1942

| 0 | Miles | 100 |
| 0 | Km. | 100 | 200 |

CHINA

BURMA ROAD

to Chungking

INDIA

Kohima

Chindwin

Myitkyina

MANIPUR

Tamu

Lashio

Irrawaddy

Ava   Mandalay

BURMA

Yenangyaung

Salween

Prome

Sittang

Pegu   Biling

JAN. 20
JAPANESE
LAUNCH MAIN
ATTACK

Rangoon
MAR. 8

Moulmein

THAILAND

Bangkok

JAP. 15th ARMY
(Iida)

Tavoy

Tenasserim
mid-DEC.

Chumphon

GULF OF SIAM

Nakhon

JAP. 25th ARMY
(Yamashita)
from Hainan

THAILAND
Kra
Isthmus
Singora   Patani

Jitra
KEDAH

Penang

Kota Bharu

Kuala
Trengganu

Ipoh
MALAYA
Kampar

Slim

Kuantan
JAN. 6

SELANGOR
Kuala Lumpur
JAN. 11

Tampin JAN. 13   Gemas

Malacca

JOHORE

Endau
JAN. 21

Johore
Bahru

FEB 15
BRITISH & EMPIRE FORCES
END RESISTANCE

Singapore

Kra
Isthmus

Nakhon

Singora

SUMATRA

for the invasion of Java. A combined fleet of British, Dutch, and American warships attempted to intercept and block the Japanese force. In this surface engagement the Japanese utilized their Type-91 "Long Lance" torpedoes. This oxygen-driven torpedo had a speed of 32 knots at a distance of 40,000 meters and could do 50 knots at a range of 20,000 meters. The Allied ships were hit before they could come within gunnery range of the Japanese attackers. As ships exploded around them Allied sailors believed they had run into a minefield and were amazed that the Japanese sailed through the supposed minefield without damage. It was not until long after this engagement that the remarkable quality of the Japanese torpedoes was revealed. Unfortunately, particularly for the American submarine fleet, the Allied forces were not to develop a torpedo of that range, speed, and efficiency during the war.

The Battle of the Java Sea, February 27-28, 1942, was a disaster for the Allied fleet. The Japanese sank two Dutch light cruisers and a destroyer and a British destroyer. The next day, at Sundra Strait, the Japanese sank three Allied cruisers. On March 1, in another battle of the Java Sea engagement, the Japanese sank one British cruiser and two destroyers. The few ships that remained of the Allied fleet fled the scene. On March 6, 1942, the Dutch East Indies became yet another territory of Japan's expanding Southeast Asian Co-Prosperity Sphere.

In April 1942, a Japanese attack force commanded by Admiral Nagumo scattered the British naval build-up in the Indian Ocean by attacking the harbor at Colombo, Ceylon (Sri Lanka). The April 5th air strike by carrier-based planes resulted in the loss of two British cruisers and the dispersal of the small British force in the Indian Ocean. On April 9, 1942, Nagumo's force attacked the British naval base at Tricomalee and sank several British vessels including the aircraft carrier *Hermes*. The Japanese thrust into the Indian Ocean appears to have been defensive in nature and designed to protect her build-up of forces in Burma, but the British became fearful of Japan's move into the Indian Ocean and seized the port of Diego Suarez on the northern tip of Madagascar in May 1942. In September, the British occupied the French colony of Madagascar. The Madagascar venture was ill-received in France. The invasion of the island coupled with the British attacks on the French fleet, harbored at the North African ports of Mers-El-Kabir and Oran in July 1940, convinced many in France that Great Britain had designs on her colonial empire. The British justified their actions on the logical assumption that French possessions and the French fleet might be used against Britain by the Vichy government— which was viewed by London as a puppet regime of the Germans. Distrust of British intentions was but one of the complexities the Americans and British had to deal with in their attempts to gain French cooperation for the North African landings (Operation Torch) in 1943.

For the United States a bright note was sounded in April 1942. A small carrier force, commanded by Admiral Halsey, carried a contingent of B-25 bombers within striking range of Tokyo. The bombers were under the command of Lieutenant Colonel James (Jimmy) Doolittle and were launched from the aircraft carrier *Hornet*. The *Enterprise*, an integral part of this Task Force 16, was to furnish air support for the carriers. The Japanese detected Force 16 before it had reached the optimum distance for the attack launch. However, the decision was made to launch the bombers. The planes were able to reach their targets before the Japanese had prepared for the attack, and aircraft losses over the home islands were minimal. So to, the carriers were able to escape damage and sailed back to Pearl Harbor unscathed.

The bomber force hit the cities of Tokyo, Nagoya and Kobe but did little real damage. All of the American planes, however, ran out of fuel and went down because the landing field promised to the operation by the Chinese Nationalist Government was not operable. Of the 82 flight personnel involved, 12 were killed in the raid. Three of those lost were captured and executed by the Japanese for war crimes; that is, the bombing of civilian populations. Some of the airmen drowned when their planes, out of fuel, ditched into the ocean; but a majority of crewmen either parachuted to safety on land or survived a ditching at sea. Four additional crewmen who survived the loss of their aircraft were captured by Japanese authorities in China and later executed. One air crew made it to the Soviet Union where they were interned for the duration of the war.

Though the Doolittle raid was little more than a nuisance attack from the military point of view, the attack on the Japanese home islands was to pay a major dividend to the Allied cause in the Pacific War. The raid had several immediate effects. First, it greatly boosted American morale. President Roosevelt, replying to reporters' demands for the name of the base from which the raid was launched, told them it was a secret base named Shangra-La, which happened to be the name of a mystical kingdom in a popular novel of that time. The raid and the President's wry quip seemed to buoy American spirits long depressed by numerous defeats in the Pacific. Second, and more importantly, the Japanese high command was stung by the attack which came so close on the heels of a brilliant succession of Japanese victories. Most historians agree that the Doolittle raid led to a hasty acceleration of Japanese plans to complete their Pacific strategy. The Japanese fleet, wearied from months of continuous action, hurried to carry out a complex plan that called for simultaneous attempts to neutralize Australia (the Battle of the Coral Sea) and to destroy America's naval strength through an elaborate naval operation that came to be known as the Battle of Midway.

As of April 1942, Yamamoto's plan had been a success. However, to paraphrase his own words, Japan could run wild for a year, but if the war went beyond two years all was lost. In less than a year Japan had nearly attained her objectives, but her fortunes were to turn for the worse in the summer of 1942 with the American victories in the Coral Sea and Midway. Despite those victories to come, the Pacific War was to be a long and costly one.

Summary

By the summer of 1941 it was obvious to informed observers that the United States and Japan were on a collision course. The United States abandoned its neutral stance and attempted to aid Great Britain without actually going to war. The popular consensus seemed to favor this "every thing short of war" policy, for in spite of evident support of the British fight against nazism, the idea of American involvement in a European war was not popular in America. Attempts by the U.S. to force Japan to give up her interests in Southeast Asia convinced Japan's militarists that war was a necessity if Japan was to assume her proper, dominant place in Asia. War plans were drawn up that called for a neutralization of America's naval and military presence in Asia. The American fleet was to be destroyed; American, British, and Dutch territory was to be overrun, and Japan would then set up a formidable defensive ring in the Pacific to guard her new "Co-Prosperity Sphere" in Asia.

The attack on Pearl Harbor came as a surprise to the United States. The raid, though successful, did not destroy America's carrier fleet. For the time being, however, this did not seem to matter. The American colonial territory of the Philippines was invaded. By May 1942 Corregidor fell. Quickly the Japanese moved to secure Hong Kong. That British colony fell in eighteen days. Malaysia was also a Japanese target. By December 10, 1942, Japanese aircraft had destroyed the British naval defense force, Z Force, in the Gulf of Siam. Moving down the Malay Peninsula they out-maneuvered and out-fought the British defenders. Superiority in air power plus greater skill in jungle warfare gave Yamashita's forces the determining edge in this conflict. The British forces were pushed back to the island of Singapore. Attacking from the landward side, Japanese forces penetrated the island's defenses on February 8, 1942, and the great port of Singapore was surrendered to the Japanese one week later.

Burma was subject to a Japanese attack in mid-December. By March 1942 Rangoon was abandoned, and the long retreat of the Allied forces (largely British, Commonwealth, and Chinese troops) began. By May, Burma, too, had fallen, and India was threatened.

However, the Tokyo raid, a carrier-based bomber raid on Japan's homeland, gave Japanese military planners pause for thought. The homeland's vulnerability to attack prompted Japan to divide its naval forces to accomplish the twin objectives of cutting off Australia and neutralizing the United States naval presence in the Central Pacific. This division of forces was to result in two naval battles which were to be crucial in the war in the Pacific.

Suggested Reading

Ito, Masonori. *The End of the Imperial Japanese Navy*. New York, 1984. This is a far-ranging book which deals with Japanese naval history, strategic thinking, and strategic failures before and during World War II. It is a very readable account written from the Japanese point of view.

Layton, Edwin T., Roger Pineau, and John Costello. *And I Was There*. New York, 1985. The book covers Pearl Harbor and Midway, and it is particularly informative regarding the code, code-breaking, and internal politics in the U.S. Navy during this period.

Prange, Gordon W. *At Dawn We Slept: The Untold Story of Pearl Harbor*. New York, 1981. This is one of the best studies done of the Pearl Harbor attack. His coverage of the Kimmel-Short story is revealing. Prange also wrote (with Donald M. Goldstein, and Katherine V. Dillon), *Miracle at Midway* (New York, 1983). This is a study of a most complex battle presented clearly and in great detail.

Toland, John. *The Rising Sun: The Decline and Fall of the Japanese Empire, 1939-1945*. New York, 1970. This writer has written three books on the Pacific War including, *Infamy* (New York, 1982). He has done much to present the revisionist view of the Pearl Harbor controversy and is well worth a comparative read with Prange and Layton.

Willmott, H. P. *Empires in Balance: Japanese and Allied Pacific Strategies to April, 1942*. Annapolis, Maryland, 1982. Willmott gives an overview of the Pacific strategy and calls into question the thinking of the leadership in both camps.

6

The War in the Soviet Union
June 1941 to June 1943

itler's forces invaded territories of the Soviet Union on the morning of June 22, 1941. This operation, "Case 21" or "Operation Barbarossa" in the German war plans, was designed to secure vast territories for the Third Reich, thus realizing Hitler's long-cherished dream of *lebensraum* (living space) for aryans at the expense of the slavic peoples of European U.S.S.R. The controversial point of this decision is why was the attack unleashed at that particular point in time? The Soviet Union, in spite of its aggrandizement of territory in Eastern Europe in 1940, had begun to follow a conciliatory policy regarding her German neighbor and "ally." Diplomatic sources in 1941 tended to indicate that Stalin went to almost any lengths to avoid war with Germany at that point in time.

Hitler, on the other hand, tended to maximize the supposed dangers to the Third Reich posed by Stalin. Soviet acquisitions in Rumania in 1940 were seen by Hitler as proof positive that Stalin had designs on Rumanian oil fields; fields vital to the interests of Germany. Every incident of Soviet acquisition in Eastern Europe was used as proof that the Soviets were preparing for war with Germany. Some historians see the creation of a Soviet nemesis as but a device Hitler used to convince his somewhat reluctant General Staff that a quick war against the Soviets was necessary for German security. This point of view has merit for there was a reluctance among German military leaders to launch such an attack while England was still in the war. After all, such an operation would place Germany in the same position as in 1914—involved in a two-front war.

In the past, Hitler had acted audaciously to secure what his military leaders deemed impossible. Therefore, it is little wonder that he seemingly threw caution to the wind and, in July 1940, ordered that plans for the invasion of the Soviet Union be formulated. Yet, caution figured heavily in planning Operation Barbarossa. It was Hitler's hope that the Red Army could be neutralized, even obliterated as a fighting force in a few months. European U.S.S.R. with its vast riches in agricultural products and raw materials would then be in German hands, and that part of the U.S.S.R. which remained under Soviet control would be forced to capitulate or establish some sort of an agreement with the new ruling power, the Third Reich. It was not an unrealistic plan. After all, Germany had been able to accomplish part of this in 1918. The Treaty of Brest Litovsk, negotiated between Germany and the newly-founded Soviet Union in 1918, might well have been in Hitler's mind as he ordered the planning of Operation Barbarossa. Though Brest Litovsk ostensibly gave autonomy to the Ukraine and other territories which had been part of the old Russian Empire, it in fact established German hegemony in Eastern Europe. Hitler's plans were more ambitious, certainly more racist in nature, yet they were not too far removed from the pan-Germanic expansionism inherent in that 1918 agreement.

The Barbarossa Plan clearly shows that Hitler did not want to become involved in a long war in the Soviet Union. He did not desire to duplicate Napoleon's error and be drawn into the vastness of that country. Yet, the strategy which the Germans employed was to involve them in ever-deepening penetrations of Soviet territory. It is surprising, given the success of the Panzer attacks in Poland, the Low France countries, and the Balkans, that Operation Barbarossa called for the orthodox strategy of the "pincer movement" as opposed to the deep penetration maneuver used by Guderian and others in 1939 and 1940. In that sense, caution and orthodoxy prevailed. In order to avoid a deep involvement in the vast space of the U.S.S.R., Hitler and his generals followed Napoleon's concepts, and, like him, were frustrated in their attempts to win a quick victory by entrapping and destroying the Soviet army.

In 1941, however, Hitler was convinced that a May or June invasion of the Soviet Union could bring victory before winter. This was crucial as a longer involvement there might mean that Great Britain would be able to hold out and eventually gain support from the United States. That fear proved justified. Germany's failure to secure a quick victory in the Soviet Union was to involve it in a two-front war against opponents which possessed greater resources and evidenced a greater commitment to continuing the conflict than had been the case in World War I. To accomplish this supposed rapid victory it was deemed necessary to use three Army Groups. Army Group North, commanded by Field Marshal Ritter von Leeb, would strike through Prussia toward Leningrad. Army Group Center, the strongest of the three forces, would drive on a line north of the Pripet Marshes, take Minsk, Smolensk, and, finally, Moscow. Field Marshal Bock was given charge of this important Army Group Center. Field Marshal Rundstedt would direct the attack of Army Group South. Units of this group would attack through Poland toward Kiev while others would drive through Bessarabia north toward Kiev. Once these objectives were taken and the Soviet's western armies destroyed, German forces would drive east toward the Volga, north toward Archangel, and south through the Ukraine toward Stalingrad. Once established there the Luftwaffe could pummel Soviet factories in the Urals, and victory would be secured.

Incorporated with the military aspect of Operation Barbarossa was *Plan Oldenburg*. This plan called for the systematic exploitation of Soviet resources. Therefore, OKW, the Armed Forces General Staff, had made extensive preparations for both the attack and the utilization of territory gained from the invasion. As noted in a previous chapter, the May 1941 date for the attack was not met. Weather and other factors postponed the attack until June 22; 129 years and one day from the date of Napoleon's invasion of Imperial Russia.

One event of May 1941 is deserving of note. On May 10, Rudolf Hess took off in an unarmed Messerschmitt fighter on a dramatic flight to Great Britain. Hess parachuted from his plane onto British soil, thus embarking on one of the more bizarre diplomatic missions of the twentieth century. Apparently, Hess felt that he could persuade the British to join with Germany in destroying bolshevism. He urged cooperation between the two powers and an end to the senseless war between racially related peoples. Hitler was to denounce Hess' mission with fury, but it is interesting that Hess, who had once been very close to Hitler, took such a risk to accomplish what was to be a fruitless mission. The British, of course, paid no heed to his plan, and Hess was interned. Yet, it is intriguing that an ardent Nazi and a member of the inner circle of that party risked all in a vain, even insane, attempt to eliminate the dangers inherent in Hitler's plan to invade the Soviet Union while Great Britain remained an active and dangerous enemy. Few have doubted that Hess was a mental case and so the British judged him, but his fears were well-based as Hitler's actions were to place Germany in a two-front war.

As Germany prepared for invasion, information from various sources was forwarded to Moscow warning of an impending attack. For reasons which still have not been explained these warnings were ignored by Stalin. Sources which he would later rely upon—Richard Sorge, his spy in Tokyo whose information would aid him in the Battle of Moscow, and "Lucy," that Switzerland-based fount of information which would forewarn him of the Battle of Kursk—were equally ignored. The Polish underground forwarded information to London that the movement and disposition of troops along the new Nazi-Soviet border of what was formerly Poland indicated an attack. Stalin was apprised of this through British sources, but again discounted the information. There is even some evidence to indicate that pro-Soviet sources at Bletchley forwarded information from Ultra Secret regarding their Enigma intercepts of German military plans for invasion. The official Soviet history of World War II condemns Stalin for his blindness and even accuses him of being naive. Obviously, Stalin was neither, yet he stubbornly held to the notion that the Germans, whom he distrusted, would not attack at this date. Why he held to this view is a matter of speculation. Yet, the fact remained that even on June 21 when it was apparent that an attack was imminent, he still argued with Zhukov—the general who brought him the news that trunk telephone lines to the West had been cut and a German deserter swore the invasion would begin Sunday, June 22 at dawn—and seemed to think that it was all a misunderstanding which could be solved by negotiations. It is a credit to Stalin that, in spite of his gross errors in anticipating the attack and his failure to organize his forces in a defensive posture, when the German fury was unleashed he was to respond quickly and decisively. As the disaster spread, he sought out those who could fight and used every means at his disposal to organize the Soviet state to meet the challenge of a war which was to become known as "The Great Patriotic War."

Invasion of the Soviet Union

Hitler's forces, approximately 135 divisions, attacked with stunning force. The Red Army, whom the Germans estimated as having forces in excess of 200 divisions, proved no match for the German armor. However, the Soviet resistance was surprisingly stiff. Though the Germans were able to "pinch off" huge pockets of Soviet forces, great numbers of troops were able to filter out of these traps. Poor roads hampered movement, and the vast spaces involved allowed relatively large groups of Red Army troops to escape encirclement and regroup. Even when surrounded the Soviets tended to fight to the death. This was something of a shock to the German troops who were used to the relatively weak resistance offered by troops in similar circumstances during the campaigns of 1939 and 1940. Therefore, time was consumed in destroying pockets of resistance. Commanders were also amazed at the rapid mobilization of new divisions by the Red Army. By August, German intelligence had counted well over 300 active Red Army divisions. In spite of dramatic reversals the armies of the Soviet Union were far from being demoralized.

By July 10, German forces were attacking Smolensk, 200 miles from Moscow. Resistance was tenacious, and Guderian's Panzers suffered heavy losses, yet by August 4, Smolensk had fallen. In less than two months of

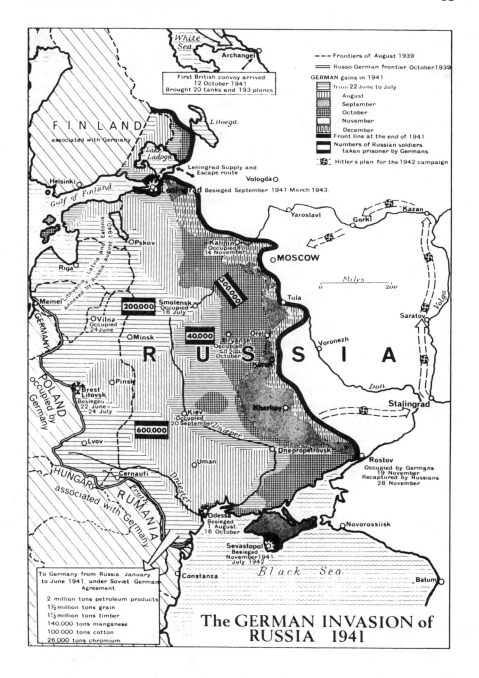

The GERMAN INVASION of RUSSIA 1941

campaigning, the Wehrmacht had captured or encircled nearly two million Red Army troops, yet the Soviet army was far from collapse, and none of the three German Army Groups had reached their objective. From August 4 to 24, time was wasted in a command muddle. Hitler chose to shift troops to gain advances in the North and the South while Bock's Group Center stabilized and straightened the front lines. It was not until September 6 that Hitler finally decided to make Moscow the primary objective of the offensive. However, the plan of attack called for splitting Bock's forces into three groups, one to the north of Moscow, one to the south, and a third to be a frontal thrust on Moscow.

The division of Bock's forces ultimately proved to be a mistake, but in its initial phase the attack seemed a glorious success. However, by mid-October the rains came, bogging down the German transport system and slowing the advance. Winter was not far off, and Hitler's generals feared what could happen if winter came early to an army unprepared and ill-equipped to face its full fury. In November cold weather came, freezing the roads and allowing the tanks and trucks to move forward. By December 2, 1941, advanced German units were within sight of the spires of the Kremlin, yet the intense cold took its toll. As the mercury plummeted the German attack ground to a halt, and frantic calls were made to Berlin to supply winter clothing to the freezing troops. The Soviets, however, were well prepared to fight in winter. On December 6, Zhukov, now a Marshal, committed his reserves to a counterattack catching the German forces by surprise. Hitler ignored demands for a general retreat to a winter line. Instead, he ordered the creation of elaborate strong points, called *hedgehogs*, wherein the German forces could hold out during the long winter. The hedgehogs held during the winter, but in many places the Red Army made large advances. Never again were German forces to come so close to Moscow.

In November, Leeb's forces lay siege to Leningrad cutting off all lines of supply to the city save one, Lake Ladoga. From September 1941 to January 1944, the siege of Leningrad took its toll of victims, but the city held out. One problem which Leeb faced was with his Finnish allies. Though the Finns cooperated with the Germans in fighting the Red Army, it was Field Marshal Mannerheim's contention that the Finnish army fought only to secure the Karelian Peninsula territories that Finland had lost during the recent war. Denied support of his ally in battle, Leeb could not bring sufficient force to completely cut-off the Leningrad garrison.

In the South, Rundstedt's forces had taken Kiev and all of the Ukraine, and his exhausted army reached Rostov on the Don River as winter set in. Rundstedt requested a withdrawal to a winter line. The request was refused, and Rundstedt was allowed to resign his command. During the winter, Soviet forces regained some territory in the south, but, in general, the Germans maintained control over most of the territory. However, as with the front of Army Group Center, the southern armies often discovered that the front boxed the compass.

As already noted, the winter of 1941 has been seen by many writers as the beginning of the end for Hitler's armies. Bad weather, poor planning, and stiff Soviet resistance are credited with stemming the German tide. Stalin, informed by Richard Sorge, a Comintern spy well connected in high diplomatic circles in Tokyo, was assured of Japanese quietude on the Manchurian border. Therefore, he was able to draw off his crack Siberian divisions and bring them west for the defense of Moscow. This, of course, contributed to the stiffening of the defense. However, one must not ignore the fact that Hitler's ever-changing strategy confused and slowed the attack. Likewise, the German transport system relied on wheeled vehicles. This reliance was to be ill-advised in a country where rudimentary roads turned to swamps at the first heavy rain, where trucks could be frozen in the mud after an overnight freeze, and ice and snow made roads too slippery and dangerous for efficient motor transport. Therefore, command indecision and oversight in logistical planning must also be considered as factors which aided the Soviets.

For the long-term, it should be noted that the German economic plan for the Soviet Union did a great deal to rouse the Soviet antipathy toward the invaders. In the Ukraine, particularly, the Germans were initially looked upon as liberators. This euphoria did not last long. In the interest of so-called economic efficiency the Germans retained the hated collective farm, and the SS employed its murderous methods of eliminating Ukrainian intellectuals and potential political leaders. In short, Hitler's economic and racial policies served to alienate peoples in the occupied territories. Faced with the brutality of their German occupiers, Ukrainians and others who had reason to hate the Soviet government were to find that their new rulers were even more cruel and ruthless than their Soviet masters had been.

Therefore, the Reich's policy in these occupied territories fostered the growth of anti-German, partisan activity. It should be noted, however, the individual army commanders, often acting in direct violation of policy, were to recruit and use Soviets as laborers, drivers, and skilled workers to aid the Wehrmacht. Hundreds of thousands of Soviets worked for the Germans. Millions of others were rounded up to serve as slave labor in the fields and factories of Germany. Still others, starving in German prison camps, were recruited as soldiers. In the later years of the war intensive pressure was mounted to recruit Soviet prisoners of war for a new Soviet division of the German army. Participation by such an army in the war against the Soviets would be rewarded with the granting of political freedoms and certain national aspirations when victory was obtained. Though the possibilities for recruitment were seen as enormous by partisans of the scheme, Hitler refused to allow the creation of such an army. He distrusted the idea on the basis that such an army might turn against the Germans, and he also refused to allow any changes in his policy toward Soviet territory. For him, the peoples and territories of the Soviet Union were for the use of the Reich. There was no thought that semi-autonomous national states would be allowed to exist in the east. Thus, Hitler's inherent racialism was to alienate the initial goodwill of peoples such as the Ukrainians and eliminate any possibility of large scale cooperation of Soviet citizens opposed to Stalinism.

The entry of the United States into the war meant that, as of December 1941, the Soviet Union and the United States were linked in a common alliance. American aid grew from a trickle to a veritable flood and benefitted the U.S.S.R. materially throughout the war. To their own credit, the Soviets showed remarkable versatility and a willingness to accomplish the impossible in developing their war production. Factories were moved from danger areas, set up, and were in production in a matter of days. In a state-controlled economy such as the Soviet Union's war production became the principal goal, and Soviet production far surpassed that of Germany in the output of tanks, planes, and guns.

The Soviet army, too, underwent changes. The command structure was reshuffled to allow for more initiative of individual theater commanders, and cooperation between district (theater) commanders was stressed. From the test of combat, competent leaders began to emerge. Inept officers were weeded out and able commanders promoted. Discipline was rigid for officers and soldiers alike; cost in casualties was less important than obtaining the objective. The losses the Red Army absorbed both amazed German field commanders and demoralized them. For it seemed no matter how many waves of attackers were stopped or turned back, there were always new levies waiting and new tanks and guns available for yet another assault.

As early as November 1941 plans were being made for the German spring offensive of 1942. Though some generals felt that the 1942 offensive should be directed against Moscow, Hitler listened to the arguments of his economic experts who stressed the necessity of securing the oil resources of the Caucasus. Capture of that area would secure a land route to the Middle East and possible access to Suez. Therefore, the offensive of 1942 was to be carried out by Army Group South, redesignated as Group A and Group B. Group A, under Field Marshal Wilhelm List, would attack the Caucasus; Group B under Bock and later General Maximillian von Weichs, would strike at Kharkov and head for the Volga River. Securing the Volga would block off Stalingrad and stop the flow of supplies and reinforcements to that area, thus eliminating any flank attack on List's Group A. A secondary offensive was planned to carry Leningrad, but, in general, the main attack was to be to the south.

The success of the attack was facilitated by Marshal Timoshenko's offensive in the Kharkov area in May. Timoshenko's forces were too weak to accomplish their objective. The attack was met by a counteroffensive which destroyed two Soviet armies and badly mauled two others. By the end of May Soviet strength in that sector was depleted thus facilitating the German drive to the Don.

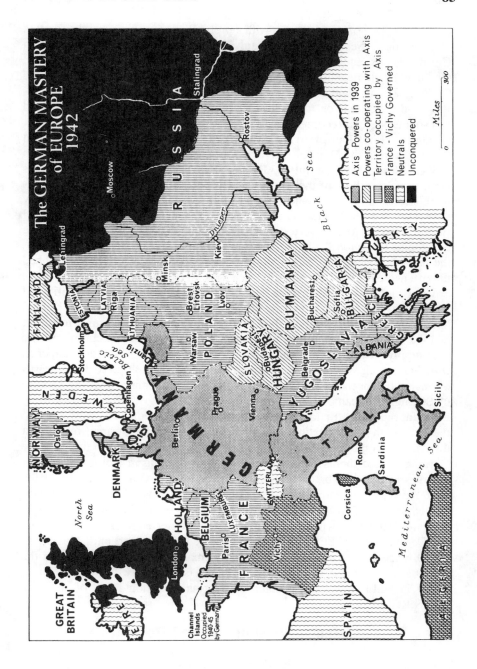

The GERMAN MASTERY of EUROPE 1942

Axis Powers in 1939
Powers co-operating with Axis
Territory occupied by Axis
France - Vichy Governed
Neutrals
Unconquered

Miles
0 300

RUSSIA

Stalingrad

Moscow

Rostov

Black Sea

FINLAND

Leningrad

ESTONIA
LATVIA
Riga
LITHUANIA

Minsk

Brest
Litovsk

Dnieper

Kiev

Lvov

TURKEY

POLAND

Warsaw

Danzig

Stockholm

SWEDEN

Baltic Sea

Copenhagen

NORWAY

Oslo

DENMARK

North Sea

Berlin

GERMANY

Prague

Vienna

SLOVAKIA

Budapest

HUNGARY

RUMANIA

Bucharest

Sofia

BULGARIA

YUGOSLAVIA

Belgrade

ALBANIA

GREECE

ITALY

Rome

Sardinia

Corsica

Sicily

Mediterranean Sea

GREAT BRITAIN

EIRE

London

Channel Islands Occupied 1940-45 by Germany

HOLLAND

BELGIUM

LUXEMBURG

Paris

FRANCE

Vichy

SWITZERLAND

SPAIN

ALGERIA

On June 7 the offensive began with a preliminary attack against the fortress of Sevastopol. Sevastopol fell on July 4. The whole of the Crimea was in German hands, and the Soviet Black Sea fleet was deprived of its major port. On June 10 elements of Group B gained passage across the Donetz River. On June 28 the main attack of Army Group B was launched in the Kursk-Belgorod sector, and on July 6 Voronezh was taken. The attack force wheeled in a southeasterly direction along the Don toward Stalingrad. In the meantime, Group A's First Panzer Army under Field Marshal Ewald von Kleist had attacked across the Donetz, drove toward Chertkovo, and wheeled south to cross the lower Don. On July 23 Rostov fell, and by August 9 Kleist's forces were in the foothills of the Caucasus. Here the attack slowed. Supply lines were stretched and the route difficult, and supply by sea was precluded by the presence of the Soviet fleet. Increased resistance slowed the advance still further, and as forces were diverted from the Caucasus to be used in the developing battle for Stalingrad, the Caucasus offensive ground to a halt. Thus, the secondary objective, Stalingrad, became the prime objective. This robbed the offensive of its primary purpose; that is, securing the oil reserves of the Soviet Union and thus depriving the Soviets of their source of fuel. Stalingrad was seen as a danger to the Caucasus operation for from there an attack could have been launched to cut off the German forces in the Caucasus. However, had the Germans concentrated on securing the Caucasus and cutting off the fuel supply, it is doubtful that a major offensive could have been launched from Stalingrad. Whether or not Stalingrad posed a major threat to the Caucasus offensive has been seriously debated, but the fact remains that the capture of Stalingrad became Hitler's obsession.

Stalingrad was a major industrial city stretching along the west bank of the Volga. In concentrating the attack on the city, the German forces lost their maneuverability. As Paulus' Sixth Army was drawn into the city, the Germans found themselves involved in close fighting in a city which their enemies knew much better than they. General Vasili Chuikov, leader of the 62nd Army, led his forces well. The bitter street fighting raged as the Germans moved slowly to drive the defenders into the Volga. This was alarmingly close to realization when, on October 14, a Soviet counterattack stemmed the German attack. Still, the defenders were hard pressed until November 19-20 when winter weather hampered German operations and allowed the Soviet armies to begin that maneuver which was ultimately to entrap the Sixth Army in Stalingrad and endanger the German position in all of southern U.S.S.R.

Defeat at Stalingrad and Retreat

In mid-December Manstein, then commander of Army Group B, tried to break the encirclement. In spite of a deep penetration of the Soviet forces surrounding Stalingrad, the attempt failed. This failure was largely the result of Hitler's orders to Paulus to hold the city. Therefore Paulus made no effort to counterattack and linkup with Manstein's forces. Though Paulus' forces were urged to hold out, and pledges to continue supplying the trapped army were made by the Luftwaffe, they could not hold, and on January 31, 1943, Paulus and most of his remaining forces surrendered. By February 2, all German resistance at Stalingrad ceased.

The impending defeat at Stalingrad threatened to cut off Army Group A. This fact was not lost on the German commanders, but as late as the first week of January, Hitler was ordering a "no retreat" policy. Some writers have argued that, even if cut off, German forces in the Caucasus could have held out and even captured the Soviet oil resources. However, the Soviet fleet still roamed the Black Sea making the resupply of Army Group A most difficult, doubly so as German air power in the Caucasus was insufficient to protect the forces from air attack, let alone guard possible shipping lanes for the transport of supplies and the shipment of oil. In any case, Hitler changed his mind, and Army Group A was ordered to withdraw from the Caucasus. What followed was a race which, ultimately, was won by the retreating Germans.

In large part the German retreat owed much to the skills of Manstein's Panzer forces which held open the Rostov gate against Soviet pressures and allowed for the escape of the German 1st and 17th armies. The race was close, and the Germans suffered heavy losses, but by February, the German lines conformed roughly to those that existed before the June 1942 offensive. However, Soviet forces had made a huge bulge in the original line by the creation of a deep indentation, or salient, in the Kursk sector. This threatened German control of Kharkov. However, Soviet attempts to drive the Germans from Kharkov failed, and in March a limited German counteroffensive stabilized the front. But the Kursk salient remained, and by April 1943, Hitler was envisioning the possibility of a great offensive against the Kursk salient which would avenge the defeat at Stalingrad and bring forth a victory so resounding as to shock the world.

Such hopes would seem ludicrous in the light of what had transpired in January and February, but German successes in stemming the Soviet attack in February and March had given Hitler cause for hope. The Soviets, too, were conscious that Germany was far from beaten. This fact is underlined by a relatively little known conference. German Foreign Minister Ribbentrop and Soviet Foreign Minister Molotov met in a small Soviet village to discuss the possibility of a peace agreement. The discussions foundered on the issue of German territorial demands and were ended when news of the separate peace talks were leaked to the Soviet Union's western Allies. Such a meeting seems to indicate that the issue was yet to be decided. Leningrad was under pressure and German forces controlled the Moscow to Minsk radius, though Moscow itself was no longer threatened.

In spite of the stunning defeat at Stalingrad, which, for a time, drove Hitler

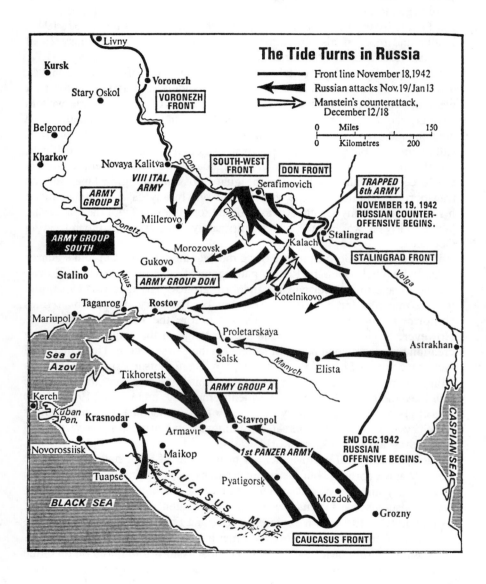

The Tide Turns in Russia

▬▬▬	Front line November 18, 1942
◀▬	Russian attacks Nov. 19/Jan 13
▷▬	Manstein's counterattack, December 12/18

0 — Miles — 150
0 — Kilometres — 200

from his military headquarters to the seclusion of Berchtesgaden in Bavaria, he still believed that victory could be his. This victory was to come by pinching off the Kursk Salient, destroying the Soviet forces there and thus opening the way to securing the oil rich Caucasus region. Hitler's belief in this plan, originally developed by Manstein, led him to involve himself in the planning and operational stages to the overall effect of delaying and ultimately dooming this, his last great hope for victory in the East.

Summary

On June 22, 1941, Germany attacked the Soviet Union. The German thrust was three pronged. One army group (North) attacked toward Leningrad; a second (Center) had as its objective Moscow; the third group (South) had as its general objective Kiev and beyond. The overall objective of this attack was to destroy the Soviet armies of western U.S.S.R. and to establish German hegemony over Soviet territory from Archangel to the Caucasus. In the beginning greater weight was given to Bock's Army Group Center, but in the course of the attack Hitler began to shift forces back and forth, weakening the central attack in support of the southern and northern campaigns. The attack on Moscow slowed to a halt in August, and for a few weeks the indecision of headquarters command kept that army in check. In late August Hitler decided to press an attack on Moscow, but the delay had been crucial and the plan of the final attack faulty. Rains in October slowed the advance, and by November winter had come with an unexpected intensity. The German army was stopped before Moscow. Neither were the Germans successful in taking Leningrad. However, siege was laid, and Leningrad was to be under steady pressure by its besiegers until January 1944. Kiev was taken, but Rundstedt's Group South fell far short of reaching the Volga.

Soviet losses had been very heavy, but German losses were to grow as the result of the harsh weather and stiffening Soviet resistance. Hitler was urged by his generals to retreat to a winter line. Instead he ordered a ''no retreat'' policy and called for establishing a series of strong points (hedgehogs) from whence the German army could resist the Soviet attack. During the winter, Soviet forces lapped around these strong points.

Though the winter had been costly for his armies in the Soviet Union, Hitler planned for a strong offensive in the spring of 1942. The objective of this offensive would be to seize control of the Caucasus and block off possible Soviet counterattacks by securing control of the Volga. The city of Stalingrad was thus a secondary objective of the campaign but was soon to become a primary one. The battles in the south began in May, but the main offensive was to wait until the end of June. Army Group South was divided into two groups; A and B. The objective of B Group was to secure the Don-Volga area; Group A's objective was to seize the vital oil fields of the Caucasus.

The campaign went well through August. The progress of Group A in the Caucasus was slowed by supply problems, rough terrain, and stiffening opposition. The battle for Stalingrad, however, was creating ever increasing problems. The Soviets fought desperately for Stalingrad, drawing the Germans into street fighting where their powers of mobility and maneuver were minimized. By November a great Soviet build-up in the area allowed for a counterattack, and Paulus' Sixth Army was trapped. By December the situation was desperate, and the Stalingrad build-up threatened to cut off Group A in the Caucasus. An attempt was made by the Germans to relieve Stalingrad, but there was not sufficient force to penetrate the defenses, and Paulus, acting under orders, made no attempt at a breakout. By February 2, 1943, all resistance at Stalingrad ended. Paulus' army had been destroyed. German losses at Stalingrad were in excess of one-quarter million troops killed, wounded, or captured.

Army Group A had been ordered to evacuate the Caucasus in January. Thus the Germans began a desperate race to escape the threat of entrapment, while the Soviets pressed the attack to bottle-up and destroy Army Group A. The Germans won the race but were thrown back to their original starting point of May-June 1942. Losses had been considerable, and the German army was greatly weakened. However, Soviet over-extension in attacks in February-March led to a limited German counteroffensive. This counteroffensive reestablished German control in the Kharkov area but did not eliminate the huge Kursk salient threatening that position. In spite of the defeat at Stalingrad, Hitler still felt that the spring offensive of 1943 would bring victory, and plans were formulated to cut off the Soviet forces in the Kursk salient. Victory at Kursk would mean that all of southern U.S.S.R. would be at the mercy of the Germans.

Suggested Reading

Bialer, Seweyrn. *Stalin and His Generals: Soviet Military Memoirs of World War II*. New York, 1969. Contains personal narratives of Soviet participants.

Carell, Paul (Trans. Osers, Ewald). *Hitler Moves East, 1941-1943*. Boston, 1965. An English translation of *Unternamen Barbarossa*. An account of the campaign as seen through German eyes.

Salisbury, Harrison E. *The 900 Days: The Siege of Leningrad*. New York, 1969. A vivid account of the effects of the siege on the inhabitants of Leningrad.

Werth, Alexander. *Russia at War, 1941-1945*. New York, 1964. A complete account written from the point of view of a social history more so than a strictly military account of the campaigns.

Zhukov, Georgy Konstantinovich (Trans. Theodore Shabad). *Marshal Zhukov's Greatest Battles*. New York, 1969. First published in Moscow, it gives a more or less official account of all Zhukov's campaigns.

7

The War in North Africa and the Mediterranean
March 1941 to July 1943

In March 1941, Rommel launched his combined German, Afrika Korps, and Italian forces in an offensive that was to sweep the British forces back from the gates of Tripoli to Tobruk. General O'Connor, who had commanded the Western Desert Force, was captured, and the port of Tobruk was put under siege. Thus began the so-called *Desert War* which remains a subject of fascination to students of World War II. This is due, in large part, to the type of warfare fought in the desert—tank warfare—and the personalities of the two principal leaders of this sun-drenched theater: Erwin Rommel, "The Desert Fox," and Bernard Montgomery, "Monty," the leader of the British Eighth Army, also known as the "Desert Rats."

The struggle in the desert of North Africa overshadows the other campaigns of the area of Middle East Command. General Wavell was well aware that the Suez could be threatened from the backdoor. Therefore, in early spring of 1941, operations were begun to insure that the Suez Canal would not be subject to attack from the east. The pro-Axis leader of Iraq was deposed in

April 1941; despite a revolt sparked by Axis agents, the British secured Baghdad in June 1941. Free French and British forces invaded Syria and Lebanon, threw out the Vichy regime, and by July 1941 had secured control of Syria. In August 1941 Soviet and British troops jointly occupied Iran, dividing the country on a north-south axis, thus assuring that Iran would remain in the Allied camp. This occupation was to be temporary, that is, for the duration of the war and six months afterward. The United States was to join in this agreement at the Tehran Conference in December 1943. Turkey alone remained neutral, selling supplies to both sides, therefore posing something of a problem to Middle East command.

By closing the "backdoor," however, the British were not assured of safeguarding the Suez Canal. In fact, the real danger to Allied control of the Middle East came from the west. Since the end of World War II, numerous writers have pointed out that had Hitler changed his line of operation, had he concentrated forces in North Africa and driven the British from Egypt, England might have been forced to come to some sort of an agreement with the Third Reich. This argument hinges on the fact that control of the Suez and of the Mediterranean would have effectively cut one of Britain's major lifelines leaving her no choice but to come to terms. Certainly, Winston Churchill realized the importance of Egypt and the Mediterranean and beggared other theaters of operation to reinforce this strategic area. However, North Africa and the Mediterranean were not seen as major theaters of operations by Hitler and his General Staff. Rommel was dispatched to North Africa to preserve the hard-pressed Italian presence in Tripoli. In spite of supply limitations and restrictions imposed upon his operations by both Mussolini and Hitler, Rommel nearly accomplished the task of securing Egypt. In the end, however, overextended and outnumbered, his threat to overrun Egypt was ended at El Alamein. There, Montgomery's Eighth Army turned the tide in favor of the Allies in North Africa.

When Rommel arrived in Tripoli in February 1941 the Italian forces had come to near total defeat in North Africa. The British forces pressing the attack were, however, depleted by demands for troops to shore up defenses in Greece. The ill-fated Greek adventure was to lead to heavy losses for no gain. Though apologists have argued that the Balkan adventure led to the delay of Operation Barbarossa, and, therefore, influenced the campaign on the Eastern Front does not seem to be substantiated by the facts. The weakening of British strength in North Africa was a plus for the beleaguered Italian forces, and, no doubt, contributed to Rommel's early successes. Still, Rommel did not wait for numerical superiority to attack the British forces in Cyrenaica. On March 26 he launched an offensive which drove the British 400 miles back to the Egyptian border. The offensive led to the loss of one of the ablest of British commanders, General Richard O'Connor, who was captured by Rommel's troops. By April 11, 1941, Rommel's forces had taken Bardia and Sollum and were inside the Egyptian border. Only the port city of Tobruk held out. From April to December 1941, Tobruk was to be isolated and under constant attack; however, her defenders, the Ninth Australian Division plus elements of the Seventh Australian and units of the Royal Tank Corp, held out until relieved.

In June 1941 General Wavell's forces sought to sweep Rommel's Afrika Korps from North Africa by destroying his fortified positions at Halfaya Pass, Sollum, and Fort Capuzzo. Then the plan called for the British to drive on to Tobruk and, after linking with that garrison, press Rommel back to Tripoli. The attack began on June 18 and ended three days later with the British in retreat. In great part the British defeat was due to Rommel's superior defensive tactics. Rommel utilized "tank traps" to defend crucial passes and ridges. These traps consisted of concealed 88mm antiaircraft guns hidden in positions in advance of the German tanks. The tanks were deployed to cover and defend the 88's. For some time the British were convinced that German tanks were vastly superior to their own—largely because the British mistook shell fire from the hidden 88's as fire from German armor. It was some time before the British realized the effectiveness of such a mobile defense in tank warfare.

As many British tank commanders were convinced that the German tanks out-gunned them and were generally superior to their own armor, so too did they begin to think that Rommel was indeed everywhere at once. In fact, Field Marshal Rommel did spend a great deal of his time on the battlefield. In viewing the battle from the actual scene he was able to send back messages to his headquarters redistributing his forces and taking immediate advantage of the changed circumstances on the battlefield. This manner of operation was to both serve his forces well and unnerve his staff. It also contributed to his growing mystic as the "Fox" of the desert campaign.

By applying the precepts of rapid movement, flexible and mobile defense, and by directing the battle from the line and not some rearward headquarters, Rommel was following the tenets laid down by the theorists and practitioners of modern, mechanized warfare. With all his talents he was not successful in reducing the garrison of Tobruk, nor could he solve the supply problem which kept his forces short of replacements and equipment. This problem resulted in part from the existence of the British sea and air base at Malta. The base was used to interdict the supply lines to Tripoli. British ships and planes preyed upon the Axis supply route with great success, in some cases destroying as much as 60 percent of the supplies sent to the Axis forces in North Africa. The inability to protect these convoys of supply ships was partially due to the fact that British aircraft ruled the air space around Malta. But, Rommel's problem may have been exacerbated by the fact that Hitler kept the Italian fleet short of oil. Perhaps, had Hitler trusted the Italian fleet to protect the Axis convoys losses could have been cut. This is conjectural, but historians have now noted that even with ample supplies, Rommel's long, overland supply route—1500 miles from Tripoli to Egypt—contributed to his chronic supply shortages.

The British, on the other hand, were able to bring in supplies indirectly via the Suez route or by running the gauntlet through the Mediterranean. Consequently, as Rommel's success grew his supply line lengthened while that of the British shrank. As time went on, and, as U.S. aid was funneled into the British pipeline, the supply war favored the British. Time was to favor the defenders of Egypt, but until the time when the British Commonwealth forces could find an able commander to harness their considerable assets they would remain hard-pressed by Rommel's coalition of German and Italian soldiers.

The failure of the June offensive led to the sacking of Wavell. His replacement, Field Marshal Claude Auchinleck, began planning for a new offensive. Auchinleck garnered reinforcement to the point of obtaining an overall two-to-one advantage in armor, manpower, and aircraft. The British offensive, termed "Crusader," began on November 18. Tobruk was relieved on December 10. On December 24 Benghazi was in British hands. But Rommel gathered what forces he had available and launched an attack on the British flank. The attack threatened to cut off the British advance, but Auchinleck, realizing the weakness of the German attacking force, refused to break off the advance. Pressured by the British and robbed of any hope of reinforcements Rommel was forced to withdraw. By the end of December, the British advance had been stopped at El Agheila. On January 11, after receiving supplies, including about 100 Mark III tanks, Rommel's forces drove the British back to El Gazala. There the British began constructing a defensive line stretching from El Gazala to Bir Hachim. This line, actually three defense "boxes" — El Gazala, Knightsbridge, and Bir Hachim — was constructed and improved from February to May 1942.

While the British were constructing their defensive line, Rommel asked for and received supplies and reinforcements for his spring offensive. Though Malta remained a formidable obstacle to Rommel's Mediterranean supply route, the Luftwaffe began to systematically pummel the island. Constant bombardment kept the defenders busy; therefore, resupplying the Axis forces in North Africa became somewhat less difficult. The Luftwaffe could not continue this pressure indefinitely. The Reich's resources were stretched by the spring offensive in the U.S.S.R., and, eventually, the attacks on Malta subsided. The North African theater, though fraught with possibilities, was of secondary importance in the grand strategy of the war as envisioned by OKW, and Rommel's forces were to again suffer neglect.

On May 21, Rommel directed his attack to flank the southern end of the British defense line. Then, he wheeled north, and tried to cut off the British forces at El Gazala. However, the British counterattacked and seemingly penned Rommel's forces in an area which became known as the "Cauldron." Fighting with their backs to the British minefield defenses of El Gazala, Rommel's advanced forces seemed doomed to destruction. In spite of repeated air bombardments and British counterattacks, Rommel's forces held firm.

On June 14, the British withdrew from the El Gazala line. The Knightsbridge and Bir Hachim boxes were abandoned, though the Free French forces at Bir Hachim were to put up a brilliant delaying defense. In spite of the delaying action, on June 11, 1942, Tobruk fell, and the British retreated toward El Alamein. The collapse of the El Gazala line and the fall of Tobruk was one of the worst British disasters of the war in the desert. In large part Rommel's victory was due to the skill of his defense at the Cauldron. Likewise, Rommel had the ability to move quickly to exploit any advantage developing on the battlefield. With the collapse of the "box" defense strategy, the British again resorted to the practice of retreating back into Egypt.

This victory prompted a debate between Rommel, who wished to press onto Cairo, and his superiors—German and Italian—who urged caution and pushed for a more limited commitment to the desert war. Rommel, who was considered headstrong by his detractors, was able to enlist Mussolini's support for this adventure. On June 24, he gave Rommel permission to press on to Egypt. On June 30 Rommel's advance units were near El Alamein, but Rommel delayed the attack until his Italian allies were brought up to the line. This delay allowed the British to look to their defenses.

The El Gazala defeat had led to the firing of Auchinleck and the appointment of a new command structure. Field Marshal Sir Harry Alexander was given Middle East Command and General (later Field Marshal) Bernard Montgomery was given command of the Eighth Army. Montgomery, who had performed well as a division commander in Belgium and France in 1940 was better known as a staff person. He had made a reputation as an instructor in various staff colleges but was not a well-proven commander of such a large field force. He was to prove to be a different sort of commander than his predecessors. In his post-war memoirs he notes that he approached the situation in a studious way. Looking over the situation he came to the conclusion that the only way to stop Rommel's advance was to channel the attack along a predictable line—via the use of extensive minefields—and destroy the advancing forces by using the vantage point of Alam Halfa Ridge to rain artillery on the German advance. The defenses at Alamein were to be quite formidable and posed a real problem for the attacking Axis forces. In part, Montgomery's plan was aided by the existence of the Qattara Depression. This area served as the southern anchor of the line. Since the terrain of this depression was unsuitable for tank warfare, Rommel had no choice but to try to breach the British defense line. Precluded from a sweeping flanking operation, the German Panzers ran into difficulty in the attack of July 2 against the British defense at Deir el Shein.

The presence of Rommel's forces only 60 miles from Alexandria caused panic there and in Cairo. The British fleet was sent from Cairo through the Suez Canal and into the Red Sea. Headquarters personnel began the task of destroying documents, and refugees began pouring from the cities. However, the British line of defenses held throughout July. By August, Rommel had yet to break through.

Rommel was well aware that the British were prepared to meet an attack at Alam Halfa, but he hoped speed and timing would give him an edge of surprise. However, the attack of August 30 was slowed by a deep minefield, and the strong British defense bogged down the attacking force. By September 3, the Germans began a withdrawal. On September 6, Axis forces were establishing defensive positions only a few miles east of the line they held on August 30. The battle for Alam Halfa had cost Rommel dearly in both men and material. Replacement of these losses became more and more difficult as Malta-based ships and planes, freed from the constant Luftwaffe bombardment, once again attacked the Axis shipping lanes in the Mediterranean.

The credit for this defensive victory has been given by some of Montgomery's detractors to the pre-planning of his predecessor, Field Marshal Auchinleck. Auchinleck denies this and gives full credit to Montgomery for the defensive plan. Others have noted that Montgomery capitalized on the information gained from Ultra as to Rommel's attack plans. Montgomery dismisses the allegation and contends that the nature of the battlefield revealed the plan. In short, prior to any access to Ultra, he contended, the direction of Rommel's attack was ordained by the terrain. The defensive plans sprung naturally from that fact. Though Montgomery possessed a strong (some say overbearing) ego, the fact remains that he did carry through his plans to the letter.

Of a meticulous demeanor, Montgomery saw the problems facing him as commander of the Eighth Army. Morale was sagging, and he saw in his troops too much admiration for the enemy commander. For the next seven weeks, Montgomery worked at putting his stamp on the Eighth Army. He visited units, addressed his troops and stressed the importance of the victory of El Alamein, and exuded confidence that the forthcoming British attack would result in a conclusive victory against their redoubtable enemy. In spite of pressures from Churchill, who wished for a quick victory over Rommel to aid the Allied plans for "Torch" (the Allied invasion plan for French North Africa), Montgomery would not be rushed. Supplies were stockpiled and reinforcements were methodically deployed for the attack. Staff planners found Montgomery to be a difficult man to please. He demanded and received carefully prepared staff work. Though his long preparation time unnerved the anxious Churchill, his assumed confidence served to fend off the demands of his superior for quick action. He was to later note that this confidence was more supposed than real.

On the Axis side of the line difficulties grew. Resupply became difficult. Fuel was in very short supply, and food rations were low. Illness spread through the Italian forces; dysentery and jaundice reduced the effective strength of both Italian and German forces. Rommel himself, worn out by constant campaigning, took this opportunity to return to Germany for rest and treatment. General Summe was placed in overall command during his absence while General von Thoma was given command of the Afrika Korps. Both officers were inexperienced in desert warfare having recently returned from the campaign in the Soviet Union. When Montgomery launched his attack on October 23, 1942, Rommel was not in command. When he returned on October 25, Rommel found his defenses badly bent by the British attacks and half of his tank force destroyed in counterattacking the superior British forces. Summe was dead of a heart attack brought about when his staff car sustained a near miss from an artillery shell, and Thoma, who blamed himself for what he saw as impending defeat, was captured when he sought a hero's death on the battlefield.

The Alamein offensive opened with a massive artillery barrage on Friday night, October 23. Montgomery's strategy was to feign an attack to the south in the hopes of drawing German forces from the north, the real center of attack. The ruse did not induce a shift in the German defense and he was not able to punch his way through the enemy's defensive line. By October 26 the British advance had been checked. On October 28 a second attack became ensnarled in minefields and the advance halted. But the defense was costing Rommel's forces heavily and losses were impossible to replace.

On November 2, Montgomery resumed the attack. Losses were again heavy as the attacking force was slowed by minefields, and the German defense was both skillful and determined. Officials in London were disappointed by the failure of rapid progress. Even Montgomery felt less than confident about prospects for victory. However, Rommel's resources were stretched to the limit. His tank force was severely depleted with less than 30 tanks left to fight a British force of 600. It was with this in mind that Rommel decided to withdraw to a new defensive position near Futa. He ordered the withdrawal, but the order was countermanded by Hitler on November 3. Twenty-four hours later, Hitler agreed to a withdrawal. By that time, it was no longer possible for Rommel to organize an effective defense at Futa. For the next several days, Montgomery's Eighth Army attempted to cut off the German withdrawal, but each time Rommel's forces made good their escape. By the end of December 1942, Rommel's forces were established in a defensive position at Buerat in Tripolitania, hundreds of miles from the Eighth Army positioned at Benghazi.

In spite of Rommel's successful withdrawal, the days of the Afrika Korps were numbered. The success of "Operation Torch" placed the German forces in North Africa between the jaws of a vise. When, in the spring of 1943, the jaws were to meet in Tripoli the Axis presence in North Africa came to an end. Rommel was to escape the fate of his army and fight against the Allies in France. However, his name and fame rests on his exploits in the war in the desert. It is a testament to his skill and the fair mindedness of his enemies that he was admired by friend and enemy alike.

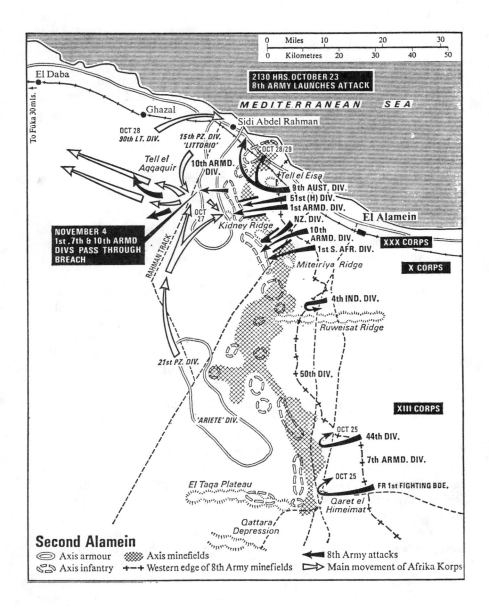

Second Alamein

Axis armour   Axis minefields   8th Army attacks

Axis infantry   +–+ Western edge of 8th Army minefields   ⟹ Main movement of Afrika Korps

"Operation Torch"

While the British Eighth Army was struggling to defeat the Germans in the Egyptian desert, the Allies had launched an invasion of French North Africa. "Operation Torch" was the first major amphibious operation launched by the Allies in the European Theater. North Africa is not Europe, and American military leaders were not enthusiastic about the operation. General George C. Marshall, Army Chief of Staff, favored a 1942 cross-Channel invasion of France. His opinion was shared by other American military planners. However, the British felt that a cross-Channel operation would be too risky a venture in 1942. In the end North Africa was agreed upon as a target. Though it was hardly the "second front" operation that Joseph Stalin had been demanding of the Allies, it was an offensive maneuver, and both the British and American leaders wanted some such action in 1942. Finally, the North African operation was enthusiastically endorsed by Stalin who hoped that it would help take the pressure off the Eastern Front.

American strategic planners were less enthusiastic and were to argue then and later that the North African operation was a step toward committing the Allies to a Southern European strategy. Such an operation, they argued, diverted men and material away from the more strategically important cross-Channel operation. This division of opinion was one of many which arose during the course of the war. The "rights" and "wrongs" of these differing opinions have made for some lively and ongoing controversies and indicate that, in spite of the Allied commitment to victory against the Axis Powers, the "how" of victory was a subject of debate.

Preliminary to the amphibious operation which was "Torch," diplomatic contact arranged by Robert Murphy, the United States representative to the Vichy government, was made between representatives of the Vichy French forces in North Africa and General Mark Clark, United States Army. The meeting was held in an isolated villa on the Algerian coast. Clark arrived via submarine and was paddled ashore in a rubber boat. The meeting did show that there was some willingness on the part of the French to cooperate. However, it was not then clear how cooperation was to work and whether all Vichy commanders in French North Africa would willingly cooperate. The principal concern of Vichy officials was what would be the German reaction to any such obvious cooperation with the Allied invaders. It must also be remembered that British actions during the early years of the war had been interpreted by some of the French as inimical to the interests of the French empire. There was concern among some Vichy leaders that the Allies might harbor secret territorial designs upon France's North African colonies.

The operation, launched on November 8, 1942 was a joint American-British undertaking. Landings were made at Casablanca, Morocco, and at Oran and Algiers in Algeria. Algiers surrendered on the first day, resistance was greater

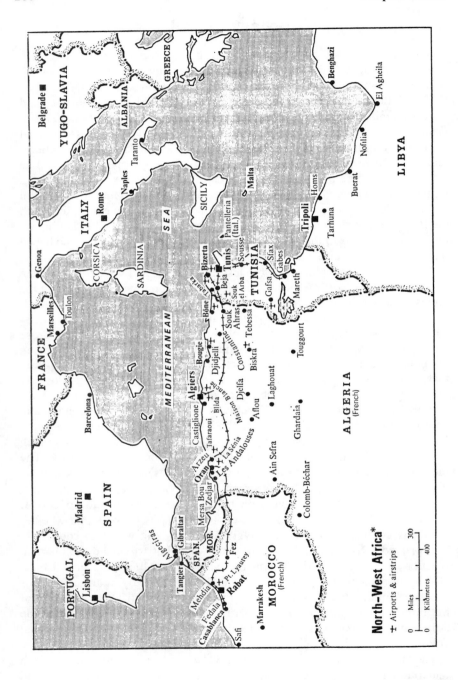

North-West Africa*

✝ Airports & airstrips

at Oran, but it and the naval base at Mers-El-Kabir fell on November 10. The Casablanca landing was the most difficult. The French naval batteries and warships fired on the invasion fleet. The Allies prepared to lay siege to the city, but on November 11 all fighting ceased.

Admiral Darlan, Petain's successor designate, was in North Africa at the time of the invasion. His position in the Vichy government afforded him legitimacy in the eyes of many French commanders. When the invasion came, he was in touch with the government at Vichy. After many false starts and changes of mind, he ultimately issued the order to stop the fighting. This order came about, in part, because Germany moved to occupy Vichy territory in violation of the armistice of June 1940. Later, when German forces tried to seize elements of the French fleet anchored in Toulon harbor, the French Admiral Laborde ordered the ships scuttled in harbor.

In an attempt to establish some semblance of political order, General Dwight Eisenhower, commanding the Anglo-American forces and soon to be named Supreme Allied Commander, appointed Darlan as the political chief of North Africa and General Giraud as military commander. This was hardly the best of solutions. Giraud was not well accepted and the Gaullists were angry at being excluded. Some of the difficulty was alleviated when Darlan was assassinated in late December. Eventually, Charles de Gaulle was to be accepted as the leader of "Free France," but this was accomplished only after long and bitter negotiations. De Gaulle is often depicted as a "difficult" person by the Allied officials who dealt with him during the war, but he was well aware of his rather tenuous position and was ever sensitive to French interests and the honor of France.

As the Allies made preparations for an attack on Tunisia, an important meeting took place at Casablanca in January 1943. The most important personalities at the conference were Prime Minister Churchill and President Roosevelt. Joseph Stalin was not present in the flesh, but much of what was decided at the conference bore directly on Stalin's repeated demands for more action from the Allies. The conferees decided that a centralized command structure was necessary. Eisenhower was named Supreme Allied Commander; Sir Harold Alexander was designated his deputy. Differences in overall strategy was evident at Casablanca as American military leaders voiced a reluctance to become overly involved in a Mediterranean strategy at the expense of delaying the cross-Channel attack. Churchill's idea of attack via the so-called "soft underbelly" of southern Europe prevailed. Plans were made for an attack on Sicily. The hope was that action in the Mediterranean would drain off forces from the Eastern front, knock Italy out of the war, and persuade Turkey to join the Allies. The conferees also agreed to launch a cross-Channel attack as soon as possible, to step up the air war against Germany, to intensify the antisubmarine campaign in the Atlantic, and to increase the volume of supplies to the Soviet Union. It was also decided that pressure would be maintained in the Pacific and Burma would be recaptured. However, the Pacific War was given a definitely secondary priority. Although it was decided that submarine activity against the Japanese would be intensified, the British evidenced a concern that the American navy was too prone to allocate its surface resources to the Pacific Theater. Victory in Europe was the first goal, and to this the two leaders agreed. However, the voices of criticism raised against the U.S. navy's leadership over allocation of resources were not to be silenced by the Conference of Casablanca.

The most surprising development of the conference came at its end. Almost as an afterthought, President Roosevelt announced a policy of *unconditional surrender* toward the Axis Powers. Citing the example of Ulysses S. Grant during the American Civil War, Roosevelt's policy statement meant that the Axis Powers would be forced to admit defeat and would not be able to negotiate terms for surrender. Churchill was surprised by the announcement but went along with it in the interests of Allied harmony. No other Allied policy made during the war has been more criticized than that of unconditional surrender. Total defeat was seen as total destruction. Critics contend that faced with that alternative, the only resource of the enemy was to fight on. Thus, unconditional surrender was seen as an important factor in prolonging the war and increasing the death toll. One plus of the policy was that it should have allayed Stalin's fears that his Western Allies might sign a separate peace with Hitler leaving the Soviets holding the bag. But Stalin was ever a suspicious man; his words and actions indicate that even unconditional surrender statements did not convince him that the Allies would not side with Germany to destroy communism. So the criticism remains. Few have defended Roosevelt's policy; yet the fact remains that in actual practice the Allies were to make some slight concessions to their vanquished foes, the Italians. The Soviets, in fact, ignored unconditional surrender in dealing with Bulgaria and Rumania, and even the United States issued some clarification regarding the fate of the Emperor to the Japanese before their surrender.

Many critics of the policy of unconditional surrender argue that it prolonged the war by discouraging the anti-Hitler element within the Third Reich from overthrowing the dictator and asking for a separate peace with the Western Allies. Certainly, as we see from the works now being released, there were those within the inner-circles of power who favored a separate peace with Germany as a bulwark against the spread of Soviet power in East and Central Europe. The argument against unconditional surrender flowered in such circles. However, if one looks at the facts, this argument becomes less clear. For example, three of the supposedly six plots to assassinate Hitler occurred after the January 1943 policy statement issued from Casablanca by Roosevelt and Churchill. Two occurred in March 1943, both of which were, of course, unsuccessful. The most famous attempt, July 1944, was nineteen months after the policy was announced. All this is by way of saying that the unconditional surrender policy seemed not to have stilled the plots against the Führer. Unfortunately, most of these plotters were discovered and executed, but the fact remains that plots were hatched, no matter how ineptly, after the policy of the Allied Powers was announced.

As we shall see, decisions of military strategy were equally important in determining the course of the conflict and the timetable of victory. For the concept of a speedy victory rests on the ability of arms to bring the enemy to its knees. The involvement in the long, destructive, and frustrating conflict in Italy is a case in point. Many strategists argue that the "soft underbelly" approach overstretched the resources of the Allies and hindered the planning for the more direct approach. Others argue that the ponderousness of Allied strategy also played a part in delaying the march to victory. In all, the controversy over unconditional surrender is but one of the promitories of disagreement which complicated what was, in essence, a successful joint effort between British and American strategic planners during the course of this long, destructive war.

In January 1943 victory was hardly within view. The move to compress the Axis forces in Tunisia did not occur without problems. The British, rightly it appears, were doubtful of the combat readiness of the untested Americans. Supply and transport problems plagued the Allied armies in their attack on Tunisia, and Rommel was far from ready to give up. In January, the German commander launched an armored attack from the Faid Pass. The American forces were pushed back through the Kasserine Pass, and Rommel's armor threatened to cut the advancing armies in two. The American response was massive; reinforcements were rushed to the front; trucks hauled tons of supplies, and Allied air power was employed to slow, then halt, the armored advance. But the Battle of Kasserine Pass cost the American forces 10,000 casualties (German losses were 2,000), and gave credence to those who had discounted the capabilities of America's untested forces. However, experience is a hard teacher, and American field commanders were to learn from such costly lessons. After the defeat, field command was given to General George S. Patton, Jr. who was to gain a reputation as an able leader during the Tunisian campaign.

In Southern Tunisia Rommel constructed a defense barrier, the Mareth Line, blocking the British advance. Montgomery's Eighth Army was to halt there in January, and it was not until March 1943 that Montgomery tried to breach the line by launching a frontal attack on the line while dispatching a part of his forces to sweep around its southern flank. The fighting moved from one mountain range to another. On May 7, 1943 the British First Army under General Anderson finally took Tunis, cutting the Axis army in two. On that same day the American Second Corps—which included some French units— took Bizerta. On May 13, 1943, General von Arnim, Rommel's successor, surrendered all Axis forces in Tunisia. The defense of Tunisia had cost the Axis dearly. In all, the Desert War had cost the Axis nearly one million men killed, wounded, or captured.

Invasion of Sicily

The next step for the Allies was to be the invasion of Sicily. Herein, the art of deception helped in the success of the Sicily operation. The British, using fake documents planted on the supposedly drowned body of a British courier set adrift in Spanish waters, led the Germans to believe that the next attack would be in Greece. Though the subterfuge was doubted by some generals such as Kesselring, Hitler was convinced that the purported documents were genuine and acted accordingly. This elaborate act of deception was one of the more successful of the war. Certainly never before or since had a corpse, dead from natural causes, played such an important role in a military campaign.

The strategy to be followed in the Sicilian campaign was a simple one. After some debate and disagreement, Allied leaders decided that the main objective was to be given to the British Eighth Army under Montgomery. The British were to land on the southeastern tip of Sicily and proceed northward to take Messina and cut off the Axis withdrawal from the island. The secondary screening role was given to the American Seventh Army under command of General Patton. Patton, who had enjoyed success in the North Africa campaign, was considered by Eisenhower to be his best field commander. The secondary role did not suit the flamboyant Patton, and he used every opportunity to stretch the letter of his orders to expand the Seventh Army's role in the Sicilian campaign.

Preliminary to the Sicilian invasion the Allied forces invaded the Italian held islands of Pantelleria, Lampedusa, and Linosa. By June 13, 1943, the islands were in Allied hands. To keep the enemy guessing Allied bombers attacked Sicily and Sardinia while Allied naval maneuvering suggested an attack on Greece. On July 9, 1943 the invasion fleet assembled. Fortunately, due to inclement weather, coastal lookouts on Sicily assumed no invasion would be likely for the day of July 10, and no watch was kept. After midnight, the weather abated. The Allies, using amphibious landing craft, proceeded with the landing. Preliminary to the amphibious landing, glider and parachute troops were sent to seize the southeastern beach (the British landing area) and the south coast, Gela area (the American landing). Unfortunately, high winds made glider landing difficult, and parachute troops were widely scattered in the drop. In the confusion of the battle, "friendly fire" from vessels of the invasion fleet exacted a toll on the Allied airborne forces. The confusion of battle and the inexperience of transport pilots added to the wide scattering of paratroops over the drop zone.

In spite of these difficulties, the ship to shore landings on both the British and American sectors of the beachhead went well. At Gela, however, the Americans were subject to a vigorous attack from the Panzers of the Hermann Göring division. The July 11 German attack was stopped at the beach by naval shellfire and air attacks, and the American Seventh Army began its move inland.

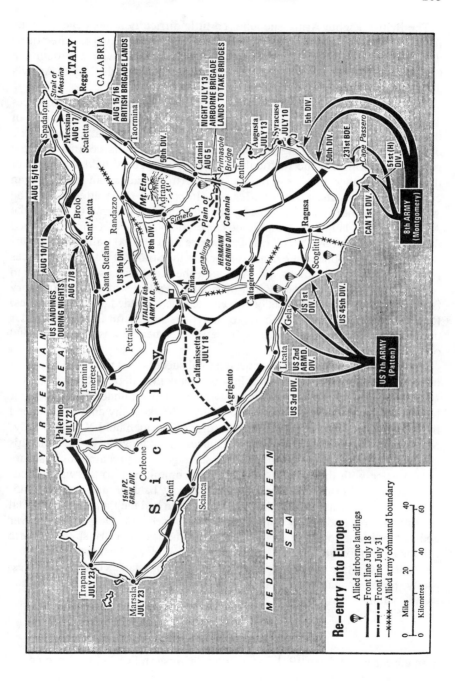

Re—entry into Europe

Allied airborne landings
Front line July 18
Front line July 31
Allied army command boundary

The British Eighth Army encountered little difficulty at the beach, but its forward advance was checked at Primasole Bridge on July 14. After three days fighting, the bridge was taken, but Montgomery's advance through the Catania plain was slowed by stiff resistance which blocked the Eighth Army's direct route to Messina.

The American Seventh Army had moved rapidly inland. Patton's forces captured Palermo on July 22. A second force drove through the center of the island to link with Montgomery's forces near Mount Etna. Yet, the Axis defense was skillful. Using the terrain, rear guard units commanded the roadways making advance difficult. While the rear guard held the speed of the Allied advance to a slow march, the German and Italian forces began evacuating across the Strait of Messina. In spite of three attempts by the American Seventh Army and one by the British Eighth Army to cut off the Axis retreat by launching amphibious operations, the Axis forces escaped the trap. More than 39,000 German and more than 70,000 Italian troops plus equipment and supplies were evacuated across the Strait before Patton's forces reached Messina on August 17. Although the Americans were the first to reach the objective the enemy had decamped. Patton's brief light of glory faded as a result of his treatment of two enlisted men "battle fatigue" casualties. Resultant publicity led Eisenhower to shelve his successful field commander until after the invasion of Normandy (June 1944), when he was given command of the U.S. Third Army.

The Sicilian campaign had not been a total success, yet the likely prospect of the fall of Sicily prompted the Fascist Council to depose Mussolini. On July 25 Mussolini was shorn of his powers and placed under custody. Later he was rescued by a commando force led by Otto Skorzeny and was to spend the remainder of the war as the puppet ruler of German held Northern Italy. Marshal Badoglio was named as his successor. Badoglio pledged that his government would continue the war, but secretly made preparations to secure an armistice with the Allies. As the Italian commitment to the war waned, it was to be the Germans who made Italy the bloody battleground of 1943-1945.

From a military standpoint the Sicily campaign had taught the Allies a vital lesson; the soft underbelly was tougher than it seemed. Despite manpower and material superiority, more than 480,000 American and British troops were used in the campaign; skilled defensive forces, utilizing the terrain, frustrated the Allies' objective of blocking the evacuation of the island's defending forces. Sicily, however, had been won, and that island was to serve as the stepping stone to Italy.

Summary

In the early months of 1941 Great Britain's Western Desert Force had nearly ousted the Italians from North Africa. In Syria, Iraq, and Iran, measures were taken to safeguard these areas from Axis hands, thereby giving some protection against an eastern approach to the Suez. But the real danger to Egypt and the Suez came from the West. In March 1941, General Erwin Rommel was sent by the Germans to aid their Italian allies in North Africa. Though the North African campaign never was seen by the Germans as their major area of operations, the so-called Desert War became the main theater of land operations for the British during this period. In the spring of 1941 Rommel launched an attack against the British forces and pushed them back from Tripoli into Egypt. Attempts to force Rommel back were made in June, but it was not until November that a British force managed to drive the Axis forces from Egypt. In May of 1942, Rommel again attacked and forced the British back into Egypt. His bid to take all of Egypt failed after his repulse at Alam Halfa Ridge, and in October 1942, British Field Marshal Montgomery launched his offensive. After much hard fighting, Rommel's forces were pushed back to Buerat. Rommel's bid for Egypt had failed.

In November 1942 a joint British-American operation, *Torch*, was launched against French-held North Africa. After negotiations and some heavy fighting, the Allies established control over the area and fighting ceased on November 11. The Allied strategy was to push from west to east, bottle up the Axis forces in Tunisia, and destroy them. This was not easy to accomplish. By January 1943, the American forces had suffered reversals at Faid and Kasserine, and Montgomery's forces were held in check by the German line at Mareth.

Meanwhile, in Casablanca, a major Allied conference was being held. Principal among the decisions made at this January conference was the development of a Mediterranean strategy to knock Italy out of the war. However, the most famous (some might say fateful) decision made there was the announcement of American President Roosevelt of the Allied policy of "unconditional surrender." Whether or not this policy was wise or unwise has been seriously debated. Though disagreements as to Allied strategy continued, the coalition was to remain sound and firm in its resolve.

After the winter rains, the battle for Tunisia began again. By early May, the Axis forces there were cut in two, and on May 13 Axis forces surrendered. The battle for North Africa had been won.

The next phase of the Mediterranean strategy called for the invasion of Sicily. Allied landing forces hit the beaches of Sicily on July 10. The American beach at Gela was threatened by an Axis counterattack, but that attack was rebuffed. For the next 39 days Allied forces attempted to secure Sicily and to block the evacuation of Axis forces from the island. On August 17, 1943 the American commander, General Patton, reached the Allied objective of Messina shortly before Montgomery's Eighth Army but not before the Axis forces had succeeded in withdrawing their troops and most of their equipment across the narrow Strait of Messina.

The campaign had taught the Allies that campaigning in difficult terrain favors the defenders and that such operations might well prove to be long and costly ones. The victory in Sicily led to the overthrow of Mussolini. He was deposed by action of the Fascist Council in July 1943 and his replacement, Marshal Badoglio, secretly began to explore ways which Italy could secure an armistice with the Allies. By August 1943, the Mediterranean was largely under Allied control. However, difficult years lay ahead, and the Mediterranean strategy proved to be a most controversial one for the Allies.

Suggested Reading

Blumenson, Martin. *Rommel's Last Victory: The Battle of Kasserine Pass*. London, 1968. A prolific writer on the subject of famous battles, he covers the intracies very well. See also his, *Salerno to Cassino* (Washington, 1969).

Hamilton, Nigel. *Monty, The Making of the General (1887-1942)*. New York, 1981. The first of a three-volume biography, it provides insight into Montgomery's character, though Hamilton is less critical than most who have written about the famous Field Marshal.

Montgomery of Alamein, Bernard Law Montgomery. *The Memoirs of Field Marshal the Viscount Montgomery of Alamein*. New York: New American Library, 1959. Though he has been accused of selective memory by some writers, his memoirs are interesting and revealing to a discerning reader.

Patton, George S. *War As I Knew It*. New York, 1947. This book is a short one, but one which is a delight for what it says and does not say.

Pogue, Forrest C. *George C. Marshall: Ordeal and Hope, 1939-1942*. New York, 1966. This second volume of Pogue's work deals with the material in this chapter and is the most interesting of the three.

Pyle, Ernie. *Ernie's War: The Best of Ernie Pyle's World War II Dispatches*. New York, 1986. Pyle followed American troops from North Africa, Sicily, and Italy to the Pacific where he was killed by a Japanese sniper. He was one of the few war correspondents who lived with and understood the life of a front line soldier.

Rommel, Erwin. *The Rommel Papers*. (ed. B.H. Liddell-Hart). New York: Harcourt Brace, 1953. Accounts of his triumphs and defeats in North Africa from his personal letters and other papers.

8

The Pacific War
April 1942 to June 1943
and Other Theaters of Operation
1941-1943

The Tokyo Raid played an important part in prompting the Japanese to complete the extension of their perimeter by neutralizing Australia and destroying the American Pacific fleet. The plan to put Australia within range of air attack necessitated the establishment of Japanese control over Port Moresby, New Guinea. This Japanese plan was to lead to an air-naval battle known in history as the Battle of the Coral Sea.

In April 1942, the hard pressed Allies had decided that the huge Pacific area should be divided into theaters. The British were given the responsibility over the Indian Ocean area; the United States took over the rest of the Pacific area. The Americans further divided this area. General Douglas MacArthur, now commanding from Australia, was charged with the Southwest Pacific. Admiral Chester Nimitz, stationed at Pearl Harbor, was given charge of the vast Pacific area from the Solomons to the Arctic.

It is of interest to note that the Japanese move to cut off Australia involved establishing control over the Solomons. These islands constituted the dividing line between the two American theaters, and rivalry between the two strong American commanders prompted some writers to observe that the war of 1942-1943 became something of a war between the U.S. Army and the U.S. Navy as well as a war against the Japanese.

Since the Pacific theater had been classified as secondary to the war against Hitler (by mutual but not unanimous agreement), reinforcements and supplies were necessarily short. Therefore, rival commanders struggled very hard indeed for a larger slice of a rather smallish pie.

In April the Japanese began assembling their combined forces and invaded Tulagi on May 3. The force then steamed east of the Solomons into the Coral Sea. Fortunately for the Americans, the Japanese code was known to them and Admiral Nimitz, therefore, had a good idea of their plans. Two carriers had been dispatched into the area, the *Lexington* and the *Yorktown*; this carrier force was under the command of Admiral Frank Fletcher. The Japanese invasion force was screened by a carrier force comprising two large carriers, the *Zuikaku* and the *Shokaku*, under command of Admiral Takeo Takagi. Nimitz was to dispatch two other carriers to the battle, the *Enterprise* and the *Hornet*, but they arrived too late to join in the battle.

In essence, what the Americans attempted to do was to block the Japanese invasion of Port Moresby, but the resultant battle was more groping than planned, and luck played a large part in deciding the issue. On May 7 American and Japanese carrier forces were in search of each other, and Admiral Fletcher's force managed to find and sink the light carrier, *Shoho*. The Japanese invasion fleet was called back from their approach of Port Moresby as both sides searched for the crucially important carrier force.

On May 8, the rival forces came into contact. American pilots spotted and attacked the *Shokaku* and seriously damaged her. However, due to heavy cloud cover, the other Japanese carrier, the *Zuikaku*, escaped detection. At the same time, Japanese aircraft attacked the American carriers, *Yorktown* and *Lexington*. Unfortunately, Admiral Fletcher's fleet operated under clear skies, and the Japanese attack planes saw and pummelled the *Lexington* and the *Yorktown*. The *Yorktown* was hit but not so severely as the Japanese thought; the *Lexington* was so badly damaged that it was abandoned.

In total, Coral Sea was an American victory, though a close one. American aircraft losses were approximately 74 while Japanese aircraft losses numbered 80. The Japanese lost more men in the battle than did the Americans, but the Americans suffered the sinking of one of their fleet carriers while the Japanese only lost one light carrier. But, the attempt to take Port Moresby had been foiled. Thus, for the first time in the Pacific War the Japanese were forced to turn away from an objective.

Battle of Midway

For the United States the greater victory was to come in June at the Battle of Midway. The Midway attack was part of an elaborate Japanese plan engineered by Admiral Yamamoto to draw the American fleet into the jaws of a gigantic trap. The bait for this trap was an attack on the Aleutian Islands and the bombing of Dutch Harbor, Alaska. Yamamoto reasoned that this would bring the American carrier fleet north while the Japanese invaded Midway Island, some 1,200 to 1,500 miles from Oahu, Hawaii. Caught between the jaws of a trap the American force would then been destroyed. However, by committing themselves to a fixed point attack, and by tying fleet movement to slower transport speeds, Yamamoto's plan became somewhat inflexible. The greatest fault of this elaborate plan was that it was not to come as a surprise to the Americans. Nimitz was aware of the Japanese objective at Midway. Piecing together information from radio intercept reports and aided by the secret fact that American code specialists had knowledge of the Japanese naval code, Nimitz was able to position his carrier force near Midway.

Fortunately for Nimitz, the Japanese air-submarine reconnaissance patterns were such that his fleet escaped chance detection. The Japanese, assured of the element of surprise, continued with their operation. The first phase began on June 3 with the bombing of Dutch Harbor. Then, on June 6, three invasion landings were made in the Aleutians. On June 4 Nagumo's carrier planes began bombing Midway. His carriers came under attack from Midway-based planes, so a second wave was ordered. Nagumo's reconnaissance detected American ships 200 miles away; the Admiral assumed them to be conventional warships. Later it was revealed that a carrier was among the approaching fleet. Nagumo altered course and avoided the first wave of American dive-bombers; however, American torpedo planes found his carriers and attacked them. The planes began their attack at approximately 9:30 in the morning. Less than an hour later the attacking force had been almost completely destroyed. Destruction of the American torpedo planes convinced the Japanese that they had won the engagement. But, a few minutes later, American dive-bombers attacked the Japanese ships. Nagumo's carrier, *Akagi*, was badly hit and later abandoned. The carriers *Kaga* and *Soryu* also were hit and eventually sent to the bottom. The only Japanese carrier left intact was the *Hiryu*. Her planes attacked the *Yorktown*, and that ship, damaged at Coral Sea, was abandoned in the afternoon. However, planes from the fatally damaged *Yorktown* exacted vengeance on the *Hiryu*, and on June 5, the *Hiryu*, abandoned and lifeless, sank beneath the waves of the Pacific.

The Battle of Midway which was to have destroyed American carrier forces ended with the destruction of Nagumo's task force. The losses in carriers, planes, and personnel were to prove disastrous for the Japanese fleet. Yet, the Japanese navy was still powerful and it would be some time before the United States could attain air and sea superiority in the Pacific. Still, the

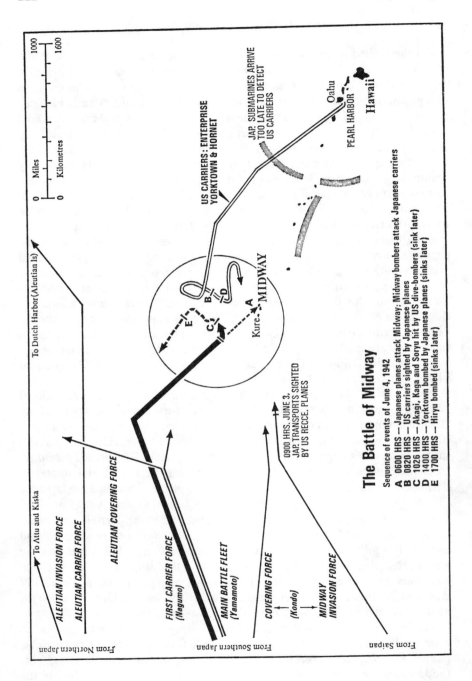

The Battle of Midway

Sequence of events of June 4, 1942

A 0600 HRS — Japanese planes attack Midway; Midway bombers attack Japanese planes
B 0820 HRS — US carriers sighted by Japanese planes
C 1026 HRS — Akagi, Kaga and Soryu hit by US dive-bombers (sink later)
D 1400 HRS — Yorktown bombed by Japanese planes (sinks later)
E 1700 HRS — Hiryu bombed (sinks later)

US CARRIERS: ENTERPRISE
YORKTOWN & HORNET

JAP. SUBMARINES ARRIVE
TOO LATE TO DETECT
US CARRIERS

Oahu
PEARL HARBOR
Hawaii

MIDWAY

Kure

0900 HRS. JUNE 3,
JAP. TRANSPORTS SIGHTED
BY US RECCE. PLANES

To Dutch Harbor (Aleutian Is)

To Attu and Kiska

From Northern Japan

ALEUTIAN INVASION FORCE

ALEUTIAN CARRIER FORCE

ALEUTIAN COVERING FORCE

FIRST CARRIER FORCE
(Nagumo)

MAIN BATTLE FLEET
(Yamamoto)

From Southern Japan

COVERING FORCE

(Kondo)

MIDWAY
INVASION FORCE

From Saipan

1000
1600

Miles
Kilometres

0
0

Midway victory had, at the very least, removed any immediate or real threat to Hawaii.

Historical hindsight helps us to realize the significance of the Midway battle, and it has led to reconsiderations of the effectiveness of Yamamoto as a great naval commander. Had the Japanese continued the fight, even after the destruction of a good part of their carrier force, their numerically superior surface fleet could have destroyed the American fleet according to some who have studied the battle. Likewise, historians note that the American naval command did not realize the implication of the Midway victory. Nor did American naval strategists understand that the Japanese would now be hard put to resupply and reinforce its vast defensive ring in the Pacific. The perspective of time allows us now to see that the Japanese fleet and, in fact, the total forces of the Emperor were not sufficient to attain the objective of the conflict which had begun on December 7, 1941. But no feeling of euphoria was evident in the headquarters of the American fleet, and rightly so. Though this summer victory of 1942 was to be a turning point in the Pacific war, those who fought the battle realized that victory had been a narrow one and the end of the conflict was still far in the future.

Defeat at Coral Sea had not forced the Japanese to abandon their strategy of neutralizing Australia. In July 1942 they launched an attack on New Guinea (Papua). The attack was designed to secure the north coast village of Buna. The final objective of the New Guinea operation was to cross the rugged Owen Stanley Mountains and secure first Kokoda and then Port Moresby. In August an additional Japanese force landed at Milne Bay on the southeastern tip of the island. There they established an airbase. Australian and American troops fought back, but it took six months of heavy fighting to drive the Japanese from Buna. The fighting in New Guinea (Papua) was far from over, but after January 1943 Japanese forces posed less of a threat to Port Moresby and Australia itself.

Allied Offensives

So far the Allied campaign in the Pacific had been more defensive than offensive. In June and July of 1942, the strategy of the offensive was discussed and debated. The war between the army and the navy had begun. Eventually, a compromise plan was endorsed which called for a three-stage offensive beginning with an attack on the Santa Cruz Islands and the southeastern Solomons, the clearing of New Guinea (Papua), and ultimately the seizure of the important Japanese base at Rabaul. In July, however, reconnaissance revealed that the Japanese were preparing an airfield at Lunga Point on the island of Guadalcanal. The development of a bomber base there was a sore threat to the American strategy. Therefore, it was decided to make Guadalcanal the first objective of the offensive. This decision was not undertaken without controversy. General MacArthur was opposed to the Guadalcanal operation. He saw it as detracting from the overall strategy of securing Rabaul. However, through the intervention of President Roosevelt, MacArthur was forced to reluctantly agree to the operation. This was not to be the last occasion when differences in Pacific strategy called for the intervention of an outside mediator—the President of the United States.

Admiral Nimitz was placed in overall charge of the Guadalcanal operation. Admiral Robert L. Ghromley headed operations, Admiral Fletcher took command of the tactical side of the operation, and Major General Alexander A. Vandergrift was named commander of the Marine landing force.

On August 7, 1942 the invasion began. Tulagi, with its 1,500-man garrison, was invaded by a force of approximately 6,000 marines. On August 8 the island was taken. The landing on Guadalcanal was hardly contested by the Japanese whose forces there consisted only of a few thousand construction workers. By the evening of August 7, more than 10,000 marines had landed on the island. The Japanese reaction was prompt; reinforcements were rushed to the island. However, since the Japanese underestimated the size of the American invading force, they tended to reinforce the island in small contingents. Each Japanese reinforcement contingent was enlarged so that what should have been a brief campaign became a protracted land and sea battle wherein American ships and planes tried to stop the reinforcement and resupply of the island while on the land marines and army troops had to hold off successive waves of Japanese reinforcements.

Though the landing on the 7th was an easy one, the Japanese response placed the marine landing force in a difficult position. On August 7 a Japanese naval task force from Rabaul sailed down "The Slot"—that is, the narrow waters between the two chains of the Solomon Islands, and struck the American ships. This night battle, the Battle of Savo Island, was a major defeat for the Americans and had the effect of depriving the American landing force of naval support. For two weeks, the Marines were bereft of sea and air support and were reduced to very short rations. On August 18 the Japanese sent reinforcements. The 1,500 men of this first wave were wiped out at Lunga Point by the American defenders. Additional reinforcements were sent in a convoy protected by three carriers and several ships of the line. This force was intended to draw out and trap the American forces. However, the Americans were forewarned. The early warning system consisted of Australian coastal watchers placed at strategic locations on the numerous islands of the Solomon chain. These men watched and reported Japanese fleet movements to the American leaders providing them with advanced information. The life of the coast watcher was often short and always dangerous, but without them, the series of naval engagements in the Eastern Solomons would have proved disastrous to the Americans. The first such engagement, on August 24, proved indecisive. The Japanese carrier, *Ryujo*, was sighted and sunk, and the American carrier *Enterprise* was damaged. The Japanese losses in aircraft were much higher

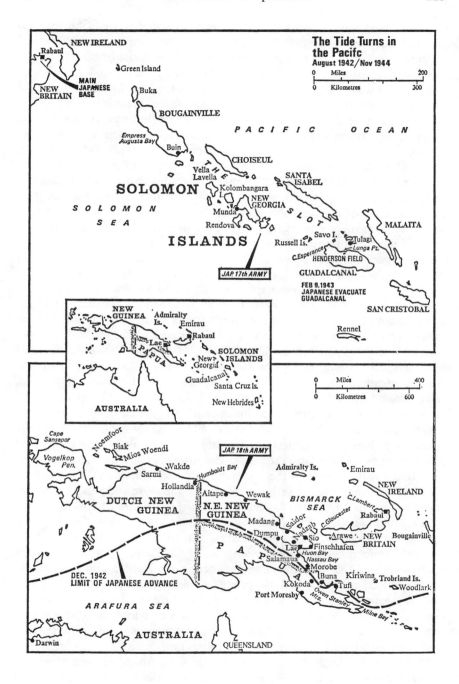

The Tide Turns in the Pacifc
August 1942/Nov 1944

than were the American, yet American air and naval supremacy in the Solomon Sea was far from being established.

On September 13 and 14 a land battle, termed the Battle of Bloody Ridge, ended with a repulse of Japanese forces. However, the military situation on Guadalcanal was still grave for the American defenders. In October, the sea battle of Cape Esperance ended with American forces claiming an edge. Yet, the Japanese were able to land a large number of reinforcements on the island bringing their troop strength on Guadalcanal to approximately 22,000. The marines, with approximately 23,000 men, were to be hard pressed. In October the naval battle of the Santa Cruz Islands ended with the Americans claiming a victory over the Japanese. In November, the naval battle for Guadalcanal ended with the loss of two American cruisers, while the Japanese lost their first battleship of the war, the *Hiei*. On November 14 the American fleet intercepted a Japanese convoy transporting troops to Guadalcanal and destroyed most of the troop transports.

Slowly the balance of power shifted. The Japanese Imperial General Staff desperately wished to hold Guadalcanal, but the constant losses sustained, losses nearly impossible to replace, forced them to consider abandoning the island. In January 1943 the decision was made, and by February 1943 the Japanese evacuated what troops they could from Guadalcanal. This American victory had cost the Japanese over 25,000 casualties plus the loss of more than 600 aircraft and 25 ships. U.S. Marine losses were 1,044 killed, 2,894 wounded, 55 missing. U.S. Army losses were 446 killed, 1,910 wounded. Naval losses in ships were the same as the Japanese, but losses in tonnage were greater for the Imperial Navy. On February 9, 1943, all organized resistance ceased. In April 1943 Guadalcanal was the base from which two flights of P-38 aircraft, one marine and one U.S. Army Air Corps, launched an attack to intercept and destroy Admiral Yamamoto's plane as it flew in for an inspection of the Japanese bases. The Admiral's aircraft was intercepted over Bougainville Island in the Solomons and was shot down. The death of Admiral Yamamoto was a serious one for the Japanese and was yet another casualty resulting from the Japanese defeat in the Battle of Guadalcanal.

The American victory was to bring about a reconsideration of the strategy for the Pacific war. This reconsideration was to occur in May 1943 at the Trident Conference, held in Washington, D.C. There, American military leaders decided that the American advance in the Pacific would consist of a two-pronged assault. One of the prongs would emanate from the Southwest Pacific theater of operation and be commanded by the theater commander, General Douglas MacArthur. The second prong, under the command of Admiral Chester Nimitz, would consist of a thrust across the Central Pacific. Both prongs would converge on the Philippines.

This division of forces was a political compromise which has been bemoaned by some military writers as being costly in time and materials. The reason for the compromise lies in the personalities of the rival theater commanders and, perhaps, an overestimation of the Japanese capability to maintain its defensive ring. This division of effort has been seen as foolhardy and the compromise, worked out under the good offices of President Roosevelt, is seen by some as a weakening of an already limited American force in the Pacific. However, from the Japanese point of view the two-pronged strategy kept them guessing and forced them to divide their already straited forces. Therefore, as a result of a clash of opinions in the inner circles of American military leadership, the enemy was put to a disadvantage and could not be sure as to when and where the next strike would come. Finally, the Trident Conference saw the designation of a third theater, the China-Burma-India theater. Command here was a bit of a compromise with Lord Louis Mountbatten named Supreme Allied Commander Southeast Asia. Lord Mountbatten also worked with General Stilwell and Chiang Kai Shek in this theater which was to be an unfortunate backwater of the main war in the Pacific.

Certainly, as American air and sea superiority grew, supply of the Japanese-held islands became increasingly difficult. The island-hopping strategy of the Americans, though costly, did serve to accelerate the Japanese decline. In committing themselves to defending such a vast area, the Japanese had counted on naval and air superiority. Losses sustained in the defensive campaigns, however, whittled away at Japanese strength. As a matter of fact, the diminution of Japanese military power allowed for the development of the American strategy of by-pass; that is, isolating and neutralizing such Japanese bases as Rabaul, which limited the need for costly invasion attempts. In general, the principal criticisms of American strategy in the Pacific centers on the eurocentric view that the allocation of men, ships, and planes in the Pacific might have been better employed in the European theater. Such writers tend to neglect the obvious fact that for most Americans the Pacific war was of prime importance. Whatever the decision of the Allied political leaders and the Allied General Staff had been as to the overall strategy of the war, it would have been politically impossible for American leadership to curtail allocation of manpower and supplies in the Pacific to the degree that Great Britain had done to her forces in Burma.

The Burma Campaign

The Burma campaign was truly a poor man's war. Short of manpower and material the British held on to the frontier defenses and planned for a counteroffensive in the Arakan region of Burma. Wavell's attempted offensive of December 1942 soon bogged down. By May 1943 the British were back where they had started. Wavell likewise employed the services and backed the concept of Colonel, later General, Orde Wingate. Wingate's plan called for developing a force which could operate behind enemy lines. Such *long-range penetration groups*, would disrupt Japanese lines of supply and communications and divert troops from the main front. In essence, these groups would be most effective during the period of a British offensive, when disruption and diversion of forces would be most crucial. Wavell supported the idea, and in February 1943 two such groups crossed the Chindwin River. By April the group had to be pulled out. The losses of Wingate's "Chindits" had been heavy and the results of their efforts small. However, the idea was not abandoned and would be attempted again in 1944.

The concept of special group operations seemed to fascinate military planners and the public alike. Though many such groups were formed most, such as the "Chindits," did not fulfill their promise or suffered grievous losses in the process of attaining their operational objective. Marauder and Ranger groups were formed in the Pacific theater and Ranger groups were to be used first in Italy in the European theater and were to suffer heavily at Salerno. In all, special, elite units operating outside of the regular military table of organization did not work well in the Pacific nor elsewhere. It has not been until very recently that the integration of such units into the overall strategy of a campaign has been accomplished. In World War II such elite formations were not well integrated into the overall operational plan.

Though Burma was primarily a British area of operation, American interest in that area was intense. The American commitment to China has been noted previously; this attachment to the China theater of operation was to continue. General Stilwell, an infantry soldier, had been made Chiang Kai Shek's principal military adviser. Though he came to distrust and even to despise Chiang, he labored to secure better supply access for the Chinese. Burma was considered to be of prime importance for reopening the Burma Road between India and China which would mean freer access to supplies. For the time being, and, as a matter of fact, for most of the war, the only real supply link between China and her Allies was via "the Hump" — that is, air supplies flown from India over some of the roughest mountain terrain in the world. It was the hope of many American strategists that in freeing Burma and supplying China that nation could become the springboard to the main islands of Japan. This, of course, proved not to be the case. The China theater was to remain an intriguing backwater of the war in Asia.

It is of interest to note that Stilwell was far too direct a person to appreciate the rather delicate position of his Chinese superior. Chiang had to contend with both the Japanese invader, his "war lord" supporters, and, of course, the menace of the communist forces under the leadership of Mao Tse-tung. Stilwell, like so many American military men and diplomats, was attracted to the seemingly democratic proclivities of the Chinese communists. They appeared a marked contrast to the corruption and apathy evidenced by those who surrounded America's ostensible ally, Chiang Kai Shek. A moralist, Stilwell was appalled by Chinese Nationalist corruption and felt that American interest lay with Mao rather than with the Chiang government. A good soldier, Stilwell did the best he could; however, his attitude was shared by other

Americans, diplomats, and soldiers serving in China. Eventually, personality and policy differences led to Stilwell's replacement. When all circumstances were taken into account China proved less fruitful a base for anti-Japanese operations than had been expected. Still, the Americans pressured the British to move into Burma and free up the Burma Road supply route. But, in 1943 at least, the Japanese were far too strong and the British far too weak for any progress in that area to be made.

Elsewhere in the Pacific only one major operation was conducted during the spring of 1943. This was to occur in the Northern Pacific. In late August 1942 American troops had occupied the Aleutian island of Adak with the intention of using it as a base to attack the Japanese-held island of Kiska. In January 1943 American troops occupied Amchika nearer Kiska. However, the plan of attack changed when it was realized that Kiska was strongly defended; the island of Attu became the new objective.

In May 1943 Attu was invaded. After two weeks of fighting, the small Japanese garrison was wiped out when Japanese troops launched a last-ditch Banzai charge against the Americans. American pressure was then centered on Kiska where more than 30,000 Japanese troops were concentrated. Under cover of fog, the Japanese evacuated the garrison. When the American attack came on August 15, the island was empty of enemy troops. The reconquest of the Aleutians has been seen as something of an over-kill operation. That arises from the fact that in order to regain these islands, substantial sea, air, and land forces were diverted from areas more strategically important to the main objective of the Pacific war. This criticism is a well-considered one; perhaps too high a value was placed on recovery of these islands at a time when men and supplies were short. However, the freeing of the Aleutians had the effect of raising American morale, and securing the Aleutian bases placed the Japanese-held Kurile Islands within range of American air power.

By the summer of 1943 substantial progress had been made by American forces against the Japanese. It is easy for one to look back on that time in the firm realization that the Japanese had spent their bolt. But American triumphs had cost dearly. Few were then farsighted enough to see a clear path to victory. The Japanese were, in spite of setbacks, in control of most of the Pacific. Their navy was still formidable; their defensive ring had yet to be breached. With that in mind there can be little wonder that the next offensive moves of the Americans in the Pacific and the British in Burma were to be cautious and prudent.

Other Areas of Operations

A world war is too complex to be explained strictly on the basis of theaters and fronts. Therefore, it is necessary now to turn from mere geographical designations to discuss other ways by which the conflict was carried on. From

1941 through 1943 the Allies were faced with a serious supply problem. England was dependent upon her shipping. As in World War I, the Germans attacked England's supply lines with surface vessels and U-boats (submarines). In reality, the German surface fleet posed less danger to Allied shipping than did the U-boat.

At the beginning of the war the German U-boat fleet was not large, nor was this fleet utilized effectively. The fleet was dispersed into the Mediterranean and elsewhere and fewer than two dozen submarines were used to harry British supply lines in the Atlantic. In spite of this, losses from U-boat attacks were very heavy in 1940 and 1941. The convoy system cut down on ship losses on the transatlantic run; even convoys, however, protected by a variety of surface craft, were not immune from attack. Ultra intercepts helped determine the general location of the U-boats, but they were difficult to detect on the surface. For it was on the surface that U-boats most often launched their night attacks. Prior to 1940 radar was far too bulky for this purpose. But developments in that year led to the perfection of *centimetric* radar. This meant that the radar operated on a very short wave, thus requiring a less bulky antenna. With naval vessels equipped with radar the small profile of the submarine became less of an advantage.

The tactical and technological advances developed by the Allies were slow in coming. For each protective development there seemed to be a countering action. For example, the Germans developed the *schnorkel*, a breathing tube which allowed submarines to use diesel power while operating under water, and the *homing torpedo*. This device enabled commanders to release torpedoes in the blind. The torpedoes would then ''home-in'' on the sound of the Allied ship's engine and screws. For a time this device was successful, but the Allies had foreseen such a development and soon outfitted their ships with a device called a ''foxer.'' This simple device was towed by the ship and emitted a noise greater than that of the ship's engines, thus torpedoes would home-in on this device rather than the targeted ship.

Air attacks accounted for heavy losses on the supply route to the Soviet Union as such convoys were subject to attack by Luftwaffe planes based in nearby Norway. Warships could and did furnish an antiaircraft defense against such attacks, but such protection was not always consistent. The greatest loss of the Murmansk run was that of convoy PQ17 which set sail for the Soviet Union in June 1942. The British Admiralty was fed false information that the German battleship, *Tirpitz*, had set sail from Norway to intercept the convoy. Therefore, orders were dispatched that the convoy should scatter. Bereft of escort vessels, the merchant ships were sitting ducks for the Luftwaffe attacks which began on July 4, 1942. Only 13 of the 36 ships survived the attack. These heavy losses led to a curtailment of convoys until September. After that, the Murmansk-bound ships were afforded the protection of small escort carriers. Air support made convoy defense more efficient, and, after September 1942, losses on the Murmansk run became more of a rarity.

In each case, for every measure there was a counter-measure, yet the U-boat seemed to be ahead of the curve. In 1943 Grand Admiral Dönitz was placed in charge of the German navy. A crash program of submarine building was introduced, and mariners from the surface fleet were pressed into service to operate the growing U-boat fleet. It was at this time that Dönitz could bring into practice his concept of the ''wolf pack.'' His idea was to use groups of U-boats to attack a convoy and destroy it. Now that he had the resources Dönitz sought to implement his attack strategy. By March 1943 Allied shipping losses were the highest they had ever been, yet, by May the tide was turned as U-boat losses exceeded Allied surface fleet losses. This reversal was the result of a combination of factors which, finally, gave British and American naval commanders the support and knowledge they needed to counter the U-boat. Convoy commanders were in direct communication with shore installations which could furnish them real-time intelligence of U-boat activity. Superior organization was to allow naval commanders to bring their forces to bear on the wolf packs and the results were astonishing. In all, 785 U-boats were sunk. Though total allied losses to U-boats were over 3,000 ships, by the spring and summer of 1943 Dönitz's force ceased to be a menace. The technological advantage of the U-boat had been lost. A great deal of credit goes to the Royal Navy whose organization skills facilitated the coordination which allowed them to keep convoy commanders current on U-boat movements. The Americans were not as willing as the British to set aside the rigid chain of command and did not allow as much direct contact between intelligence centers and captains at sea. The statistics show the results, Royal Navy sinkings of U-boats made up 60 percent of all U-boats sunk. The battle for the Atlantic had been won, and the relatively safe waters of the Atlantic were to see an armada of ships which would supply the Allied cause in the European theater.

The years 1942 and 1943 saw the beginning of what has been called the *Third Front*, the carrying of the air war to Germany. Strategic bombing was initiated by the Germans during the Battle of Britain. The RAF Bomber Command attempted to retaliate by night raids on German industrial targets. Though the RAF had every expectation that these night raids would be able to strike specific military and industrial targets this expectation was not realized. Daylight reconnaissance revealed that the margin for error in night bombing was more than 1,000 yards. By 1942, however, night bombing raids secured navigational aid from a variety of radio devices which helped them ''home-in'' on a targeted area. These devices helped the bombers find the general target area, but the idea that night bombing could be precise was scrapped in favor of striking large, urban targets. This technique, termed by some ''terror bombing,'' was perfected to the point that huge bomber streams could bombard cities with a mix of high explosive and incendiary devices and thus create a firestorm—a swirling hurricane of fire and superheated gases—which could engulf and destroy a city.

The American Eighth Air Force arrived in England in 1942 and began making small-scale daylight raids. The American strategy of air bombardment used high-level B-17 bombers equipped with precision Norden bombsights against specific military-industrial targets. An integral part of American doctrine was that bomber groups could protect themselves—as opposed to the British concept of flying independently in a bomber stream. Bomber groups, much like the circled wagons of American Western folklore, could protect one another from fighter attack. However, American losses in aircraft grew as they penetrated deeper into Germany. The largest and deepest such raid occurred in October 1943 and was directed against the precision ball-bearing plants located at Schweinfurt, Germany. In such a deep penetration the bombers were forced to do without full fighter support, and fliers soon discovered that formations could be broken up. Bereft of support, bombers became easy prey to fighter attacks. The losses for this raid were to be disastrous to the Eighth Air Force. It was not until 1944, with the development of long-range fighters able to escort and protect the bombers to and from their target, that precision bombing became far less costly and, therefore, more practicable.

To sum up this attempt at a "Third Front," the years 1942-1943 saw the application of various techniques and tactics of air warfare. Night-time raids became more and more prevalent, and urban centers within Germany were assailed with high explosive and incendiary bombs. However, precision bombing was not yet practical and would have to await the perfection of longer-range fighters before American bombers could attack the heartland of Germany with any degree of safety. The conduct of the air war has been the subject of both praise and blame. Yet, at that time, Allied political and military leaders were convinced that the allocation of vast resources in men and supplies to the air war was justifiable. This contention was to be brought into question only after the war in Europe came to an end in May 1945. Then, a detailed bombing survey revealed that production losses from air bombardment were far less than had been anticipated.

Another facet of the war was the clandestine war of espionage and deception. As the war progressed, the Allies seemed to be winning that war. The *Abwehr* (German military intelligence) operatives sent secretly to England were usually detected. Most cleverly, the British were to use them in an elaborate double cross system which furnished their ostensible employer with false information. The system proved successful. The Germans seemed unaware that their agents were in fact sending them half-truths and distortions. The most dramatic aspect of espionage is, of course, support to the underground resistance movements in Europe. Many agents were sent as operatives into occupied Europe. Special operations units supplied partisan groups throughout Europe and parachuted special teams into occupied territory to gather intelligence. These operations conducted by the American Office of Strategic Services (OSS) and British Intelligence (MI5) were often costly, and even the most successful agents (such as the leader of the *Red Orchestra*—a Soviet-sponsored espionage network operating in France and the Low Countries) ultimately were exposed.

The greatest success of the Allies was in the use of deception. That is, misleading the enemy as to intentions, objectives, and strategy. Evidence of this is seen in the successful deception prior to the Sicily invasion. The art of deception was to be constantly employed and improved by the Allies during the later course of the war. But, the greatest deception of all was in securing the super-secret German coding device known as "Enigma." The Ultra organization was to aid the Allies throughout the war in Europe. Likewise, the Americans were successful in breaking the Japanese code, and "Magic," the name given to the operation, was very useful in the war against Japan. The Allied war effort owes much to the work of the specialists who managed to break the enemy code. However, as the war progressed, particularly in Europe, the value of Ultra diminished as secure telephone and teletype communication was used. Secure land line communication meant that fewer plans were sent over the airwaves to be intercepted. This lack of prior knowledge was to have an effect on the Allied campaign in Western Europe in 1944-45.

In committing themselves to victory, the Allies used every opportunity to harass and frustrate the enemy. Yugoslavian leader Josip Broz, (also known as Tito), was supported by the British who supplied his partisan forces in their struggle against the German occupiers of Yugoslavia. Tito's forces, harried and hounded by the Germans, were given new life by the British support. To a small degree at least, such partisan activity "overstretched" German resources. However, we now know that the move to back Tito at the expense of Serbian partisans under General Draža Mihajlović was engineered by an officer in Middle East Command (Cairo) to further the ends of the communist led partisan group of Tito. The decision to back the Titoites was based on a biased reading of Mihajlović's Chedniks association with the German occupation forces and was to lead to post-war complications in the Balkans.

Commando raids were conducted against German occupied *Festung Europa*, or Fortress Europe. One of the most famous was the Canadian commando raid on Dieppe on August 19, 1942. Over 70 percent casualties were sustained by the raiders, and results were generally considered negligible. Some argue that by dismantling a new German radar installation there, the Dieppe raid proved successful. However, it does appear that a more important result of this raid was that it convinced the British that, in view of the state of German defenses, a cross-Channel invasion in 1943 was impossible. This was the view expressed at Casablanca by the British, and the one which prevailed over American demands for a "Second Front" in 1943. In all, the commando operations, most of which were small raids against specific targets, excited the home front, but for those who commanded these elite forces the experience was a bitter one. Most such commanders felt their elite units were not used in an effective way to advance the progress of the war.

On the home front, the years 1941-1943 were ones of consolidation and rationalization of productivity for the war effort. This was true among the Allied nations as well as among the Axis Powers. The mobilization of populations for the war effort took many forms. Propaganda was utilized by all participants in securing, as far as possible, total support of the nation's people for the war. Consumer items were rationed. Though most citizens accepted the restrictions of wartime, illegal trading in scarce or rationed items was common. The *black market* became a fact of wartime life.

In Germany, rationalization of industrial production for war took an extreme form. Nations under German occupation were stripped of resources and production goods to assure that Germany would not suffer unduly from the war effort. Millions of people were forced to leave their homes elsewhere in Europe to work as forced "slave labor" in German factories and farms. Albert Speer was to organize a captive labor force to keep up German war production. War plants were served by forced labor from all the occupied territories, though slave laborers fared a bit better than those in the extermination camps. In such camps, laborers worn out by short rations and heavy labor ended up in mass graves or the crematoriums of the Third Reich.

The systematic implementation of Nazi racial doctrines led to the establishment of camps for the extermination of those judged by Nazi racial ideology as inferior racial types. From 1941 onward such camps began gathering Jews, Slavs, and others judged "unfit" from all over Europe. Victims were marched in masses to gas chambers. Afterward, their bodies were incinerated in crematory furnaces on the grounds of the various camps. Clothing, personal effects, gold fillings, even hair and ashes from the crematoriums were the "products" of these death camps. Under the eyes of their SS guards, inmate laborers, themselves future victims, carried out the deadly function of the camps. Factories and repair shops were operated as satellite facilities for these camps; and workers, doomed to death, were forced to labor in them until their time came. Within the camps inmates performed the gruesome business of searching, stripping and disposing of the victims. It was to be many years before the world was to associate the names Auschwitz, Belsen, Majdanek, Sobibor, Troblinka, and other such place names with extermination camps. In 1943, due to information smuggled out of Europe by underground sources, word reached the Allies that mass murder was being practiced in these camps. Yet, it seemed so heinous that few people then believed the extent and the systematic nature of extermination employed by the Nazi's in these death camps. Even today there are those who dispute the extent of the now termed *Holocaust* but the facts are detailed in the Nuremberg Trial documents for all to see, and numerous exhibits and memorials are available for those who doubt the enormity of these acts of genocide.

Modern German scholarship, while not denying the enormity of the horror which was the extermination policy of the Third Reich, has compared it with that of the Stalinist regime. They argue that the *Gulag* (a term the Soviet author Alexander Solzhenitsyn used to describe the network of labor camps in the

U.S.S.R.) phenomenon was the model used by the Nazi's in creating their own slave labor camps, and, by association, the resultant extermination camps. Though this German thesis has been ignored by most American historical scholars it is a chilling reminder that the modern, totalitarian state has demonstrated a malignancy coupled with a ruthless efficiency that has made the cruelty of earlier state systems pale in comparison.

Summary

Early spring of 1942 found the Japanese anxious to carry out the final phase of an operation which would neutralize Australia as a base for Allied operations and would, hopefully for the Japanese, eliminate for some length of time the American carrier force in the Pacific. In May the Battle of Coral Sea frustrated the Japanese attempt to secure Port Moresby, New Guinea, and the threat to Australia was averted for the time. In June, in what became known as the Battle of Midway, a Japanese scheme to trap the American fleet backfired, and Yamamoto's forces were badly mauled by American air attacks.

The Japanese did not abandon their interest in New Guinea (Papua), but hard fighting by Australian and American troops forced them from Buna, thus threatening Port Moresby from the land. In August the Americans went on the offense, invading the Solomon Islands of Tulagi and Guadalcanal. The Battle of Guadalcanal was to be a long and bloody one. A series of naval engagements proved inconclusive. It was not until American forces were able to dominate the skies over the Solomons that the balance tipped in America's favor. The American forces on the island were able to hold off repeated assaults. By January 1943 the Japanese Imperial High Command had decided to abandon its attempts to regain Guadalcanal.

In the China-Burma-India theater British attempts to regain the offensive failed. The use of such novel forces as long-range penetration groups (the Chindits) advocated by Wingate proved ineffective; the Allies remained in place along the Indian frontier. Burma was, at that stage of the war, considered most important as a means of securing access to China. The plan, largely endorsed by the Americans, to use China as a springboard to Japan was far from being realized in 1943, and in fact, was never to be.

From May through August 1943, American forces cleared the Aleutian Islands of Japanese. Though the campaign was a success, it has been argued that it diverted too many troops and supplies to an area which was, in some minds at least, incidental to the main strategy of the Pacific war. It is with this in mind that some writers have classified the Aleutian operations as one of the most successful Japanese diversions of the war as it funneled American power away from more vital areas and contributed to the so-called summer stalemate in the Pacific in 1943.

The battle in the North Atlantic was led by German U-boats and surface raiders which chipped away at the Allied supply lines by sinking supply vessels. Losses to U-boats continued to increase until 1943 when the Allies began to use more effective detection devices. The use of radar on surface patrol craft and on patrolling aircraft reduced the U-boat menace greatly by the spring of 1943. Air attacks on convoys to the Soviet Union were likewise made more manageable by employing escort cruisers and heavily armed escort vessels. Thus, by the summer of 1943 this essential supply line was afforded greater protection.

In the air war, the British thought to carry the war to Germany via night raids. Eventually, the idea of precision nighttime bombing was forsaken in favor of bombing larger, urban targets. Civilian populations became the target of RAF night raids as the technique of nighttime bombing was developed. The Americans, preferring high-level, daylight bombing, found that without adequate fighter cover such raids against Germany were far too costly. By the fall of 1943, the American Eighth Air Force and the RAF found that they did not control the air space over Europe. Without such control, bombing raids proved less effective and more costly than strategic bombing advocates had imagined. Success on the "Third Front," the air war over Europe, so far evaded the Allies.

Commando raids, support to resistance movements, counter-espionage, and the breaking of the German "Enigma" code and the Japanese "Purple" code were the noted developments in the clandestine war.

The years 1941 to 1943 saw the industrial nations locked into a battle of production as well as a shooting war. Every industrial nation sought full war production at the expense of consumer comfort. In Germany this meant the development of huge slave labor camps to meet the labor demands of the Reich. Also, secretly, the Germans began to systematize the extermination of Jews and other "unfit" peoples by creating death camps. Though the world knew little of such camps in 1943, they were extant and functioning at that time.

Suggested Reading

Dawidowicz, Lucy S. *The War Against the Jews, 1933-1945*. New York, 1975. A thorough account of the implementation and practice of the "Final Solution" by Hitler's Reich.

Larabee, Eric. *Commander in Chief: Franklin D. Roosevelt, His Lieutenants and Their War*. New York, 1987. A view of Roosevelt as a strategist and his dealings with his sometimes recalcitrant military leaders. The problems in the Pacific theater are handled well.

MacArthur, Douglas. *Reminiscences*. New York, 1964. The General's own view of his career and well worth the reading as he was a good writer.

Masterman, John. *The Double-Cross System*. New York, 1972. Perhaps the best book on British counter-intelligence during World War II, written by a man who helped perfect and run the successful double-agent system which completely fooled German intelligence.

Potter, Elmer B. *Nimitz*. Annapolis, 1976. See also, *Bull Halsey*. (Annapolis, 1985.) Two biographies of the best-known naval leaders of the war in the Pacific.

Slim, Field Marshal Sir William. *Defeat into Victory*. London, 1956. Slim has the refreshing habit of accepting the fact that he made mistakes in his successful but frustrating Burma campaign.

Speer, Albert. *Inside the Third Reich*. London, 1970. Speer was responsible for the rationalization and organization of the German war machine fueled by slave labor from all over Europe. He was one of the few of the near "inner-circle" who has been widely read in Europe and America.

Tuchman, Barbara W. *Stilwell and the American Experience in China, 1911-1945*. New York, 1970. She writes well on a difficult subject and shows the quality of the man who, by his own admission, rued the day he studied Chinese and became our man in China in World War II.

Willmott, H.P. *The Great Crusade: A New Complete History of the Second World War*. New York, 1989. This book is particularly good on the war in the Pacific.

9

The Eastern Front
July 1943 to May 1945

The reversals of the winter of 1943 had not dissuaded Hitler from taking the offensive. Though some of his military advisors were beginning to think in terms of establishing a defensive line, the so-called East Wall, utilizing river barriers such as the Dnieper to hold back the Soviets, Hitler thought in terms of a new offensive. This offensive, termed "Operation Citadel," was designed to pinch off the Kursk salient, destroy the Soviet armies in that sector, and open the pathway to victory in the Soviet Union. The shortening of German supply lines, and the increased production of armor, aircraft, and synthetic fuel seemed to afford the Germans the edge needed to resume the offensive. "Operation Citadel" had been planned in March 1943 and was to be implemented in May, but the attack was delayed because of weather. More importantly, Hitler wished the attack force to be equipped with two new, untested, heavy tanks, the *Panther* and the *Tiger*.

"Citadel" called for a two-pronged attack to pinch off the huge, Kursk salient by attacking from the north, Orel, and the south, Belgorod. The northern attack was under the command of General von Kluge. Field Marshal Manstein was given command of the southern attack force. Whether these two commanders held great hope for victory at this late date is subject to a variety of opinions. Official enthusiasm was the order of the day; therefore, it is difficult to judge whether the two commanders were truly sanguine about their prospects. After all, the situation had changed since the days of 1941. The Soviet army seemed to have a better understanding of the tactical situation. New equipment, improved tanks, the use of multiple rocket launchers (the so-called ''Stalin Organs'') and the seemingly limitless forces gave the Red Army an advantage over the Germans. Supplies from the Soviets' allies — particularly the United States — had given the Red Army more mobility. American trucks, for example, came into wider use in 1943. These four-wheel drive vehicles better handled the mud which bogged German transport in the mire. The vital technological edge which the Germans had enjoyed in 1941 seemed to have slipped away by 1943.

As important as technology is to modern warfare, one must not ignore the fact that the German commanders, since 1941, had always endeavored to pinch off, to envelop and to cut off enemy forces. The Kursk salient lent itself, it seemed, to such an orthodox maneuver, and the Soviets anticipated the German ''pincer'' operation to the point that they laid minefields in depth along the probable line of attack. The Soviets likewise hardened their defense to channel the anticipated attack and readied a counteroffensive to begin as the German attack stalled.

On July 5, 1943, ''Citadel'' began. On the first day Manstein's forces penetrated 20 miles of Soviet-held territory. The going was relatively slow and become slower still as the attack foundered in the minefields. Thunderstorms of great intensity caused havoc with communications and rain mired the battlefield. To further complicate the situation, Hitler, worried at the progress of Allied forces in Sicily dispatched two divisions from the Kursk contingent to Italy. These circumstances were to exacerbate the already difficult situation of the attacking army. As the German attack ground to a halt, the Soviets countered on July 12 with an assault on Orel and Belgorod. On August 4 the Germans were pushed out of Belgorod; the next day Orel fell. By August 23, 1943, Kharkov was abandoned. Kursk proved to be a stunning victory for the Red Army. Hitler had thrown in 18 of his best Panzer and Panzergrenadier divisions only to see them halted and chewed up by the Soviet forces. Thus, the vaunted spring-summer offensive of 1943 was to be the last major offensive of the Germans on the Eastern Front. After Kursk, it was the Soviets who commanded the offensive edge as they moved to the attack on all fronts. The Soviet strategy from 1943 onward was one of deep-thrusting Blitzkrieg-like offensives. The Red Army punched through the German lines and moved on. They wasted little time in pinching off pockets of German troops and continued their drive until they completely outran their supply lines.

Observers noted that a Soviet offensive ran unchecked for approximately three weeks then halted to refit and resupply the attacking force. Much has been written on how little support, food, and bodily comforts were afforded the Soviet soldier. Discipline in the Red Army was—according to many observers—harsh and uncompromising and woe to the commander who faltered. All this is no doubt grounded in fact, but the losses sustained by the Red Army in its offensive in the south were to be less than those sustained during those dark years when the German army commanded the offense.

With increased mobility and room for maneuver, the Red Army moved across the Ukraine. Kiev fell in November, and though Manstein launched a counteroffensive to regain Kiev, the attack gained little. This limited, costly offensive indicated a continued German commitment to the attack. In the Soviet Union, as later in Western Europe, Hitler insisted on a "no-retreat" policy. This order had worked in 1941, but in 1943, the situation had changed. Each new Soviet offensive punched holes in the German lines and isolated German troops who often had to stand and fight until, usually too late, the order came for their withdrawal. In spite of repeated advice, Hitler clung to the idea of holding ground and steadfastly refused to make adequate preparations for a defensive line. There was some talk of an East Wall, but Hitler did little to make this wall a reality. As the front in the south crumbled, only extreme necessity brought agreement from OKW for the withdrawal of forces. Sevastopol was held until April of 1944, and the garrison was evacuated only after great losses. Yet, by that time, Soviet forces were already in the Carpathian Mountains threatening Hungary, and the Red Army was on the Bug River in what had been pre-war Poland.

By refusing to establish a defensible line, by delaying retreat to the last minute, Hitler was sacrificing his trained forces, forces which could not be replaced. Allied levies, Hungarians, Rumanians, and an Italian contingent were not the highly motivated, well-trained, and well-equipped troops of the old 1941 Wehrmacht. In fact, Hitler had little trust in his allies. Non-German troops on the Eastern Front soon realized that the Wehrmacht came first both in supply and in the allocation of transport for the retreat. As the war came to Italy and as the threatened invasion of Festung Europa came to be more of a reality, the Germans were forced to transfer troops from front to front. Likewise, recruitment was stepped up in the occupied countries. Western Europeans under Nazi rule were urged to join with the Germans in the "crusade" against bolshevism. In Eastern Europe anti-Soviets and Balts were recruited into units to aid Germany in the supposed crusade to save Europe from the Stalinist hordes.

As previously noted, the Germans had had ample opportunity to exploit the national sentiments of the Ukrainians and other peoples who detested Stalinist rule. This opportunity was lost by the ruthlessness and senseless racism of the Nazi occupiers. As early as 1942, various German officers had urged the recruitment of anti-Stalinist forces from Soviet prisoners of war. General Andrei Vlasov, defender of Kiev and Moscow and a genuine Soviet war hero, seemed a likely prospect. Captured in the spring of 1942, General Vlasov was seen by some officers of the German army as a likely leader of an anti-Stalinist Soviet Army. General Gehlen, head of the Eastern Section of the German General Staff, was a partisan of the "Liberation Army" concept. But Hitler evidenced no interest in such an idea in 1942. However, Wehrmacht officers, acting without higher authority, recruited ex-Red Army soldiers and other "volunteers" into fighting units. Hundreds of thousands, some say as many as one million, "Soviet volunteers" served with the German army both on the Eastern and Western fronts during World War II. Late in the war, Hitler allowed for the creation of the so-called Vlasov Army—two divisions were formed—but strictly for propaganda purposes. Hitler did not trust the "volunteers" and was in no way interested in promising Soviet dissidents any sort of autonomy or national status if and when Germany defeated the Soviet army. Until the end, Hitler appeared to cling to his original concept that the lebensraum in the East was to be an Aryan colony whose slavic inhabitants would have no status except that of serf or slave.

The fate of Soviet nationals who cooperated with the Nazis and served in Nazi units is difficult to ascertain in particular. Vlasov was executed for treason after the war. It is assumed that most of his followers died in the Stalinist prison camps which have been so vividly described in the works of present day Soviet dissidents. The tragedy of these people sprang from an illusion shared by themselves and by the German officers who encouraged them. The illusion was that Hitler's new European order—when and if it were created in the East—would include a better way of life for the Soviet people than that offered by the Stalinist system. Hitler had no intention of providing a place of dignity for such peoples. This was amply evidenced by his words and deeds.

As the Southern Front was battered and bulged by repeated Soviet offensives, so too the Northern Group of Wehrmacht armies were subject to repeated attack. In the North, however, the German forces had constructed a powerful defense line around Leningrad. Soviet attempts to break the siege there and to obtain control of the vital Moscow-Minsk highway were foiled by an expert German defense led by Colonel General Gotthard Heinrici's Fourth Army. Heinrici had the ability to discern the point of attack of each successive Red Army offensive, and distributed his forces to absorb the initial shelling and respond to the attack. From October to December, the Fourth Army fought off five Soviet offensives holding the highway lifeline against odds of six to one.

In January, a Soviet offensive on the Baltic Front lifted the siege of Leningrad and isolated Germany's Finnish allies, but the German northern front was to hold. In fact, it benefited by the shortening of its lines. However, the sense of isolation felt by the Finns prompted preliminary discussion for a separate peace with the Soviet Union. The discussions began in February but were broken off in March. It was not until September that the Finns accepted the Soviet terms which called for reestablishing the 1940 frontier and removing of German troops from the area. The Finns agreed to take action against any German troops on Finnish soil which remained after September 15. German forces in northern Finland were evacuated to Norway, but a German attack on the island of Hogland prompted the Finns to declare war against Germany. The German position in the Baltic area seemed precarious, but they checked the Soviet attempt to encircle their armies, withdrew to the so-called Panther Line of the East Wall, and checked the Soviet advance in March. The line was to hold until the Finnish surrender in September 1944 freed Soviet forces to attack the German line. By October the German forces pulled back to the Courland Peninsula of Latvia. There they were to stay until they were evacuated by sea at the end of the war.

On the Southern Front the great bulge created by the Soviet attacks meant that the German forces were insufficient to cover the entire front. In August 1943 three simultaneous attacks were launched against the Germans. By March 1944 the Germans were driven back to the Carpathians, and the Soviets had penetrated into southeastern Poland. In April German forces were forced out of the Crimea. Though some of the German troops there were evacuated, most were captured by the Soviets. By April Soviet forces had also reached and crossed the Pruth River, Rumania's eastern frontier, but the Soviet drive ended there. In May a successful German counterattack drove the Soviets back. This limited success prompted Hitler to order his forces to hold the territory gained by the counteroffensive. This was to prove disastrous when the Rumanians, subjected to air attacks from Allied planes flying from bases in Italy, grew disillusioned with the war. On August 23 Rumania accepted Soviet terms which called for an immediate declaration of war against its former ally, Germany. Bulgaria, which had not participated in the invasion of the U.S.S.R., was wary of Soviet intent and attempted to sue for peace with Great Britain and the United States. The Soviet Union countered by declaring war on Bulgaria and invaded Bulgaria. The Bulgarian government chose not to resist the invasion and acceded to Soviet demands by declaring war on Germany on September 9. This general collapse netted the Soviets more than 100,000 German prisoners.

The collapse of Rumania and Bulgaria, and the resultant withdrawal of German forces from Greece and Yugoslavia seemingly cleared the way for a Soviet thrust into Hungary. However, the Red Army was to have a difficult time overcoming the German-Hungarian forces there. It would not be until late December that Soviet forces invaded Budapest. On December 29, 1944 a new Soviet-backed Hungarian government declared war on Germany.

For some time, Army Group Center had been a relatively quiet sector. In June 1944, anticipating renewed attacks to the south, the German High Command transferred the bulk of Group Center's Panzers to the south. The Soviet attack of June 22-23, 1944, drove through the German flanks and pushed back its forces in the center. Hitler demanded that his armies stand fast, but a few commanders ignored the order and fell back. Others followed orders

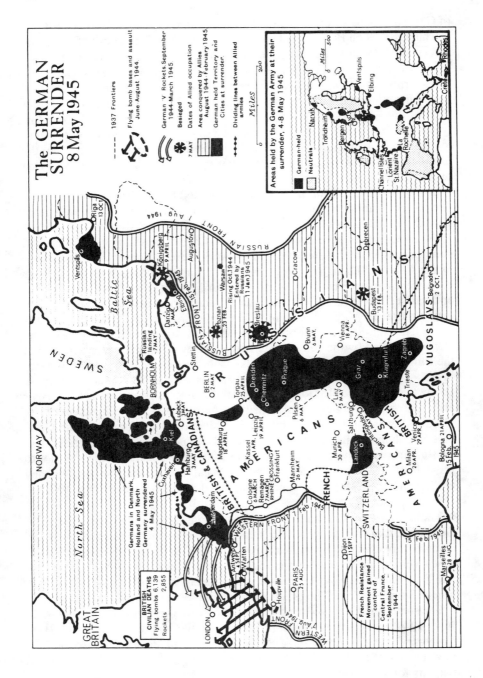

The GERMAN SURRENDER 8 May 1945

and were trapped. In a matter of two weeks, Army Group Center lost over 60 percent of its forces. In late June, Hitler combined the commands of Group Center and North Ukraine (formerly Army Group South) under the leadership of General, later Field Marshal, Walther Model. Model, a dedicated supporter of Hitler and the Nazi Party, was a man Hitler felt he could trust. But the new commander could do little to hold back the Soviet advance. The Soviet attack lapped around the German front, plunged into northeastern Poland, penetrated deep into Lithuania, and threatened East Prussia. Army Group North was now isolated. On July 14, the Red Army attacked south of the Pripet Marshes, and by July 27, Marshal Ivan Konev's forces captured the city of Lvov. Marshal K.K. Rokossovsky's drive north of the Marshes was equally spectacular. By July 26 Rokossovsky's forces were on the Vistula, and the Germans were forced to abandon Brest-Litovsk. On the 29th, Soviet columns crossed the Vistula, but four of the five bridgeheads made were eliminated by German counterattacks. By July 31, 1944, Soviet troops had reached the outskirts of Warsaw and took the suburb of Praga on the east bank of the Vistula.

The spectacular Red Army advance owes much to the increased mobility of the Red Army and the inability of the overstretched German forces to mount an effective resistance. In part, this may be explained by the fact that on July 20, 1944, Count Claus von Stauffenberg had placed an explosive device near Hitler during a staff meeting at Hitler's East Prussian headquarters at Rastenberg, East Prussia. The explosive device was contained in a briefcase which Stauffenberg carried to the staff meeting. He arrived late, placed the briefcase near Hitler who was pouring over maps on a large wooden table, excused himself, and left. The plastic explosive was detonated by a delayed action chemical fuse and was a device of British manufacture. Stauffenberg, an aristocrat and a wounded veteran of the campaign in Tunisia, had become the agent of the conspiracy to assassinate Hitler and to overthrow his regime. When the bomb exploded at 12:42, the conspiracy went into effect. Various commanders had been contacted and elaborate preparations were made to neutralize SS units, seize the reigns of power in Germany and in German occupied territory, and bring an end to the war. It was the hope of many of the conspirators that a Germany free from Hitler could sign a separate peace with the Western Allies which would allow them to direct Germany's military power against the Soviets. Interestingly enough, Stauffenberg himself favored making a separate peace with the Soviets. The plot failed as circumstances conspired to save Hitler's life. The briefcase bomb was in the way of one of the officers present so he pushed it away, thus placing the bomb on the other side of the heavy table from Hitler. The explosion killed four and wounded 20, but left Hitler alive. The shielding afforded by the wooden table and the fact that the explosion was detonated in a wooden building (the headquarters bunker was in the process of being painted and was not used for this particular briefing), saved the life of the German dictator. Had the meeting been held in the concrete bunker, where the staff meetings at Hitler's "Wolf's Lair" headquarters were often held, the explosion-implosion effect would have been fatal for most of those present. As it was, the bomb plot unleashed a purge which saw the destruction of most of the conspirators.

When the bomb exploded, Stauffenberg left the so-called Wolf's Lair. He notified his co-conspirators that Hitler was dead and the plan to neutralize the SS and round up Hitler's inner circle be carried out. But Stauffenberg's supporters seemed reluctant to act on his word alone. Verification of Hitler's death was demanded before commanders felt free to act to seize the reins of power. Conflicting information as to Hitler's demise spread confusion, but soon the news was flashed that Hitler lived. The plot had failed and the plotters proved unable to act quickly enough to seize power. This failure to implement a quick coup d'etat has puzzled some who have studied the conspiracy. Yet most agree that, no matter their attitude regarding Hitler, most of Hitler's officers were reluctant to act against their oath of personal allegiance to Adolph Hitler. Had Hitler been killed in the blast, the conspiracy would probably have succeeded; though it could have, quite possibly, provoked a civil war within Germany. It is also very doubtful that the plotters' hope of a separate peace was a realizable one. Conjecture, though interesting, is still merely guesswork. What happened, however, is brutal fact. Hitler, alive and angry, unleashed the Gestapo. The State Secret Police rounded up tens of thousands of suspects. A purge was unleashed which resulted in the brutal execution of the top conspirators who were hanged with piano wire suspended from meat hooks. According to some survivors of Hitler's inner circle, the agonizingly slow deaths of the conspirators were filmed and Hitler often screened them for his late night audience who, as staff members, were forced to listen to his ramblings.

The death of the prime conspirators, which included General Ludwig Beck, former Chief of the German General Staff, did not stop the purge. Many more were to die as a result of the conspiracy. But, more importantly, fear permeated the ranks of Hitler's generals. Any deviation from orders, no matter how unrealistic such orders might be, opened military commanders to the charge of conspiracy. The atmosphere of fear was to have a potent effect on the conduct of the war after July 20.

Field Marshal Model, the first general officer to renew his pledge of support to Hitler after the assassination attempt of July 20, was freed from this atmosphere of terror. Though the Eastern Front was near collapse in July, by August the situation changed. The Germans moved quickly to organize the front. The results of this rapid change was to have a disastrous effect on the Polish resistance movement.

On August 1, 1944, the well-organized Polish underground attempted to seize control of Warsaw. It was their expectation that the Soviets, now within sight of Warsaw, would come to their aid. On the surface it was a brilliant move. If Warsaw could be freed by Polish partisans before the Soviets arrived, the Polish government in exile, the so-called Lublin Government, would have greater political leverage within the Allied councils. Stalin, even before the Tehran Conference of November 1943 had made it clear that the post-war boundary between the Soviet Union and Poland would be that of October 1939—the date when the Soviets annexed that portion of Poland granted them in the Nazi-Soviet Pact of August 1939. Stalin also pushed for and ultimately gained a new western border for Poland on the Oder-Neisse Line. In large part, the fate of Poland had already been decided by Stalin, and the Western Allies were to agree to Stalin's demands. However, it must be said that the Western Powers did not agree to a Soviet dominated Poland. In the end, however, there was little they could or would do about it.

In short, the gallant uprising was foredoomed politically and diplomatically, but the military failure was not inevitable. On August 1, 1944, the approximately 10,000 soldiers of the Polish Home Army under command of General Tadeusz Bor-Komorowski seized most of Warsaw. The expectation of Soviet aid was not forthcoming, and on August 10 Warsaw was hit with a massive air and artillery bombardment. Fighting continued until October 2 when General Bor-Komorowski's Home Army, having lost at least half of its numbers, was forced to surrender. The German vengeance upon the population of Warsaw was ruthless in the extreme; the city itself was largely destroyed.

The controversy over the Warsaw rising centers around the failure of the Soviets, particularly Chuikov's forces encamped on the east bank of the Vistula, to come to the aid of the Polish Home Army. In part, this has been explained by the stiffening of German resistance and the exhaustion and depleted strength of the Soviet forces. Chuikov's replacements did not begin to arrive until the second week of September. The Red Army leaders, having sacrificed so many of their men to drive the Nazis from their homeland, seemed reluctant to sacrifice more of their men to aid the Poles. At least no attack was planned until the Red Army forces were more than a match for the Germans. On the other side of the coin was the refusal of Stalin to allow Allied planes to use Soviet airfields for refueling and refitting Allied aircraft sent to supply the beleaguered garrison of Warsaw. Supplies dropped by the Allies were insufficient; most were to fall into German hands. On September 13, Soviet aircraft attempted to supply the Polish Home Army, but it was a case of too little too late.

Most writers have emphasized the military realities as determining the Soviet attitude toward the rising. Others see it as a clear-cut political choice beneficial to the Soviets. For in allowing the Home Army to be obliterated, the pretensions of the Polish government in exile were diminished. By allowing the Nazis to destroy potential anti-Soviet leaders, Stalin's idea of establishing pro-Soviet politicos in power in post-war Poland was quite callously facilitated. Ultimately, the liberators of Poland were to be Soviet forces and Soviet sponsorship went to pro-communist Polish political leaders. The Polish government in exile, more or less deserted by the Western Allies, was powerless to insist upon any real authority over Soviet-liberated Poland.

It was not until January 1945 that Red Army units crossed the Vistula to occupy Warsaw. In the south, the Soviets had breached the Carpathian defenses in October 1944 and by November were fighting for Budapest. The city was to prove a difficult strong-point to overcome and was to hold out until February 1945.

Between January 12 and 14, 1945 the Soviets began an attack on all fronts. The German General Staff had been warned of a massive Soviet build-up in December, but Hitler discounted the extent of the Soviet forces arrayed against the German army in the East. The attack, when it came, swept everything before it. In Hungary, the German counterattack to regain the Danube line failed. On March 16, two Soviet armies broke through. By March 30 Soviet forces were crossing the Austrian border and on April 13 Vienna fell.

On the Northern Front, Red Army units reached the Baltic near Danzig on January 26. There they were to engage and ultimately destroy two German armies. In the Center, Soviet forces crossed the Vistula in January and by early February were on the east bank of the Oder, 36 miles east of Berlin. By March Soviet forces had cleared the Germans from Silesia and, in the north, had cleared the right bank of the Oder to its mouth.

Germany was defeated, but Hitler refused to believe it. From his bunker Hitler directed the defense of Germany. Divisions were shifted from the defense of the Rhine to hold on the Oder, but the forces were too scanty in resources and too exhausted by fighting to do much to counter the overwhelming power of the Red Army. On April 16, 1945, Soviet forces attacked from the Oder-Neisse area and on April 21, succeeded in reaching the outskirts of Berlin. By April 25, 1945, the city was surrounded. On April 27, 1945, Soviet forces reached the Elbe to link with the Americans who had been there since April 11.

In looking at the Soviet advances from 1943 to 1945 analysts have been struck by the tremendous scope of their offensive. The advance along such a wide front, the movement into southeastern and central Europe, has caused observers to note that Stalin's objective was less the immediate defeat of the Germans than of advancing the Soviet's sphere of influence. This fact was noted as early as January 1944 when President Roosevelt received a dispatch from one of his representatives in Moscow that Soviet forces were moving into previously independent states and putting in place governments there which would be sympathetic to Soviet interests. Stalin himself was to remark to Tito's second in command, Milovan Djilas, that one company of the Red Army had done more for the spread of communism than all the intellectuals of the Cominterm combined. There can be little doubt that Stalin capitalized on the tremendous sufferings caused by the war in order to give the Soviet Union greater control over European affairs — more so than ever was gained by the Tzar Alexander from his association with the victorious coalition against Napoleon in the nineteenth century.

The last few days of the Reich will be chronicled in a later chapter. However, it must be remembered that, in the final analysis, it was the Soviets who took the capital of the Third Reich. In the end, it was against the Soviets that the Germans threw most of what remained of their reserves. In that sense, the Soviets received the brunt of German resistance in April 1945. But, the ending days of the war were truly a joint venture. Though many may dispute the extent of cooperation between the Allies and even contend that continued cooperation to the end of the war might well have been a mistake, the fact remains that the defeat of Hitler's Germany was the result of Allied pressures on several fronts. The war in the East, however, had immense ramifications for Europe during the post-war years. The Soviet advance into East Central Europe was to create a new order in Europe. The effects of this Soviet victory are still seen today, despite the massive changes that have occurred in eastern and central Europe in this decade. Therefore, in discussing the progress of the war on other fronts, we must keep in mind the effects of the Nazi-Soviet conflict on the planning and execution of the war in Italy and Western Europe.

Summary

Operation Citadel was the last major German offensive against Soviet forces. The attempt to pinch off the Kursk salient proved a disaster for the Germans. From June 12, 1943 until the end of the war, it was the Red Army which commanded the offensive on the Eastern Front. In the summer of 1943 the Soviet forces in the south moved to clear German forces from the Ukraine. Kiev was liberated in November, and German forces in the south were heavily pressed.

In attempting to stem the Soviet tide, recruitment was stepped up in occupied territories where Eastern Europeans and Balts were urged to help the Germans in their crusade against bolshevism. Some German officers had tried since 1941 to convince Hitler to create a so-called "Liberation Army" in the Soviet Union. By appealing to repressed nationalism and emphasizing anti-Stalinism, they believed that millions of Soviets would flock to Germany's aid. This proved illusory as Germany's racist policies in the Soviet Union alienated the population. Most importantly, Hitler had no intentions of altering his lebensraum policy to accommodate the national aspirations of peoples whom he judged as inferior. For propaganda purposes Hitler did allow for the creation of the Vlasov Army. However, this small two-division army was never effectively employed by the Germans. In spite of official orders against such practices, Wehrmacht officers did create Soviet "volunteer" units, some of which fought in Western Europe. The number of "Soviets," i.e., Ukrainians and other nationals, in support and combat roles within the Wehrmacht has been estimated in the hundreds of thousands. This figure does not include the millions of Eastern Europeans who were to serve as slave labor within the Third Reich.

By January 1944 the Red Army managed to lift the siege of Leningrad. German forces were pushed back into the Baltic states but managed to hold on. By March 1944, the Finns, isolated by the Soviet offensive, began negotiating for a separate peace. These talks were broken off March 17, but by September 1944 Finland accepted the Soviet terms and declared war against Germany.

In the south the winter and spring of 1944 brought more Red Army successes. The Crimea was cleared. By April, Red Army forces had reached the Rumanian frontier. A German counterattack in May pushed the Soviets back, but this action proved temporary. The Rumanians, disillusioned by the way war was going, accepted Soviet surrender terms and declared war against their former ally, Germany, on August 23, 1944. Bulgaria followed on September 9. The collapse in the Balkans forced the Germans to withdraw from Greece and Yugoslavia, and a stand was made in Hungary. Budapest held out against the Soviets until February 1945 but by April 1945 Red Army troops had taken Vienna.

The June offensive of 1944 pushed back Germany's Army Group Center. By the end of July 1944, Red Army troops were at the outskirts of Warsaw. The Polish Home Army rose against the Germans on August 1 and attempted to free Warsaw from German control. The uprising was crushed after six weeks of heavy fighting. The Poles, anticipating Soviet support, were to find their hopes smashed by the inactivity of the Soviets. The failure to aid the Polish resisters has been variously explained, but the end result was that it was to be the Red Army which liberated Poland.

In July 1944 an abortive attempt on the life of Adolph Hitler created a situation of panic and fear within the ranks of the German officer class. The plot failed and the plotters were executed, but the aura of suspicion was to remain. Hitler was to intensify his distrust of his ''Prussian'' officers and to consider any officer who failed or disregarded his orders as suspect. The near collapse of the German army in July was followed by a hardening of the defense in August. In January 1945, the Red Army resumed its offensive on all fronts. In the north, German Army Group North was bottled up in Courland (Colonnade) and Red Army units were to be near Danzig by January.

Throughout the winter and spring of 1945, Soviet forces attacked westward. By early February the Red Army was on the Oder, and by April 25 Berlin was surrounded. Germany was now cut in two by the advance of the Red Army in the East and its allies in the West.

Suggested Reading

Chuikov, V. I. (Trans. Ruth Kisch). *The Fall of Berlin*. New York, 1968. The hero of Stalingrad's account of his wartime career and the last battle.

Djilas, Milovan (Trans. Michael B. Petrovich). *Conversations With Stalin*. New York, 1962. Djilas has the ability to take the reader into the mind of this most complex and ruthless man.

Manstein, Eric von. *Lost Victories*. Chicago, 1958. One of Hitler's most brilliant generals, his discussion of battles on the Eastern Front are well worth the reading.

Ryan, Cornelius. *The Last Battle*. New York, 1966. The last of his series of books on World War II. It tells of the battle from a series of perspectives. A very readable book.

Sajer, Guy (Trans. Lily Emmet). *The Forgotten Soldier*. New York, 1971. An account by a French soldier who fought for Germany against the Soviets, it is a well-written if bitter tale of the war from a soldier's point of view.

Seaton, Albert. *The Russo-German War, 1941-1945*. New York, 1971. A good account of the scope of the war in the Soviet Union and eastern Europe from beginning to end.

Tholberg, Jergen. *The Illusion, Soviet Soldiers in Hitler's Army*. New York, 1975. An account of the Vlasov situation and the reluctance of the Nazi leadership to capitalize on anti-Stalinist sentiment.

10

The Italian Campaign
July 1943 to May 1945

The Italian campaign was a frustrating and costly operation, the value of which has been vigorously defended and disputed by a myriad of participants and scholars. As previously noted, General Marshall and his supporters had always insisted that the cross-Channel operation would be the most effective way of bringing the war to *Festung Europa* (Fortress Europe) and defeating the Nazis. The British view was that Italy was a gateway not only to the German homeland, but to the Balkans as well. This fundamental difference in "Grand Strategy" did not, of course, lead to a rift between the two alliance partners; however, Anglo-American cooperation was to be severely tested during this attack on the "soft underbelly of Europe."

On July 25, 1943, the Italian King Victor Emmanuel III announced to a startled public that he, the King, had taken over command of the armed forces and that Field Marshal Pietro Badoglio was to head a new cabinet. Mussolini was placed under arrest and remained under custody until his rescue by German commandos in September 1943. The news of Mussolini's downfall came as a surprise to the Allies as well. General Eisenhower issued a statement on July 29, 1943 praising the Italians for overthrowing Mussolini. The Allied

High Command, however, was apparently not sure how to proceed. It was speculated, of course, that if Italy signed a separate peace the whole peninsula could be delivered into Allied hands. This overly optimistic view of the situation was to crumble as negotiations dragged on.

After Mussolini's overthrow, the Italian government made it clear to their German allies that they would continue to fight. Hitler did not trust Badoglio's promises. In fact, the Badoglio government immediately began secret attempts to contact the Allies hoping to negotiate a separate peace. These negotiations were hampered by the lack of a safe means of communicating with the Western Allies. Neither the British nor American liaison officers at the Vatican possessed any safe codes which they could use to notify their respective governments regarding the intent of the Italian government. In desperation, under the guise of a trade delegation, a representative was sent to Lisbon, to contact the Allies. Lisbon was, in World War II, something of the spy capital of the world, but the delegation had some difficulties in establishing liaison with the Allies. What the Italians hoped for was to negotiate a separate peace and secure a neutral status regarding future participation in the war. When finally contacted, the Allied representatives had a different agenda. They wanted Italian cooperation in the war effort against Germany. In all, the negotiations were hampered by disagreement on this point and were also bogged down by the uncompromising public policy of "unconditional surrender." What ultimately resulted was something of a compromise, a less than unconditional capitulation. The terms were harsh enough: surrender of all forces, removal of Fascists from the government, and complete demilitarization. The Allies, however, did not have control of Italy. Badoglio had some room to maneuver.

The Germans had also been active. As early as July 25, 1943 Field Marshal Rommel was ordered to prepare plans to secure Germany's access to Italy. What Hitler feared was that the Badoglio government would negotiate a separate peace, close the northern passes of the Alps, and allow the Allied forces to take all of the peninsula. During the period from July 25 to September 8, the Italian military and political leaders reiterated their support of the Axis alliance. The Germans were not beguiled. German units were moved into Italy; ultimately, they were placed in position to control Rome when and if the Italians capitulated. Hitler's suspicions were, of course, accurate. German action forestalled any hope for an easy victory in Italy. The placing of General Student's paratroopers in the Rome area foiled an Allied scheme to seize the capital with their own airborne troops. General Maxwell Taylor had made a secret journey to Rome to discuss such an action with the Italian government, but the prompt German maneuver made such a mission difficult and it was abandoned.

Meanwhile, negotiations dragged on for what seemed an interminable period. To jog the Badoglio government into action, Eisenhower ordered air raids on Rome. On September 3, 1943, Badoglio signed the document of surrender.

The signing was kept secret, but arrangements were made for a public announcement of surrender on September 8, the date for the launching of Operation Avalanche—the invasion of Italy at Salerno. While Badoglio signed the documents in secret, the Allies had already commenced operations against the Italian mainland. Operation Baytown, Montgomery's attack on the toe of the Italian boot, was launched on September 3. The war for Italy had begun.

On September 8, 1943, a public announcement of surrender was made by the Badoglio government, which then promptly fled the country. On September 16, 1943 the now "government in exile" called on Italians to resist the Germans and, on October 13, 1943, signed a declaration of war against Germany making Italy an official co-belligerent in the war against Germany. However, their was no real Italian government in Italy. No orders were given to the military as to how to act and, in fact, the commanders of the Italian military had fled with the government to a safe haven. This abandonment meant that any resistance would be in the hands of very junior officers. German forces moved quickly to secure Rome and to crush any opposition to German control. Some Italian units, aided by enthusiastic patriots, attempted to fight against the German takeover, but such actions proved both costly and futile. With German control, Nazi racial policies were put into force, and Italy's Jewish population was to suffer the loss of more than 9,000 people under Nazi rule. In all, the actions of the Italian government left Italy without any semblance of legitimate government. Allied occupation authorities set up a military government apparatus, but outside Allied areas of control Italy was governed by the Germans and/or partisan factions. In the north, the puppet regime of Mussolini's Republic assumed authority, but it was challenged by partisan groups of various anti-fascist political persuasions. In all, Italy was in political and social disarray until the end of the war brought an elected government. Even then, animosities fostered by fascist rule and wartime partisanship assured the continuation of strident factionalism long after the guns ceased to fire.

Thus on September 8, 1943, the Allied hope that Italy would be out of the war was realized, but the fantasy that Italy would fall into Allied hands without a struggle was destroyed by the realities of the German occupation. Critics of the campaign indicate that the Allied objectives in Italy were exaggerated. From a military standpoint, the Allies needed the port of Naples and the airfields at Foggia. From a political standpoint, the capture of Rome was an important objective. These three objectives were to be obtained only after hard fighting. The march of the Allied armies became, in reality, a muddy, bloody, inching crawl up the peninsula. Therefore, it has been argued that operations after Rome were but folly leading to an overstretch in the Allied commitment and, therefore, something of a logistical impediment to military operations in Western Europe in 1944-1945.

Partisans of the campaign argue that Italy proved to be an overstretch for the Germans. Despite a spirited and diabolically clever defense, Hitler had to commit divisions to Italy which would have been employed either in the defense of Festung Europa in the West, or on the Eastern Front. Thus, by tying down such forces, Operation Overlord, the Normandy invasion of June 1944 was facilitated. Diversion of forces from the Eastern Front, where German forces were already overextended, is considered by defenders of the Italian campaign as an important factor in facilitating the breakthroughs made by the Red Army in January 1944. Certainly, as we have seen, bombing of Rumania by Allied bombers based in Italy was a factor in convincing that nation to abandon her alliance with Germany.

These are, in broad outline, the pros and cons of the Italian campaign, but the real controversy centers on the actual conduct of the campaign. What might have been and what actually happened has produced a spirited debate. Therefore, let us turn our attention to the conduct of military operations in Italy from September 1943 to May of 1945 when the guns fell silent in Europe.

Montgomery's Eighth Army was to conduct the operation known as Baytown to secure the Strait of Messina by establishing beachheads on the Reggio di Calabria. He was then to proceed to engage the enemy, thereby drawing German forces southward to facilitate the ease of the main invasion operation, Salerno. Montgomery felt that the orders he received from Field Marshal Alexander, the overall commander of the Italian operation, were rather vague and less than thoroughly coordinated with General Clark's Fifth Army operations scheduled for September 8. In launching Baytown, Montgomery amassed hundreds of artillery pieces to bombard the Italian beaches. In reality, this softening-up operation was unnecessary as only a few German troops were in the area and these units were at least ten miles from the beach. The invading forces encountered no opposition on the beaches and little farther inland, but Montgomery moved cautiously to consolidate his forces before engaging in any race up the boot toward Salerno. Critics of Montgomery note that his preoccupation with amassing all his forces before moving forward was completely unnecessary or cautious to the extreme. One group of correspondents drove from Montgomery's headquarters in Reggio to Salerno, avoiding German patrols on the way, to illustrate that a linkage could have been made. Such adventurism was a bit extreme, yet the criticism of Montgomery's caution continued and grew in volume during the campaign in France and Germany in 1944-1945.

Salerno, a point which coincided with the range limits of Allied aircover, was an obvious target for the invasion. However, General Clark was convinced that the Salerno operation would catch the Germans by surprise. To facilitate the imagined element of surprise, General Clark overrode all attempts of his fleet commanders to initiate a preliminary bombardment of the Salerno beaches. This overconfidence was to be dashed suddenly when Clark's force was met with a ready and able enemy who almost succeeded in throwing his forces from the beaches of Salerno. The British sector of the beachhead was concentrated a few miles south of Salerno, while U.S. Ranger units and British Commando forces were landed north of Salerno to seize the high ground and

The ALLIED INVASION
of ITALY
1943 – 1945

SWITZERLAND

GERMANY

Mussolini executed by
Italian partisans
28 April 1945

Brenner
Pass

US
troops
met 4 May

Vipiteno

Dongo
L. Como

New Zealand troops
entered 2 May 1945

Trieste

Salo

Milan
26 April

L. Garda

Verona

Venice
29 April

YUGOSLAVIA

Turin

Allied Advances
20–30 April 1945

Genoa

Bologna

Ravenna

US Advance
20–30 April 1945

WINTER LINE
JAN–APRIL
1945

Zara

Florence

Adriatic Sea

Liberated by Free
French forces
September 1943

by 4 August

Elba
Occupied
18 June

CORSICA
Revolt of Resistance
Movement, summer 1943

ROME
Entered
4 June

by 9 June

Termoli

Monte
Cassino
18 May

WINTER LINE
1943–44

Anzio
Beachhead
22 Jan
22 May 1944

by 8 October

Bari

Naples

Salerno

Brindisi
by 14
Sept

Occupied by
Anglo-American
troops
autumn 1943

by 25 September

Taranto
9 Sept

SARDINIA

Tyrrhenian

Sea

Mussolini overthrown 25 July 1943
Italy surrendered 3 September 1943
Germans occupied Italy September 1943
Italy declared war on Germany 13 Oct 1943
Germans in Italy surrendered 29 April 1945

9 Sept 1943

by 14 Sept

9 Sept 1943

Entered 17 Aug

Messina

Palermo

3 Sept

Miles

0   100

by 23 July

by
17 August

Catania

ANGLO-AMERICAN
occupation

Tunis

AMERICANS

Licata
by
15 July

Syracuse

10 July 1943
Landings from
NORTH AFRICA

BRITISH

cut the Salerno-Naples road. These units managed to secure ground overlooking the road but were blocked in their attempt to secure the road by quick German counteraction. The main British landing was a few miles south of Salerno. This landing was met by enemy fire, but naval gunfire protected the landing craft, and a light preliminary bombardment softened the beach defenses somewhat. Still, confusion abounded. The beach became congested and resistance stiffened. Though the British forces reached the beaches more or less on schedule — 3:30 a.m., September 9 — by the end of the day, they had not secured their objectives and were able to advance only two miles inland from the beach.

The American sector, south of the Sele River, ran into difficulties from the beginning. In spite of intense fire from the beach, Clark persisted in his no-fire policy. The assault force, consisting of the 36th American Infantry Division, was to experience a severe baptism by fire both on their approach to the beaches and after the landing. Orders were then given for naval covering fire, and by the end of the day, the Americans had penetrated five miles inland. The 10th of September was a relatively quiet day. The American forces were able to land the reserve division, the 45th, and expand their perimeter of control. The British were able to take Salerno by the evening of the 10th, but the gap between the American and British sector of beach had yet to be closed. By the end of the third day of operations, the Allies had approximately five divisions on the beach but were still confined to two separate "toe-holds." The Germans exploited the gap between the Allies with a well-placed Panzer attack. By first turning the British left flank and then pushing back the American right wing to the point that, by the 13th, a few Panzer units were able to come within a few thousand yards of the beach.

The threatened collapse of the beachhead prompted General Clark to order the evacuation of Fifth Army headquarters from the beach and issue preliminary orders to shift the American point of landing to the British sector. This, of course, would have been a disaster, but Clark's fears of what might happen stimulated higher headquarters to rush reinforcements to Salerno. Airborne troops were sent to close the gap in the lines. Unfortunately, lack of gunfire discipline aboard the Allied vessels led to the loss of several planeloads of Allied airborne troops to what is euphemistically termed "friendly fire." The reinforcement of the beachhead, plus increased naval bombardment and innumerable sorties of Allied aircraft stopped the German attack. The beachhead held. On the 16th, the last German counterattack was stopped by combined naval, air, and land-based fire. Among the many losses at Salerno was that of the newly created force called the U.S. Rangers. This elite, lightly armed, two-battalion force had the bad fortune of defending part of the left flank of the Salerno battlefield. They were to be dessimated by a Panzer attack and 600 of the survivors were marched through Rome as a prize of "victory" before imprisonment in a German POW camp.

Field Marshal Kesselring, charged with defensive operations in the south of Italy, had failed to drive the Allies from the beaches. Now with Montgomery's Eighth Army advancing toward Salerno the Germans were forced to withdraw and to establish a defensive line north of Naples. The withdrawal was a gradual one and was to stop at the Volturno River where Kesselring hoped to hold back the Allied advance for at least a month. Kesselring, who was ultimately to take command of German forces in all of Italy, proved a very skilled practitioner of the art of defense. His success prompted Hitler to allocate more and more forces to Italy despite advice from other military leaders, including Rommel, who wanted to pull back German forces to a defense line in the rugged mountains north of Rome. In a sense the slowness of the Allied advance and the skill of the German defense was to produce the overstretch effect which many see as the most important aspect of the Italian campaign.

The Salerno invasion almost became another Dunkirk, but in the end, superiority in forces and firepower was to save the day. In all, the Allies were to discover that the campaign in Italy would require much more of the same than had been anticipated. Clark's misplaced optimism at Salerno was, no doubt, a reflection of the general misapprehension in higher headquarters that an Italian capitulation would greatly facilitate the conquest. No one, except the Germans, seemed to have anticipated how ruthlessly and how rapidly they could react to take over Italy and defend it against Allied attack.

While Operation Avalanche was being launched, a lesser known invasion (Operation Slapstick) was taking place against the heel of the Italian boot. The objective there was to seize the naval base at Taranto. The invasion force landed on September 9 without encountering opposition as the Italian fleet had left the port and was enroute to Malta to surrender. If the operation had been better planned and equipped, the British forces might have been able to advance rapidly northward and to take the important air base at Foggia. However, the lack of adequate transport meant that the advance was delayed. Further delays resulted as operations on the east coast were carefully prepared. These delays ultimately allowed the Germans to shift some of their forces from the west to the east coast and thus forestall any rapid Allied advance.

The breakout from Salerno was hardly a rapid one. It took the Fifth Army three weeks to take Naples and another week to reach the German defenses on the Volturno. Stiff German resistance, bad weather, supply problems, and the general difficulty of the terrain led to a severe check on the Allied advance. Clark's attack on the Volturno line met stiff resistance, and the Germans held back the Allied advance until October 16. On that date Kesselring ordered a withdrawal to a strengthened defensive line running along the Garigliano-Rapido-Liri rivers and their tributaries. Behind this line, another more permanent defensive position was being constructed. The latter line, which included the Garigliano-Rapido river systems, was commanded by the pivotal defensive point, Monte Cassino. This line, the Gustav or Winter Line, presented a frustrating check to the Allied advance toward Rome.

Clark's attack on the first of Kesselring's defensive lines began on November 5. For ten days, the Fifth Army attack was to batter against the German defenses. Some small gains were made, but these were achieved only at heavy cost. The attack was broken off and was not resumed until December. On November 22, 1943, Kesselring's skillful defense prompted Hitler to appoint Kesselring commander of German forces in Italy. Rommel, who had commanded German forces in Northern Italy, was superseded and, later, was sent to France where he was charged with shoring up the defenses of the so-called "Atlantic Wall" of Festung Europa.

Clark's frustrations were soon to be shared by his more famous colleague, Montgomery, and the British Eighth Army. Montgomery's forces proceeding up the eastern coast and across the rugged central spine of Italy encountered similar reversals. General Alexander's plan for the Italian campaign had emphasized the capture of Rome. For Montgomery, whose forces had been engaged in Italy since September 3, Rome would have indeed been a prize. By November 1943 Montgomery was ready to launch his Sangro offensive. The object of this attack was to push the Germans from Sangro, crack the Gustav Line, and seize the Rome-Pescara highway. This action would threaten the German flank and prompt a withdrawal from Rome. Unfortunately, bad weather, difficult terrain, and strong German resistance foiled his plans. The offensive ground to a halt in late December with the Eighth Army only slightly beyond the Moro River less than halfway to its objective. The situation was in stalemate when in January 1944 Montgomery handed over command of his forces to General Oliver Leese and returned to England to help plan and prepare for the cross-Channel invasion of Normandy. Liddell-Hart notes that this was a good career move for Montgomery, for little glory or prestige was to come to those who served in the frustrating campaign in the Italian theater of operations.

On December 2, 1943 Clark's forces resumed the offensive, but by the second week in January 1944 they had succeeded in reaching only the outer defenses of the Gustav Line. In over four months of fighting neither the Americans nor the British had been able to fulfill the basic objectives laid down for the campaign. Losses had been heavy and successes minimal.

Meanwhile, at the Tehran Conference in November 1943, Italy proved to be a topic of disagreement between the British and American Allies. It was decided, however, that while "Overlord," the code name for the Normandy operation, was to have overriding importance, Italy should not be neglected. Rome remained a prime objective, and beyond Rome, the Allies agreed to proceed as far north as Pisa. In all, it was the British who seemed most sanguine as to the value of the Italian campaign. Pressure in Italy, it was argued, would contribute more to Hitler's problem of "overstretch" and facilitate the success of Overlord. The Americans were far less optimistic and considered Italy a strain on resources which might force the delay or even the cancellation of the planned "Anvil" operation. Anvil was to consist of an attack on southern France. This invasion would occur at the same time as the Overlord attack and would help draw off German forces from northern France. Anvil, to the Americans, seemed more of an asset to Overlord than the Italian campaign, but after due deliberation, continued efforts in Italy received joint Allied support. The British preoccupation with the Italian theater was to lead to clashes between Eisenhower and his Overlord planners and Churchill and his generals. In the end it was Anvil that was to suffer from this strategic debate.

It was also agreed at Tehran that the only way to end the stalemate in Italy was to crack the Gustav Line. Therefore, the Allies conceived a plan of coordinating a renewed attack on the line with an amphibious operation behind the German lines. The spot selected for this amphibious operation was the small port city of Anzio. Kesselring, who realized the Allies capability for such an operation, had long considered that they would try to strike north of Rome. Anzio was not, in his estimation, a primary target for attack. Allied planners, however, chose Anzio as a point far enough behind the Gustav Line to be an effective base from which German supply lines could be attacked and disrupted. Disruption of supply would force a German withdrawal thus opening the road to Rome.

On January 22 a combined British and American force of two divisions landed at Anzio. During the next week, General John Lucas, commander of the operation, spent his time consolidating the beachhead and gathering forces for a move inland. His hesitancy to move, his failure to take advantage of the light resistance first encountered at Anzio, prompted his removal from command when Anzio became a bitterly contested battleground. In concentrating on the logistics of the campaign, Lucas' forces had neglected to gain command of the high ground. It was from the commanding heights that the Germans began to pour fire onto the crowded beaches of Anzio. Elements of eight German divisions were rushed to Anzio, and by January 30, when the American forces launched their scheduled attack to gain the Alban Hills, they were halted by a solid ring of German defenses.

On February 15, 1944 General Eberhard von Mackensen ordered the German attack which, he hoped, would obliterate the beachhead. By the 17th, the German command felt that victory was near as a gap began to develop in the Allied lines. However, air and naval support broke up the German Panzer attacks of February 18 and 20. General Lucian K. Truscott, who replaced General Lucas, had conducted a superb defense, and though the Germans were to continue to launch attacks in late February and early March, the Anzio beachhead was secure. However, the Allied forces there were bottled up by a ring of five German divisions. Anzio was saved, yet the Anzio forces, whose objective had been to outflank and weaken the Gustav Line, found themselves doomed to wait under shell fire and air attack until a breakthrough of that line would bring them relief from their enemies on the heights above the beachhead.

The heroic defense at Anzio is often emphasized, yet the fact remains that the Anzio operation was a failure. Though General Lucas is usually blamed for this lost opportunity, his mode of operation was determined in part by the advice and orders of his superiors. In fact, the careful preparation, the agonizingly slow build-up for an attack was more typical of Allied strategy in Italy and, later, in Western Europe, than that of the rapid advances envisioned by Winston Churchill, a staunch supporter of the Anzio operation and the principal critic of the commander who had failed his expectations.

The attack on the Gustav Line, launched in conjunction with the Anzio landing, began on January 24, 1944. A combined French and American force was sent to attack the commanding heights of Monte Cassino, but this direct attack faltered and failed. On February 11, the attack was abandoned. But Monte Cassino was the focal point of the attack to break the Gustav Line. The check at Cassino produced the controversial decision to destroy the historic Benedictine monastery of Monte Cassino by aerial bombardment. Though it is now evident that the Germans were not using the monastery as an observation post, such was the Allied supposition. The Germans had, in fact, expressed concern about the monastery and long before the Allied forces threatened Monte Cassino many of the manuscripts, art objects and priceless relics had been shipped to safety in Rome. However, three truckloads of material destined for Rome were supposedly diverted to Germany and to the collection of insatiable acquirer Hermann Göring.

That the Germans were not using the monastery and were seemingly protective of its structure and contents was either not known to the Allies or was, most probably, beside the point. From the view staring up at the hill, the massive stone structure was a symbol of continued resistance. Therefore, it seems it was as much for psychological as military reasons that clearance was given for the destruction of the ancient structure. On February 17, the monastery was bombed into rubble, but the defense of Monte Cassino continued. In fact, the Germans moved into the ruins and used the rubble to construct even stronger defensive positions on the mountain. Repeated direct attacks failed to dislodge the defenders, and the Allies were again checked.

The battle for the Gustav Line continued in the councils of higher command. The check at Cassino prompted some to urge the minimization of effort on the Italian front and to shift forces to Operation Anvil, the attack on southern France. The opposite council won the day, partly because Churchill favored the Italian operation and partly because there was a real need to relieve the harried defenders of Anzio. Therefore, resources allocated to the Anvil operation were reassigned for the attack on the Gustav Line. This would, of course, mean a delay in the attack on southern France. Ultimately, the Anvil operation was downgraded, renamed Dragoon, and launched on August 15, 1944.

On March 15, a third attack was launched against Cassino. For the second time, the New Zealand division and the Fourth Indian division attacked the

German First Parachute regiment. Halted again, the battle was called off after heavy losses had been sustained by the assault force. It was obvious to the Allied commanders that Cassino had to be taken in the general spring offensive. Direct attacks had proved fruitless in the past, but it was thought that, as part of a broader plan of envelopment, Cassino could be taken. The British Eighth Army was given the charge of taking Cassino, and the American Fifth Army was to aid their efforts by thrusting across the Garigliano River. Likewise, a breakout from Anzio was planned. The six American divisions there were to cut through the five divisions of enemy defense forces and attempt to gain control of the main road to Rome, Route 6, at Valmontone. This was easier said than done as the German defenders would call upon four more divisions stationed in reserve at Rome.

On the Gustav Line, sixteen Allied divisions faced a German force of seven divisions. When one considers that at this stage of the war an average German division comprised a force of less than two-thirds of an Allied division, it is obvious that the attack force had vast numerical superiority. German defenses were, however, formidable, and though the odds favored the Allies, victory was not a foregone conclusion.

The hardest assignment of the campaign was given the Polish Corps which consisted of two divisions under the command of General Wladyslaw Anders. It was to be the Poles who pressed the direct attack against Cassino. The spring offensive opened on May 11, 1944, with a massive artillery barrage. At first, little progress was made by any of the attacking force. However, the French Corps, under General Alphonse Juin, broke through. Moroccan troops (Goumiers) used their skill in mountain fighting to pierce the Hitler Line in the Liri valley. This collapse on one flank jeopardized the German position, and the whole line began to collapse. However, Cassino was to hold out until the 17th of May. On that day, the Polish flag was hoisted over the ruins, but the victory had cost Anders more than four thousand casualties.

What happened next evoked a storm of controversy. Alexander's plan called for the Fifth Army to secure Route 6 and trap the German Tenth Army as it retreated from the Gustav Line. The Anzio breakout began on the 23rd of May, and on the 25th, the Americans had taken Route 7. Clark then ordered four divisions to head straight for Rome leaving only one division to take Route 6. The Germans blocked the attack on Route 6, and the Tenth Army ultimately made good its withdrawal to defensive positions north of Rome. The failure to bag the Germans has been ascribed to Clark's hungering after the glory of liberating Rome. Certainly, Alexander's plan had been ignored by General Clark, and the British had every right to be annoyed. The British contention has been that Clark's actions prolonged the war in Italy and assumes that the German army could have been encircled and trapped. But later, at Falaise in France, Allied forces had a much better opportunity to trap a German army and failed. Therefore, if one wishes to engage in speculation, one must take into account the track record of the Allies in North Africa, Sicily, and

Italy to 1944. Certainly, the Germans had shown greater skill in extracting themselves from such traps than the Allies had shown in springing them.

Clark's march to Rome was less than easy. German forces on the so-called Caesar Line, south of Rome, attempted to block the advance, but the line was breached. On June 4, Rome fell. The fighting in Italy was to continue, but Italy became more and more a backwater of the war as Allied forces in Italy were stripped to meet the personnel needs on the Western Front. For the foot soldier (and the Italian campaign *was* an infantryman's war) the Italian campaign had been and would continue to be a nightmare of bad terrain, bad weather, and stiff resistance. One more river to cross and one more mountain to climb was the theme of the Italian campaign since 1943, and it was to continue so until 1945. After Rome came the Transimene Line, the Arno Line, the Gothic Line, and, by late September 1944, Kesselring's forces held a defense line stretching from Florence to Rimini. There his forces stayed until April 1945.

It was during the winter of 1944-1945, a trying and difficult time, that the morale of the Allied soldiers reached its lowest point. Though it is hardly noted, old campaigners insist that the winter brought a virtual mass desertion. Seasoned campaigners went Absent Without Leave (AWOL) to the fleshpots of the city, and harried commanders sent green troops to maintain the bleak, mountainous front. In April the offensive began again, but this time German resistance collapsed. The Allies then moved rapidly northward reaching the Brenner Pass in May 1945. Thus, the war in Italy came to rapid conclusion only after Germany, cut in two by Allied forces, was itself beaten.

Benito Mussolini, whose puppet government of Northern Italy vanished with the German retreat, was captured by partisans and, along with his mistress, Claretta Petacci, was executed on April 29. The photographs of their bullet riddled bodies displayed hanging head down and reviled by crowds of armed partisans is graphic and is hardly an end he could have imagined. Yet the cruelty shown that vanquished dictator and his mistress seems to typify the harshness of the battle for Italy in that it cost so much and resulted in so little gain to the Allied cause in Europe.

Summary

The overthrow of Mussolini in July 1943 was hailed by the Allies as an event which might possibly lead to a dramatic reversal in the balance of power. The hope that Italy would be knocked out of the war was realized when secret negotiations between the Anglo-American Allies and representatives of Marshal Badoglio's government reached an agreement. However, the Western Allies did not anticipate how rapid and how thorough the German reaction would be. Hitler, suspicious of Badoglio's pretensions of support to his Axis partner, ordered preparations made to secure Italy in the event a separate peace was signed. When the surrender was announced on September 8, 1943, the German reaction was prompt. The Allied invasion of Italy had begun on September 3 when Montgomery's forces attacked the toe of the Italian boot. The main invasion, Avalanche, came on September 9 when amphibious landings were made near Salerno.

At Salerno, Clark's forces were almost overwhelmed. However, Allied naval and air support kept the beachhead from being overrun. By September 17, the beachhead was secure. The swift German action had surprised the Allies and marked the beginning of a series of checks and subsequent frustrations which made the Italian campaign a source of friction between the Anglo-American Allies.

A third operation, Slapstick, was launched against Taranto on September 9. The operation met no resistance, and the port was taken. However, the British forces were unable to exploit the initial weakness of the enemy. Delays allowed the Germans to form a defense line, and the movement up the east coast of Italy was to be a slow, laborious one. On the west coast, the advance was not a rapid one. Naples fell, but the Fifth Army was checked by German defenses. By October the Fifth Army, under General Clark, had reached the first line of German defenses shielding Rome. On the 16th General Kesselring ordered the German forces to withdraw to the more permanent Gustav or Winter Line.

Kesselring's holding operation had been so successful that Hitler named him overall commander of the Italian theater and sent additional forces to Italy. The check posed by the Gustav Line frustrated both Clark's Fifth Army and Montgomery's Eighth Army. Allied leadership was equally disturbed by the lack of progress. The division of opinion as to the wisdom of carrying on an Italian campaign was renewed. However, it was decided at Teheran that Rome was a prime objective of the campaign. As long as the Italian campaign did not jeopardize either Overlord or Anvil, the efforts there would continue. Ultimately, Anvil, the invasion of southern France, was delayed and downgraded because of the lack of progress and escalating costs of the Italian campaign.

To facilitate breakthrough on the Gustav Line, an amphibious attack on Anzio was launched on January 22, 1944. The operational objective was to disrupt supplies to the Gustav Line, and thus weaken it. The landing met with little opposition, but delays in moving from the beachhead allowed the Germans time to pin the Allies on the beach. Though the Germans were to be unsuccessful in destroying the Anzio beachhead, Allied forces there were contained. Therefore, rather than aiding in the cracking of the Gustav Line, the Allies now had to break through that line in order to relieve the beleaguered forces at Anzio.

To break through the Gustav Line, it was necessary to take the commanding heights at Monte Cassino. Costly attacks were launched against Cassino in January, February, and March. Each attack was repulsed, and it was not until the spring offensive of May 1944 that Cassino was taken and the Gustav Line breached. The success of the spring offensive was less than complete. Failure to cut off the retreat of the German Tenth Army has been blamed on the American action of racing for Rome rather than blocking Highway 6 and trapping the retreating Germans. Whether or not the Germans could have been trapped remains conjectural. Rome was taken on June 4, but the operations in Italy continued. The Germans retreated northward to a series of lines which were to hold back the Allied advance through the rest of 1944. In April 1945, the collapse of the German defenses allowed for a rapid movement northward. In late April Mussolini was captured and executed by Italian partisans. By May 6, 1945, the Allies had reached the alpine passes of northern Italy.

Suggested Reading

Clark, Mark. *Calculated Risk*. New York, 1960. The Fifth Army commander's own view of the campaign.

Davis, Melton S. *Who Defends Rome?* New York, 1972. This book details the complex intrigues surrounding the overthrow of Mussolini and later negotiations between the Badoglio government and the Western Allies.

Eisenhower, David. *Eisenhower at War, 1943-1945*. New York, 1987. This voluminous book deals in detail with Eisenhower's many decisions, but the Anvil-Dragoon facet of strategy is particularly interesting.

Mauldin, William H. *Up Front*. New York, 1968. This book of cartoons and comments by a soldier, cartoonist, and correspondent best illustrates the enlisted man's view of the campaign in Italy.

Moorehead, Alan. *Eclipse*. New York, 1945. A candid account by a very talented writer and war correspondent. His reflections on the Italian campaign and its effects are but part of this important chronicle.

Mowat, Farley. *And No Birds Sang*. New York, 1989. This is a paperback reprint of an earlier published work by the well-known Canadian writer who fought in Italy. It is a grim and clear picture of the war from the point of view of a small unit commander.

11

The Western Front
June 1944 to May 1945

T he invasion of Western Europe had long been contemplated by the Allies, and by the fall of 1943 serious planning was underway to make a "second front" in Western Europe a reality. But the logistical problems of launching a cross-Channel invasion were staggering. Detailed planning was carried out by a veritable army of specialists and was overseen by a Supreme Allied Commander. Eisenhower was picked for the job of Supreme Commander; Montgomery, in command of 21st Army Group, was named group commander for the invasion. Eventually, after the beachhead was established and a build-up for "breakout" began, Montgomery was to relinquish overall ground command to Eisenhower, and he and General Omar Bradley would be co-equal commanders of their respective Army Groups. Bradley would head what came to be known as 12th Army Group and Montgomery the 21st. Concern about who was to have ultimate authority seems unimportant when speaking of the Overlord Operation, but clarification of the chain of command was to be most crucial. Occasionally, in the course of liberating Western Europe, friction developed between rival commanders and egos and national pride became bruised. Through all this General

Eisenhower emerged as a Supreme Commander of immense tact and leadership. With the chain of command established, the immense job of logistics, training, and other such preparations moved ahead. At the Tehran meeting of November 1943, it was made clear that Overlord would be ready for implementation in May or June of 1944.

The Germans, too, made preparations for an expected invasion. In November Rommel was given the job of readying the "Atlantic Wall." Rundstedt was to be in overall command of military forces in the West. Rommel, who had run his own show in Africa, assumed he would have tactical command of the operation when the invasion came. However, command responsibilities remained unclear, and, of course, no German commander was free of interference from Hitler. Though Rommel threw himself into the job of strengthening the coastal defenses, there was a fundamental difference of opinion between him and Rundstedt as to how to respond to an invasion. Rommel believed that an invasion must be met on the beach. To accomplish this, Panzers were to be positioned near the coastal defenses to respond quickly to an invasion. Experience in North Africa had shown that the enemy's command of the air made movement difficult during an attack. On the other hand, Rundstedt believed that the invading forces should be held to a beachhead, and then, after they had committed themselves, Panzers should attack and destroy the forces in detail. Ultimately, the disagreement was settled by Hitler who compromised by positioning German infantry near the coast while the Panzers were positioned in rearward areas. In fact, commitment of Panzer reserves was to be left to Hitler himself. This compromise was to prove to be an important factor in the success of Operation Overlord.

Though the Germans anticipated an attack on the Atlantic Wall, they could not be sure where and when such an attack would fall. To confuse the Germans as to the Allied plans, elaborate deceptions were practiced. Phony intelligence reports were sent to the Germans by agents who were in British custody or who had been "turned" into double agents. These deceptions included establishing ghost armies in the north of England and Scotland. Patton, who had been in the dog house since Sicily, was in charge of just such a shadow army. To flesh out these "ghost" units, radio nets carried military traffic for divisions which did not exist. Security restrictions were stringent, and any breach of security was met with prompt disciplinary action. At least one American General went home a Colonel for carelessly speaking about invasion plans.

The Germans were to prove more credulous than Allied planners had hoped. They became convinced that the main Allied attack would be launched in the Pas de Calais area. So convinced were they of that fact that a whole army, the 15th, was kept in that sector long after the landing in Normandy. In this way they overestimated the Allied forces, for the Allies had neither the personnel nor the resources to launch such a second invasion. In fact, it took tremendous effort and pressure to assemble the shipping necessary for the single Normandy invasion.

To aid Operation Overlord, tactical bombing was employed to disrupt communication and transportation links to the French coast. Allied fighters, fighter-bombers, and heavy bombers concentrated on stopping all transportation in that general area. The French rail system was rendered a shambles and movement on the cratered highway was safe only at night. In this way air power was to accomplish what Rommel had feared, the blocking of a rapid German response to an Allied invasion. To gain this advantage had not been easy. Air power advocates protested the diversion of bombers to fight the tactical battle. To both British and American fliers the strategic battle over Germany was far more important that the disruption of communications in France. However, Eisenhower, with the help of Churchill, prevailed over the strategic bombing advocates and sufficient air power was allocated to disrupt transport and communication in France. It was not an easy thing to do as railroad lines could be easily repaired, bridges were hard to destroy given the "iron" or "dumb" bombs of the day. Likewise, targeting rail centers would have meant heavy civilian casualties as they were located in population centers. Therefore, the disruption of rail transport and roadways was not as simple as Dr. Frederick Lindemann, Churchill's scientific adviser, had outlined in his plan to dismantle supply routes. However, the job was done and redone with sufficient consistency to render rail transport dangerous and unpredictable. It was unfortunate that this activity was to be constantly criticized by those who still believed that the war could be won by destroying Germany's industrial base.

Operations Overlord and Dragoon

What came to be known as the Normandy invasion was launched against the Cotentin Peninsula-Caen area which included the important port of Cherbourg. The Allies had considered the Brest area, Calais, and even the coast of Holland as possible invasion points. For various and sound reasons Cotentin (Normandy) was selected. Though the operation was scheduled for May, it was to be postponed until early June. As late as the 4th of June, it was doubtful that weather conditions would allow for a June 6 invasion. The inclemency of the weather deluded the Germans into complacency. Heavy seas, clouds, and fog kept German reconnaissance inactive, and the massive invasion fleet sailed undetected toward its objective on June 5.

In all, five assault divisions were allocated to the attack. The U.S. First Army was assigned two beach areas, code-named Utah and Omaha, while the British Second Army landed nearer Caen on three beaches designated Gold, Juno, and Sword. Juno was largely a Canadian operation consisting of one infantry division and one armored brigade. A paratroop drop was scheduled in advance of the after-dawn invasion with the objective of seizing bridges and roadways to aid in sealing the beaches. The wide scattering of the airborne

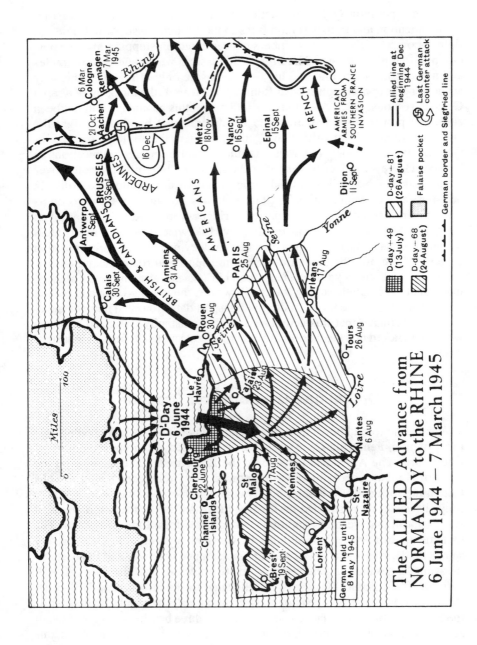

The ALLIED Advance from NORMANDY to the RHINE
6 June 1944 – 7 March 1945

forces proved something of an asset as reports of widely scattered air drops led some German commanders to feel that the Allies were engaged in a diversion. The sighting of the fleet on June 6 disabused local commanders of that idea, but for the better part of the day of June 6, senior German commanders remained unconvinced that the Normandy operation was anything more than a feint to cover an impending invasion elsewhere.

At dawn on June 6, naval gunfire was used to help silence coastal defenses, and assault craft made their way to the beaches. Although there were difficulties encountered on all beaches, Omaha proved the most troublesome for various reasons. The defenses there were much stronger, and delays were encountered in clearing the obstacles blocking access to the beach. Critics of Bradley's handling of the Omaha attack contend that he and his subordinate commanders did not take advantage of the many specialized vehicles and weapons employed by the British on their beachhead. These weapons included tanks with flails to explode mines, flamethrower tanks, track laying tanks, and other such devices which aided the British in storming the beaches. The fact remains, however, that at Omaha Beach the Americans had to face forces more numerous and more experienced than those encountered on Utah and the British-Canadian beachheads. In spite of difficulties all landing points were secured by the evening of June 6.

The immediate objectives of the invasion included the seizure of Caen, but Caen was strongly defended and was to fall only after weeks of fighting. However, the Allies did link up from their beachheads and began to secure the Cotentin Peninsula. Also, it had been hoped that Cherbourg would be quickly secured to enable the Allies to stream in supplies and reinforcements for the "breakout." The failure to secure the ports had been anticipated by Overlord planners, and an artificial breakwall was constructed at the beachhead and portable breakwalls and docks, termed Mulberries, were towed over from England to create instant ports for the invasion. In spite of these measures the lack of adequate port facilities created problems for the Allies throughout the year. Lack of ports led to a constant supply pinch which in turn placed limitations on Allied strategy in Europe in 1944.

On the German side, the success of the invasion was most disturbing. Rundstedt was of the opinion that the Allied success meant that Germany should try to negotiate a settlement in the West. This view was unacceptable to Hitler. Rundstedt was relieved of command and General von Kluge was placed in charge. On June 15 Rommel was caught in a strafing attack and severely injured. Responsibility for the German defense then rested with Kluge who took command with an enthusiasm soon to be dissipated by events both at the front and at Hitler's Wolf's Lair headquarters. For after the July 20 assassination attempt, Hitler distrusted his Prussian generals and watched their every move. Rommel, whose involvement in the plot against Hitler has been exaggerated, nevertheless was aware of discontent over Hitler's conduct of the war and countenanced a change in leadership. Thus, Rommel fell under suspicion and was allowed to commit suicide on October 14. Kluge was to fail in blocking the Allied breakout. Kluge was out of touch with Berlin for several days and ignored Hitler's urging to move quickly to contain the beachhead. His actions attracted Hitler's suspicion and Kluge was recalled. Kluge, aware of his probable fate in Berlin, committed suicide in August. Thus, the July plot was to have a severe impact on the conduct of the war on the Western Front to a greater degree than was the case on the Eastern Front.

Initially, the Allied plan had called for a breakout from Caen. That city, however, was a focal point for the German defense, and Montgomery's forces became involved in a holding operation. Therefore, the breakout from Normandy, when it came, was to be on the American part of the line at Avranches. Montgomery has been criticized as being too cautious in his attacks on Caen, but it is also argued that by drawing German forces into the defense of Caen, Montgomery's forces facilitated the American breakout from St. Lo-Avranches. In that sector the hedgerows of Normandy proved to be defensive barriers against American tanks. Fortuitously, a clever American ordinance sergeant developed a device made up of four horn-like steel protrusions to be fitted on the American Shermans. This device permitted the tanks to drive into the hedgerows, the horns gripping into the dirt and roots of the rows, and plow through them. Now prepared, the breakout from St. Lo-Avranches was begun on July 26.

The bombing attack which preceded the breakout proved effective; however, short drops inflicted heavy casualties on American forces, and it was to be a long time before coordination between air and ground reached a point where such "accidents" were minimized. In spite of these difficulties, by August 1, the American attack had broken through at Avranches. Forces were sent to liberate Brittany and secure the port of Brest. Meanwhile, the main American force, including Patton's Third Army, pushed toward LeMans. To plug the gap in the line at Avranches, Hitler ordered a counterattack. This attack drew in the German forces and made it possible for the fast moving American armor to threaten a cut off of German forces at Falaise. As the German counterattack was halted at Mortain, Canadian forces from the north converged on Falaise, while the Americans held Argentan, 15 miles from Falaise. Through this small hole the shattered remnant of numerous German divisions were to pass. On August 20 the gap was closed, and an estimated 70,000 Germans, a larger part of 19 German divisions, were killed or captured in the Falaise pocket. Failure to close the gap sooner and trap the German forces, including much of the 15th German army, led to an acrimonious debate. The British blamed Patton and Patton blamed the slow movement of the Canadian forces, yet the fact remains that there were too many tasks assigned to forces which were not as coordinated and battle-trained as was their enemy. For even in defeat the German forces were elusive and formidable.

The destruction of large numbers of German forces at Falaise opened the door to the liberation of all of France. On August 15 Operation Dragoon began.

This invasion of southern France was accomplished with comparative ease. Though German resistance at Toulon and Marseilles continued for two weeks, the Allied landing on the Riviera was something of a walk through. Joined by member of the French resistance movement, American and Free French forces moved quickly northward. One interesting sidelight of this campaign was the claim by observers that, in the vine country, the French were careful to only attack through vineyards of lesser quality. In spite of this criticism, if such it be, by mid-September the combined American and French forces had linked with Patton's Third Army near the German frontier. The rapid movement of the Allied troops to the Seine opened Paris to attack. Though not a strategic objective, this great city was a prize which the Free French forces hoped to gain.

In Paris the resistance had begun open warfare with the Germans. To avoid the destruction of the city by the German garrison, an arrangement, carried out by the Swiss Consul General, was made with the German commander, General Dietrich von Choltitz, to surrender the city to an Allied military force. The French Second Armored Division, commanded by General Jacques P. Leclerc (J.P. Hauteclocque), was assigned the task. On August 22 the Second Armored headed for Paris, and on August 25, von Choltitz's formal surrender was made at the Agre Montparnesse. The liberation of Paris was more of a parade than a battle. Once in Paris, threats had to be used to get the French Second Armored out of the city and back to the campaign. But, by August 25, de Gaulle and his Free French forces were in control of France. In fact, from the very beginning of the beachhead at Normandy, de Gaulle's political organization had taken over control of liberated territory. This had not been foreseen by Allied planners who had expected to establish a military-type government until a new, non-Vichy, regime could be installed. De Gaulle's political skills and acumen were to frustrate this plan and left him in undisputed control of France.

The startling success of the breakout from Avranches presented problems to the rapidly advancing Allies. Part of the Overlord plan called for the use of the port of Brest. The liberation of Brittany, however, proved a long and costly operation. Brest, finally captured on September 19, was to prove unusable as a port. Elsewhere, two small Brittany coast ports, Lorient and St. Nazaire, were held by the enemy until the end of the war. Therefore, the diversion of forces into Brittany brought little return, and the ports there were never to serve as founts of supply for the advance into Germany. Eventually, Montgomery's advance in the north led to the liberation of Channel ports, yet most of these were so damaged that it took a good deal of time to repair and clear them before they could function to ease the Allied supply problem. Therefore, to supply the two Army Groups with their various armies became a determinant in the campaign.

From the beginning of Overlord, the northern advance was considered to be the crucial one. The argument was simply this: those who control northern

Germany control Germany. Montgomery's task was to move along the northern axis, through France and Belgium, secure the Rhine, and attack northern Germany. Montgomery moved cautiously in comparison to the fast dash of Patton in the south, but demanded and received the lion's share of supplies. It was certainly proper to allocate Montgomery's force higher supply priorities, for such had been the overall plan. However, the collapse of German resistance in France had come as a surprise. Eisenhower sought to exploit this development by adapting the Overlord plan to meet the situation. Therefore, he ordered a two-pronged thrust, the main one in the north and a second one to the south.

By mid-June 1944, the Germans had begun V1 (flying bomb) attacks on England. These flying bombs termed "doodlebugs" or "buzzbombs" were more psychologically threatening than militarily destructive, but they were given high priority status as objectives. The V1 launch sites lay along Montgomery's attack route. Therefore, a deviation from the single northern attack plan was to cause problems between Montgomery's command and the 12th Army Group under Bradley. In September, the Germans began to use the V2 missile or rocket bomb against London and, later, Antwerp and Liege. Therefore, Montgomery felt that all effort should be made in clearing the coast of these sites. In bowing to what Montgomery construed as American pressure, Eisenhower seemingly weakened the force of the northern advance. From the American point of view, specifically that of General Patton, Eisenhower was favoring the British at the expense of the rapidly advancing American Third Army. It was quite possible, during the month of August, that Patton's Third Army could have reached and breached the Rhine. However, his force literally ran out of gas short of the German border. The failure to supply Patton's army brought a halt to the advance in September. In spite of logistical wonders such as the Red Ball Express—a steady stream of truck transports—the inadequacy of the cross-Channel pipeline to supply an abundance of fuel meant that the advance could not be sustained.

Priority given to Montgomery over Patton in allocation of supply was part of the problem, but other factors deserve consideration. Both Eisenhower and Montgomery planned leap-frog airborne jumps to cut off the enemy retreat. Allocation of supplies, particularly gasoline for troop carriers meant limiting supplies to armored units. For the most part these drops were not carried out because the advance on the ground was so rapid. However, supplies were stored for these projects, and the supply pinch grew. Likewise, most commanders demanded more supplies than were really necessary. The divisional slice, i.e., the tonnage needed to keep a division on the attack for one day, was quite large on the Allied side. Whereas the Germans seemed able to keep moving and fighting on less than 200 tons per day per division, the figure for the Allies averaged 400 to 450 tons per day. Few commanders chose to risk inadequacy of supply to force the pursuit. Patton tried to operate on a smaller slice, but even the Third Army had to halt when its armored units ran out of gasoline.

In early September the supply problem seemingly found its solution in the capture of Antwerp, a major Belgian port. However, access to that port is by way of the Scheldt River, and a tenacious German force controlled this access. It was not until November 26 that Canadian units cleared the approaches to Antwerp. It was to be weeks before the port of Antwerp could function at anything like full capacity. As the Allies rapidly outran their supply lines and the advance ground to a halt, the German resistance stiffened. This stiffening of resistance led to the failure of Operation Market-Garden. This operation was Montgomery's audacious plan to use airborne troops to secure access to the Meuse, the Waal, and, finally, the Rhine. The farthest drop at Arnhem in Holland was carried out by the Second British Airborne division and ended in disastrous failure. The attack was launched on September 17, and by September 25 less than one-third of the 9,000 men dropped in the Arnhem attack filtered their way back to Allied lines. Thus, Montgomery's hope that ''Market-Garden'' would open an easy path to the Rhine proved an illusion.

By September the Allied drive had slowed, and it would not be until the supply problem was eased that an offensive could be resumed. Meanwhile, Eisenhower continued to hold that the major thrust would come from Montgomery's 21st Army Group and would be directed into the industrial heartland of northern Germany. However, contrary to what Montgomery had hoped, the Supreme Allied Commander also approved a second offense by the 12th Army Group to force a double envelopment of the Ruhr. Such plans called for a disposition of forces which deliberately left a thin screen of troops to guard the Ardennes, concentrating forces north and south of that forested region in anticipation of a winter drive on the Rhine. Bad weather in November and stiff enemy resistance slowed the American offensive. To the south, Patton's army had secured a toehold in the Siegfried Line, but the advance to the Rhine fell afoul of flooded rivers, overcast skies, and stiff enemy resistance.

Ardennes Counterattack

As the Allies moved in a slow advance, word was received that a mystery Panzer army was assembling near Cologne. It was supposed that the Germans hoped to use this army for a spoiling attack to cut off any advance across the Roer, but, in reality, German forces were assembling for a much larger purpose. This purpose, the Ardennes offensive, was largely Hitler's plan designed to split the Allied armies, capture Antwerp, and reestablish German control on the Western Front. Few of his generals believed such an attack would have such grandiose results, but they dutifully prepared for the offensive. The plan called for a force of three armies, 25 divisions, and was to be carried out in three parts: a holding operation on the southern shoulder of the Ardennes sector, a Panzer attack on the northern shoulder against St. Vith and Malmedy, and the third, a Panzer army, attack against the weak center defenses of the

Ardennes. To aid this offensive thrust, Hitler called upon Otto Skorzeny to lead a force to disrupt Allied communication and spread confusion. This force included groups disguised as Americans to spread confusion behind the lines.

Heavy cloud cover meant that the Allies were largely unaware of the impending attack which came with fury on December 16. It is also true that combat intelligence was impaired by the lack of Ultra intercepts as German military dispatches were now being sent via secure land lines. Likewise, the euphoria of the Allied camp, the discussion of sending the "boys home by Christmas" seemed to blind the advancing armies to the fact that German forces could still fight and fight well. At 5:00 A.M. on the morning of December 16, the American First Army was hit at five separate points. The offensive grew in scope and momentum to the point that it bulged the American line and threatened to break it, hence the name Battle of the Bulge. In reality, the attack towards St. Vith and Malmedy by Sepp Dietrich's Sixth Panzer Army made little headway, and the so-called "northern shoulder" of the bulge held. Fighting there was close and bitter, and the Sixth Panzer Army was unable to secure its objective. The Fifth Panzer Army, led by General Hasso von Manteuffel, struck at the center of the Ardennes defenses, and drove on toward the Meuse. Manteuffel's forces skirted strong points and drove toward the important town of Bastogne. Elements of the Ninth and Tenth Armored Divisions holding the town were reinforced by the 101st Airborne Division, commanded by General MacAuliffe. By December 19 the town was surrounded. Since Bastogne was an important highway center, the Germans desperately needed to control it. On December 22 an ultimatum was sent to the American defenders demanding their surrender. General MacAuliffe's reply to the ultimatum, "Nuts," became the most famous quote of the entire battle.

Faced with American intransigence, the Germans tried to destroy the town and its defenders. Relief, however, was already on the way. Patton's forces were ordered north to relieve Bastogne. On the 25th, elements of the Third Army broke through to Bastogne. On the 26th good weather returned, and Allied air strikes began to play havoc with the German Panzers. Lack of supplies, particularly gasoline, hampered the German plan, but, most importantly, the stubborn resistance of the American forces destroyed the timetable of the German advance. Skorzeny's commandos had spread confusion behind the lines, but word of infiltrators disguised as Americans was met with an improvised system of identity checks. Soldiers used their own system of interrogation to determine the identity of officers and men who passed through their checkpoints. Names of movie stars, baseball lore, and other bits of Americana were used to test the traveler. In some cases it meant delays, but it indicated the versatility of the American soldier in meeting unexpected challenges.

Though one may talk of the leadership of American officers in meeting the test of the Bulge, this particular battle was often a contest between small isolated American units against a massed German attack. The battle for Bastogne particularly caught public attention, but throughout the Ardennes, American soldiers, including rear echelon personnel, held out against great odds, and turned back the German attack. The German bid for breakthrough was lost on the 26th, but the straightening of the Bulge was not accomplished until January 31, 1945. As the danger faded in the field, in the press the battle went on. Prior to December 16, 1944, attitudes in America and in higher echelons in England and France were those of confident expectation of an imminent German collapse. The offensive of December 16 caught many such optimists by surprise, and the depth of the German thrust caused embarrassment, even panic, in some circles. For some time after, scapegoats were sought to explain the failure of the Allied command to anticipate a German counteroffensive. The situation was not helped by the tendency of the British press and General Montgomery to claim credit for the 21st Army Group as the savior of the Americans at the Bulge. In spite of later clarifications by Winston Churchill, ill-feeling resulted. In all, the Battle of the Bulge indicated that the Allied command had been overconfident. In stripping the Ardennes of defenses for the November-December offensive, they had risked and lost. However, Hitler's gamble had also proved a failure, and, most importantly, in risking all for a knockout punch, Hitler had stripped German defenses in the Rhineland.

Allied Push into Germany

The continuing Soviet offensive on the Eastern Front, the press of Allied forces toward the Rhine, and the constant and massive bombing raids were certain indications that Germany had lost the war. Still, resistance was to continue. Allied bombing raids destroyed cities by the score. Allied bombing techniques were perfected to the point that high explosive and incendiary bombs were used to produce fires which destroyed cities and inhabitants en masse. Synthetic petroleum plants were devastated, communications were disrupted by constant bombardment, but German war production continued. Studies made after the war by the Allied Strategy Bombing Survey indicated that the massive bombardment had not stopped production. However, lack of fuel and the virtual collapse of the German transportation system meant that much of this production never reached the front. The new jet planes which might have decimated the Allied bomber fleets sat on the ground devoid of aviation fuel.

Hitler's other "secret weapons" such as the V1 and the V2 were introduced too late to change the course of the war. Hitler, however, continued to hope that the tide would change and, incongruously, was able to infuse his supporters with a will to continue the resistance. For Hitler the only alternative to victory was complete annihilation, and the policies followed by the Reich assured that much of Germany would be destroyed. It was during these last months of the Reich that the ruthlessness and cruelty of the regime was most evident.

The "Death Camps" carried out the policy of genocide in a frenzy of murder. Continued, senseless resistance was to mean death for hundreds of thousands of Europeans in these last, tragic months of the war in Europe. On the Western Front the Allied initiative was regained in late December, but it was not until March that the Rhineland was taken.

On March 7, 1945, elements of the Ninth Armored Division, First Army, discovered a railroad bridge spanning the Rhine at Remagen. American forces were pushed across the river and expanded a three-mile bridgehead across the Rhine. According to the Allied plan, the major Allied crossing was to be in the north. However, Eisenhower had agreed to a pincer movement to secure the Ruhr, and the Remagen bridgehead was to aid in this endeavor.

Further south, Patton bridged the Rhine at Oppenheim on March 22. On March 23-24, Montgomery's major attack was launched across the Rhine. The subsequent operation pinched off the Ruhr and netted over 300,000 German prisoners. In the south Patton's forces raced through Germany and crossed over the Czech border. In the north Allied forces advanced toward the Elbe where, on April 27, they were to link with the Red Army.

The rapid collapse of Germany, and the lack of major resistance east of the Rhine has prompted many writers to criticize Eisenhower's strategy during the last two months of the war. For them, the way to Berlin was open, and Berlin should have been the prime objective. However, Eisenhower thought otherwise. Berlin was a political target but not a prime military objective. Eisenhower was much more concerned about the so-called National Redoubt which supposedly existed in the mountains of southern Germany. This Redoubt, a vast fortress system to house fanatic Nazi resisters, was the product of propaganda, but the threat it might pose concerned the Allied Commander to the point that Patton's forces were directed to search it out. The National Redoubt proved a chimera, and the pursuit of this objective at the expense of capturing Berlin is seen by some writers as a major error. However, Eisenhower, who realized that the Soviets were difficult allies at best, operated as Supreme Military Commander and as such adhered to the territorial divisions which had been decided at Teheran and Yalta. In every case where Allied armies had overstepped the tentatively delineated zones of control, Patton's move into Czechoslovakia in search of the Redoubt is a case in point, such forces were subsequently withdrawn. A point missed by all those who conjecture about what might have been is that in a shooting war, when Allied armies are pushing towards each other, the fear of ground commanders is that friendlies will fire on friendlies. Therefore, it is imperative that easily distinguished borders be established and held to avoid "incidents." Berlin posed just such a risk. Since, in the Supreme Allied Commander's eyes the city had no military significance, such a venture was both unwarranted and risky.

While Allied armies cut through Germany, Hitler stayed in his command bunker in Berlin. On April 12, 1945, he received word of the death of the American president, Franklin D. Roosevelt. He was to receive the news with enthusiasm and conjectured that Roosevelt's successor, Harry S. Truman, a midwesterner and a supposed isolationist, might well take America out of the war. Hitler placed faith in the precedence of the Seven Years' War wherein the Russians were advancing against Frederick the Great but retreated upon receiving news of the death of the Empress of Russia. This incident of January 1752 had little relevance to the political realities of April 1945 but Hitler, who now lived in a world of his own dreams and plots, felt it did. This illusion disappeared as the Allied armies continued their advance. On April 29, in a civil ceremony, Hitler married his long-time mistress, Eva Braun. The next day, as the guns of the Soviet army pounded Berlin to rubble, Hitler and his wife committed suicide. With Hitler's death, leadership passed to Admiral Dönitz as both Himmler and Göring were in disgrace. In all, confusion reigned. Army commanders, on their own initiative, began arranging surrenders to the Western Allies while frantically trying to avoid capture by the advancing Red Army. On May 2, 1945, Dönitz sent a representative to Montgomery's headquarters near Slezwig to arrange a surrender in the West, but proposed that German forces continue fighting against the Soviets. This offer was refused. On May 7, 1945, an unconditional surrender was signed at Reims, France. Four separate documents, for the four participating Allied Powers, including France, were signed by the German delegation. Thus ended the war in Europe. Yet the final, official ratification was to occur in Berlin; therefore, May 8 became the official date for ending the war in Europe.

Hitler's War, or the Nazi War, as young Germans term it, had been the most costly in history. Casualty figures for nearly six years of war are most difficult to establish, but estimates indicate that for the Jewish population of Europe and for the Slavic populations of Eastern Europe and the U.S.S.R., the cost of the war was staggering. Of an estimated population of 8 million European Jews, less than 3 million were to survive the holocaust. Approximately 20 million Soviets died in the war. Nearly half of these losses resulted from deaths under the German occupation. Polish civilian casualties amounted to 6 million and more than 1.7 million Yugoslavs perished under German rule. Though these figures are incomplete and are but bloodless statistics chronicling unbelievable human suffering, degradation, and death, they clearly indicate that for these people World War II was a genocidal conflict.

Losses sustained by the Western Allies exceeded 900,000. Yet as cruel and heavy as such casualties were for the Americans and the British, they were largely the result of combat and combat-related losses. For the Western Allies the war had been a struggle to overcome an evil, dominating political system controlling Europe. For those under Nazi occupation, particularly in the East, the war had been a struggle for survival itself. The ramifications of this war-time reality was to affect the shaping of the post-war world profoundly.

Summary

Operation Overlord, the plan to open a second front, was the result of Anglo-American cooperation and was an undertaking requiring careful organization, detailed planning, and determined leadership. Diversion and deception were used to keep the Germans in the dark as to the time and place of the attack. These actions proved valuable in diverting German forces to cover a large coastal area of Europe, and convinced Hitler that the main invasion was to come in the Pas de Calais area. Bad weather delayed the operation, but on June 5 the invasion fleet sailed toward Normandy. Airborne troops preceded the main force. Though scattered by winds and antiaircraft defenses, they helped block German access to the beach area. On June 6 a bit after dawn, the attack was launched. Resistance was heaviest on the main American beach, Omaha, but by the evening of June 6, the invasion forces were off the beaches and were beginning to link up. The original plan had called for the securing of the city of Caen, but it was held by German forces until late June. Therefore, another site was to serve as the point of Allied breakout from the confines of the Cotentin Peninsula. This was to come by way of the St. Lo-Avranches area.

By August 1 American forces had breached the German defenses at Avranches. In attempting to close the breach the Germans counterattacked. By drawing their forces in toward Avranches, the Germans, under command of General von Kluge, ran the risk of being cut off at Falaise. Canadian and American forces attempted to cut off German forces there and were generally successful. This sparked a general German retreat and opened all of France to Allied attack. Paris was liberated in late August, and American commanders were confident that the Rhine could be reached in a week. However, Plan Overlord called for the major thrust to be directed along the Channel coast toward Belgium and, ultimately, northern Germany. In allowing rapid American advance in the south, the British commander felt that the major effort was being weakened. Irked by Montgomery's slow advance, Patton, commander of the American Third Army, was convinced that Eisenhower was favoring the British over the American command. Disputes as to the proper strategy to follow would have been less important had not a supply pinch, caused by the lack of usable port facilities, determined that strategic priorities had to be established. In favoring the northern movement, the rapid advance in the south was slowed and ultimately halted. This decision provoked additional controversy and friction between alliance partners. The deliberations as to what might have been, mistakes made, and opportunities lost led to some bitterness between rival commanders, but tact and mutual interests precluded a serious breach in the Anglo-American alliance.

By September some Allied units had reached the German border, and a daring attempt to secure the Rhine was attempted and failed. It was not until November that Allied forces could launch a serious offensive. To do this, forces were taken from the Ardennes sector. The weakening of the front there prompted a German counteroffensive to split the Allied armies, capture Antwerp, and restore German power in the West. On December 16 the German attack was launched and the Battle of the Bulge ensued. Rapid advances were made in the center of the Ardennes sector, though both the northern and southern shoulders of that front were to hold off the German advance. After heavy fighting, and some rapid maneuvering by Patton's Third Army, the bulge in the Allied lines was halted. By January the front line was restored to that existing before the attack. The Allies then began to secure the Rhineland, by March the Rhine river had been crossed at Remagen, and later, at Oppenheim. On March 23-24 Montgomery's attack on the northern Rhine met with success. In a few weeks the Ruhr was taken, and Allied forces penetrated deep into Germany. By April 11 American and British forces had reached the Elbe. In the south Patton's army raced through Germany and into Czechoslovakia in search of the supposed National Redoubt.

On April 30 Adolph Hitler and his mistress cum bride committed suicide in his headquarters bunker in Berlin. On May 8, 1945, the war in Europe came to an official end. The cost of the war in loss of life was the heaviest in European history. The horror of German occupation was most fully experienced by the Slavic peoples of Eastern Europe and the Soviet Union and by the Jewish population of German occupied Europe. In these areas and among these peoples, particularly the Jewish population of Europe, the Nazi war was a genocidal conflict.

Suggested Reading

There are so many good books on this phase of the war I can give but a sample of a beginning bibliography.

Bradley, Omar N. *A Soldier's Story*. Chicago, 1978. A straightforward account of the war from one who helped make the decisions from before D-Day until May 1945. See also Bradley and Clay Blair, *A General's Life* (New York, 1983). This is a very different book and one which is less kind, whether through truth or rancor, to his wartime comrades.

Dornberger, Walter, (Trans. James Cleugh and Geoffrey Halliday). *V2*. New York, 1954. General Dornberger directed the work of German rocket scientists at Peenmunde and tells of the development of Hitler's secret weapons.

Eisenhower, John. *The Bitter Woods*. New York, 1969. There are more recent works on the Battle of the Bulge, but none better.

Keegan, John. *Six Armies in Normandy, From D-Day to the Liberation of Paris*. London, 1982. This book created something of a stir when Keegan pointed out that the German army, at this stage of the war, was still better than most units in the Allied forces.

Marshall, S. L. A. *Battle at Best*. New York, 1964. After-action reports by a master storyteller and military historian whose reputation has become somewhat tarnished of late, but this collection of reports is well worth reading.

McIsaac, David. *Strategic Bombing in World War II*. New York, 1976. An analytic study of the strategic bombing survey in one volume.

Trevor-Roper, Hugh R. *The Last Days of Hitler*. New York, 1947. Though many recent books have been released on the last days of Hitler, Trevor-Roper's work still stands as the most readable and comprehensible to date on that subject.

12

The War in the Pacific
June 1943 to September 1945

hough the balance of military power in the Pacific had shifted somewhat to the advantage of the Allies, Japan's defensive ring had yet to be breached. The task of launching an offensive action which would put Japan in a vulnerable position was to rest largely with the American and Australian contingents assigned to the Southwest and Central Pacific theaters of operations. The ultimate strategy to be employed had been laid down at the Trident Conference of May 1943 which called for the convergence of forces from both Pacific theaters on the strategic islands of the Philippines. Though differences of opinion remained between the two theater commanders—General MacArthur of the Southwest Pacific theater and Admiral Nimitz, Commander of Naval Operations in the Pacific theater— both were in agreement that their main task in the summer of 1943 was to break through the barrier posed by the Japanese control of the Bismarck Archipelago and to capture the main Japanese base at Rabaul on New Britain Island.

To accomplish this purpose a series of campaigns were initiated to clear the Japanese from the Huon Peninsula of New Guinea. The next step would be to move up through the Solomons via Rendova, Munda, New Georgia, and then to Bougainville. From there the final attack would be launched on New Britain, i.e., Rabaul. This offensive, slated to begin on June 30, was carefully planned and was expected to take at least eight months. The New Guinea operation began with an amphibious attack on the coast near Salamaua to draw Japanese attention from the main Allied objective, Lae and the Huon Peninsula. Progress was slow, and it was not until August that the Japanese were pushed back to Salamaua. Amphibious operations in the Solomons were begun on June 21, as reports of Japanese fleet movements, reported by Australian coast watchers, promoted an early invasion. Halsey's forces landed on Rendova Island and quickly overcame the small Japanese garrison there. In July an attack was launched from Rendova against Munda. This operation proved difficult and costly, and it was not until August 5 that Munda fell. Meanwhile, the Japanese garrison of more than 10,000 troops was evacuated to the adjoining island of Kolombangara.

The New Georgia operation cost the Japanese more than 2,500 men and 17 warships. American combat deaths amounted to more than 1,000, and six ships were lost. The Japanese Imperial High Command then decided to evacuate the Central Solomons and, through September and October, the Kolombangara garrison was transported in a series of night operations to Bougainville.

On September 5 General MacArthur's forces landed east of Lae on the Huon Peninsula. The attack consisted of an amphibious assault on the coast, an overland attack on Salamaua, and an airborne assault northeast of Lae. These maneuvers, termed a *triphibious* approach, was MacArthur's method of cutting off and isolating the Japanese strong points. By complex maneuvering MacArthur felt he could minimize casualties while accomplishing his objective. He was to be critical of the island-hopping maneuvers used by Nimitz in the Central Pacific, and was to contend that such direct approach operations were too costly and unnecessary.

MacArthur's complicated maneuver met with little resistance as the Japanese had decided to evacuate its forces there and redeploy them on the northern coast of New Guinea. By October Allied forces, i.e., American and Australian units, had reached Dumpu, and by the end of 1943, the important northern coast port of Madang was threatened. In fact, the advance, though behind schedule, was facilitated by a change in policy initiated by the Japanese Imperial General Staff. The cost of maintaining the outer defensive ring in manpower, ships, and planes was considered too great. American submarines were inflicting heavy losses on Japanese merchant shipping, and such losses led to a scarcity of fuel and a decline in production of war materials. Therefore, it was decided to redraw the Japanese defensive line to encompass Burma, Malaya, Western New Guinea, the Carolinas, the Mariana chain, and the Kuriles. The Solomons, the Bismarck Islands, the Marshall Islands, and most of New Guinea were thus considered nonessential. By constricting the defense perimeter it was hoped that time would be secured to build up Japan's air

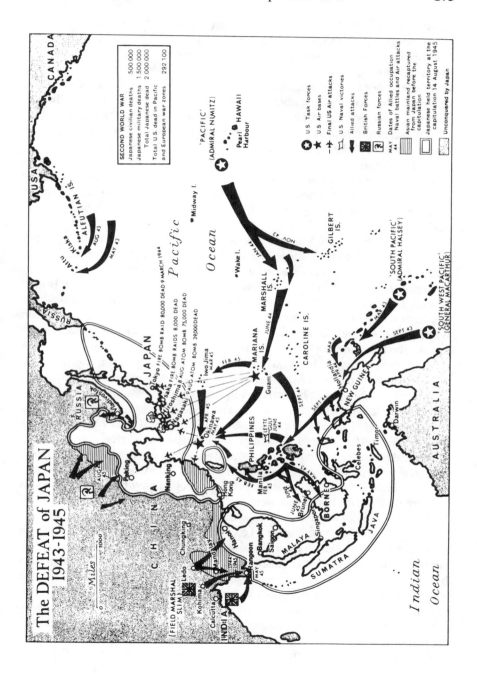

The DEFEAT of JAPAN 1943-1945

SECOND WORLD WAR

Japanese civilian deaths	500 000
Japanese military deaths	1 500 000
Total Japanese dead	2 000 000
Total U.S. dead in Pacific and European war zones	292 100

- ✪ U.S. Task forces
- ★ U.S. Air bases
- Final US Air attacks
- Allied attacks
- British Forces
- ⓡ Russian forces
- Dates of Allied occupation
- Naval battles and Air attacks
- Asian mainland recaptured from Japan before the capitulation
- Japanese held territory at the capitulation 14 August 1945
- Unconquered by Japan

and naval strength. Thus, time was to be purchased at the expense of Japanese forces scattered among these nonessential areas.

Likewise, the Allies were reconsidering their strategy. The slowness of the American advance in New Georgia had prompted a high-level division to isolate rather than take Rabaul. Still, the enemy had to be cleared through the Solomons so on November 1, 1943, the invasion of Bougainville was begun. Heavy bomber raids from planes stationed on New Guinea and by carrier-based aircraft kept the Japanese planes busy at Rabaul freeing the landing force from heavy air attack. The Japanese had expected the Americans to land on the island's southern coast, and their reaction to the amphibious attack from the north shore was equivocal. It was not until December, after American forces had established a ten-mile beachhead on the island, that the Japanese commander began to realize that the north shore landing was the main invasion point.

On New Guinea MacArthur's forces were moving up the coast. By April 1944 Madang fell to the Allied advance. In fact, Madang had been abandoned and its Japanese garrison evacuated to Wewak over 200 miles west of Madang. In the meantime, MacArthur had ordered the taking of airfields on New Britain Island. In December 1943 an amphibious attack was launched against the southern tip of the island near Cape Glouster, and the Japanese garrison withdrew to Rabaul. In February a landing was made in Admiralty Islands by a reconnaissance force. Heavy resistance was encountered, but reinforcements arrived in early March, and the Japanese garrison was defeated. However, it was not until May that the last pocket of Japanese resistance was overcome. These actions had effectively cut communication between Rabaul and the major Japanese base at Truk. The huge Japanese garrison at Rabaul was now isolated. Heavy bombardment of Rabaul and later of Truk was to destroy their effectiveness as centers of Japanese resistance.

In all, the campaigns in the Southwest Pacific had gone well, but had fallen behind schedule. The worrisome aspect of delay for General MacArthur and Admiral Halsey was that forces under their command would be diverted to the Central Pacific. For it was there that the prospect of securing island bases for long-range B-29 bombers provided the most immediate prospect of carrying the war to Japan's home islands. To crack the Japanese defense ring in the Central Pacific, it was decided to launch an amphibious attack against two islands of the Gilbert chain, Tarawa and Makin. These islands had been held by the Japanese since December 1941, and strong defensive positions had been constructed. Makin Island was attacked on November 20, 1943. The amphibious landing was not without its difficulties, but by the fourth day, what remained of Makin's 800-man garrison launched a futile and suicidal *Banzai* charge against the American attackers and were destroyed.

Tarawa proved more difficult. The island was garrisoned by a 3,000-man defense force and was heavily fortified. An atoll, Tarawa was protected by an outer reef sheltering a lagoon. It was at this reef that many U.S. Marines of the Second Division were to be wounded or killed. It had been anticipated that an unusually high tide, which was scheduled to occur between November 20th and the 22nd, would enable the invasion force to clear the reef. Although the attack was launched at high tide, it was not high enough for the landing craft to cross the reef. Many marines were forced to disembark over the gunwales of the older style landing craft and paddle across the lagoon. All this was done under heavy gunfire from the island's defenders. Some amphibious, tracked vehicles, called "Buffalos" or "Amtracks," were employed, but there was not a sufficient number of those to accommodate the waves of Marines storming Tarawa, and losses on the reef and on the beach were heavy. Though the Japanese defenders had suffered a tremendous preparatory bombardment, they met the attack with well-aimed artillery, mortar, and small arms fire. Progress off the beach was difficult, and fighting was often hand to hand. Marine losses would have been even heavier had the Japanese held to their defensive positions, but on the night of November 22, the Japanese launched repeated, massed, "Banzai" attacks and were decimated by American firepower.

Losses at Tarawa seemed excessively heavy; total dead was estimated at 1,100, wounded at 2,072. Yet it was an important victory from which was learned the hard lessons of amphibious operations. The controversy sparked by marine and navy losses led to the development of more and varied types of amphibious, armored landing craft. Therefore, the experiences of that campaign were to be utilized by the Allies in subsequent island invasions.

The next island-hopping expeditions were aimed at the Marshall chain. Admiral Nimitz decided to avoid the obvious by bypassing the most easterly of the 700-mile island chain to attack the largest island, Kwajalein. If all went well there, the most westerly of the islands, Eniwetok, would be invaded. The experience at Tarawa convinced American planners that more bombardment was necessary to soften Japanese defenses. Therefore, aerial bombardment was begun a full two months before the invasion. Carrier-based planes destroyed Japanese air power in the Marshall chain as Kwajalein and its two neighboring islands, Roi and Namur, were subject to repeated air attacks. On February 1, 1944, after a long, naval bombardment, the Americans stormed ashore. This time there was to be an abundance of tracked amphibious vehicles; rocket-equipped aircraft circled overhead to provide air cover and tanks were ferried ashore. In spite of this, however, the 8,000-man Japanese garrison proved difficult to overcome. Though air observation had noted the destruction of the island's buildings (the cratering of the island made it resemble the moon in aerial photographs) the massive bombardments had not destroyed the island's defense force. Again, however, the Japanese forsook their prepared defenses and tried to drive the invaders into the sea by direct "Banzai" charges. Such attacks destroyed the defense force, and of the 8,000 Japanese who garrisoned the island, only 264 prisoners survived the battle. American losses were approximately 370 killed. An additional 339 Americans were killed in the taking of Eniwetok, but Japanese losses there exceed 3,400. By February 22, 1944 the Marshall chain was under American control. More importantly, Truk, a major Japanese naval and air base, had been seriously damaged by sustained naval and air bombardment.

The securing of the Marshall Islands and the crippling of Japanese power at Truk aided in securing the Mariana Islands of Tinian and Saipan. These islands were to serve as bases from which B-29 bombers could strike the Japanese home islands. On June 15, 1944, two divisions of Marines attacked the beaches at Saipan. The Japanese countered by launching a carrier attack force to destroy the invasion fleet. In the ensuing air combat the Japanese lost more than 300 aircraft and, eventually, three of their carriers. This battle, called the "Battle of the Philippine Sea" or "the Great Mariana Turkey Shoot" by carrier pilots, was one of the decisive naval engagements of the Pacific War. The Japanese were never able to replace the huge losses of ships, planes, and skilled pilots and crew which were sacrificed in this engagement. In part, Japanese losses were heavier due to the fact that the commanders were not sure of the main focus of the U.S. fleet's attack. Forces were fed piecemeal into the battle until it was finally realized that Saipan, and not the Philippines or some other objective, was the real point of the American attack. This confusion as to the real objective of U.S. fleet movements is cited as an example that America's two-pronged offensive approach in the Pacific was less a hinderance to U.S. strategy than many critics have proposed.

The battle for Saipan was a long and bloody one. After three weeks of resistance, the Japanese defenders were pushed back to the northern end of the island. On the night of July 6-7, 1944, a gigantic "Banzai" attack was launched against the American 27th Division. The failure of this attack led the Japanese army commander, General Yoshitsugu Saito, to commit suicide. Admiral Chuichi Nagumo, who had been relegated to a small fleet command at Saipan, shot himself to death with a pistol. American soldiers and marines were aghast to see hundreds of Japanese civilians who worked and lived on the island commit suicide by leaping into the sea. Some were persuaded to surrender after it was made clear to them that they would not be killed. It was a shock to Americans that these Japanese civilians accepted death rather than fall captive to the foreigners whom, they thought, would torture and murder them. In all, more than 23,000 Japanese were killed and nearly 2,000 prisoners taken on the island. American losses were 3,500 killed and missing and more than 13,000 wounded. In all the weeks of heavy fighting and numerous losses the most horrifying memory for those Americans who fought the battle for Saipan was the suicides of civilians. There were to be other such mass suicides of civilians, particularly on Okinawa, before the Pacific War came to an end.

Battle for Burma

As progress was being made in the Southwest and Central Pacific, the British struggled to reverse the tides of fortune in the Burma theater of operations. The Allied strategy in Burma was that of freeing northern Burma from Japanese control and thereby opening the Burma Road to China. The Americans, in particular, still harbored the belief that by opening an overland supply route to China that nation could become the jumping-off point for a major offensive against Japan. These plans were to fail in realization. Until February 1945, China's principal supply link with its Western Allies was via "the Hump." This tenuous and dangerous air supply route through the passes of the Himalayas could furnish only limited supplies at tremendous cost. The failure to open the Burma Road in 1943-1944 and the slow progress of Stilwell to open a new Ledo Road to link with the Burma Road can be blamed on three factors: the Japanese, the weather, and the terrain. Of the three, the Japanese were to be the most pressing problem facing the British in India during the 1943-1944 period of the war.

In August of 1943, a unified Southeast Asia command was established, and Admiral Lord Louis Mountbatten was named as the commander. Naval, land and air units were placed under his command. To solve the sticky command problem presented by relations between the British in India and the Chinese and Americans in China, General Stilwell was named as Supreme Deputy Commander, an anomalous but, supposedly, co-equal position to that of the Commander, Mountbatten. Preparations were made for the launching of an offensive in 1944. A new army was formed, the 14th, under General William Joseph, later Viscount, Slim, and air and naval strength was increased. The Japanese, aware of the British build-up, anticipated an attack during the dry season. To forestall this offensive, they made preparations to beat the British to the punch. Each side began preparations for a limited offensive in the Arkan region before launching a major attack on the central Assam front. On the right, or southern front, Stilwell's Chinese forces were to launch an attack in March. This was to be preceded by a deep penetration into the Indaw area by Wingate's airborne Long Range Penetration Group, the Chindits.

The British attack into the Arkan began in early February but was met by a Japanese counteroffensive. The Japanese drove back the British forces, but they were able to forestall defeat due to General Slim's tactic of creating "strongholds" which could be supplied by air drops. The limited Japanese offensive in the Arkan was but a prelude to their main offensive on the Assam front. In mid-March the Japanese launched an attack to secure Imphal and Kohima. British air superiority was to help determine the outcome of this long struggle, and, by May, the road to Imphal was cleared. In July the British 14th Army crossed the Chindwin River. The Japanese force of 84,000, which had hoped to clear a path to India, was thrown back with a loss of approximately 50,000 of their number. British losses were put at 17,000.

On the northern front, Wingate's plan, Operation Broadway, began on March 5. Its objective was to disrupt Japanese communications and secure the Indaw-Irrawaddy area north of Mandalay. The operation was to serve as a spearhead for Stilwell's attack on the northern front and the British attack from the center or Assam front. The operation began badly and fared worse. Wingate himself was killed in an air crash on March 24. The Chindits were badly mauled by the Japanese, and it was decided to shift them northward to aid in Stilwell's advance. Though the Chindits enjoyed some success in securing Moguang, Stilwell's Chinese forces failed to attain their major objective of seizing Myitkyina.

By the summer of 1944 the British had moved from the defensive to the attack, but the Japanese hold on Burma was yet to be broken. The struggle to regain northern Burma and open the overland supply route to China was the objective of the 1944-1945 campaign in Burma. But the tremendous strides made elsewhere in the Southwest and Central Pacific relegated the Burma theater to the backwaters of the war. Eventually, Slim's forces were to push back the Japanese, but success in Burma was to come too late to have an effect on the grand strategy of the war in the Pacific.

Pacific Strategies

As we have seen, by August 1944 American air units, based on Saipan and Tinian, were within B-29 range of the Japanese homeland. The two-pronged offensive strategy of 1943 was beginning to bear fruit. American submarines, their torpedoes now somewhat more reliable, were taking a dreadful toll on Japanese shipping, and the homeland was feeling the effects of these losses. Incendiary bombing sent fires raging through the residential areas of Japanese cities. In approximate figures more than 800,000 Japanese civilians were killed by air bombardments in the 1944-1945 period. Such events had been foreshadowed in August 1944 with the loss of the island of Saipan. The Japanese air and naval defeat during the Battle of the Philippine Sea rendered Saipan and the Marianas untenable. Though Saipan did not fall until August 12, 1944, it was obvious to the Japanese that it could not be held. Therefore, on July 18, 1944, General Tojo and his cabinet resigned and a new cabinet, under General Kuniaki Koiso, was formed on July 22. The objective of this new cabinet was to develop a defensive strategy which would stem the tide of the American advance toward the Philippines.

As the Japanese struggled to develop yet another strong ring of defenses to safeguard her vital supply lines, American strategists were beginning to argue that the Philippines had ceased to be a primary objective. It was now within the capabilities of the American forces to bypass the Philippines and breach Japan's inner defensive ring by attacking Formosa (Taiwan), Iwo Jima, and Okinawa. This plan did not meet with official approval. Critics of the

Philippine strategy see it as a manifestation of MacArthur's overblown ego. Yet, the islands had become something of a symbol to the American people, and MacArthur's "I shall return" slogan seemed to capture the imagination of Americans who, perhaps, saw it less as a manifestation of individual hubris than a national pledge to free American territory. Therefore, it is probably too harsh a judgment to single out one man's ambition as the overriding factor promoting what many have come to believe was an obsolete strategy. For good or ill, the Philippines had become a popular objective in the public mind. In a total war, it would have been poor leadership indeed to have ignored the publicity advantage of securing those islands which had cost America so dearly in the dark days of 1941-1942.

The Trident Conference had approved a strategy of converging the pincer attack on the southern Philippine Island of Mindanao. Naval reconnaissance indicated, however, that the Philippine Islands, in general, were but weakly held. In the light of this information it was decided to split this weak Japanese defense by attacking the central island of Leyte, thus isolating the southern Japanese defense force on Mindanao and its main defensive units on the island of Luzon.

Before the Philippine campaign could be mounted the island of New Guinea had to be cleared of hostile forces or, at least, neutralized. To accomplish this feat, MacArthur resorted to a leap-frog approach to the attack. In April, an offensive was launched against the key Japanese base at Hollandia; Japanese forces on Wewak were thus isolated. From Hollandia, an attack was launched against Toem and Wakde islands. On May 27, Biak Island was invaded, but the invading force met heavy resistance from the Japanese defenders who, unlike previous attacks, tended to hold to their defensive positions and not engage in fruitless and costly "Banzai" charges. It was not until August 1944 that Biak Island was cleared of enemy troops. Meanwhile the leap-frog, or triphibious, advance along the coast of New Guinea was continued. Cape Sansapor on the northeastern New Guinea coast was taken in late July. Japanese forces in that sector were isolated. Thus, by August 1944 New Guinea was largely in Allied hands. Over five divisions of Japanese were isolated on the island, but they posed little threat to the Allies. Later, the Australians were to be charged with mopping-up these enemy pockets. Such mopping-up campaigns were to continue through 1945 in the Solomon Islands and elsewhere. Troops chosen for this task looked upon it as both costly and useless. Certainly, it would have been preferable to follow a policy of allowing isolated garrisons to succumb to boredom, disease, and starvation rather than clear them out with offensive action. It was little wonder then that mopping-up operations were greeted with little enthusiasm by those charged with carrying them out.

Battle of Leyte Gulf

With New Guinea neutralized the Philippine invasion could begin. In September American forces secured the islands of Morotai and Palau which provided air bases for the American attack on the Philippines. The Japanese also prepared for the impending invasion by strengthening their land forces in the Philippines. However, the Japanese strategy was postulated on the belief that the real battle for these islands would be fought at sea. The Japanese reasoned that the American invasion fleet would be screened by a carrier force. The plan was to decoy the American carriers away from the main fleet. Japanese surface vessels, particularly battleships, could then sail in and destroy the transports and other vessels of the invading force. The decoy would, of course, be Japanese carriers since it had been the American practice to see carriers as the main objective in a naval battle. In developing this plan the Japanese relied heavily on two new battleships, the *Yamato* and the *Musashi*. These two giant battleships were thought to be unsinkable and were, in fact, more than a match for any of the battleships then available to the American invasion force. But, like most plans, the Japanese plan fell afoul of circumstances unforeseen by those who had conceived the decoy concept.

Admiral Jisaburo Ozawa's carrier force was to sail south from Japan, and lure Halsey's carriers away from Leyte Gulf while Admiral Takeo Kurita's main force, divided into two unequal parts, was to trap the unprotected American transports in Leyte Gulf. Ozawa announced his departure by sending out uncoded messages which he knew the Americans would intercept. Meanwhile, Kurita's force was to sail, in secrecy, toward their target. However, two American submarines detected Kurita's force and managed to sink two Japanese cruisers and damage a third. News of the impending attack was flashed to the American fleet on October 23. Waves of American planes engaged the fleet and managed to sink the battleship, *Musashi*. Kurita turned about and steamed away. Halsey, basing his actions on what were overexaggerted estimates of Japanese losses, assumed the battle had been won.

When reconnaissance reported sighting Ozawa's carrier force, Halsey sailed to the attack. In the meantime, Kurita's force, which had sustained the loss of one battleship and severe damage to a cruiser, turned about to attack Leyte Gulf. Halsey discounted reports that Kurita's force was turning again to the attack and continued his pursuit of Ozawa's carrier force. Meanwhile, a detachment of Kurita's force approaching from the southwest was detected and blocked in a night action wherein American radar proved successful in directing fire control. By the dawn of October 25 Kurita's southern detachment had been eliminated. Yet, the battle was not over for in the midst of sending congratulations to those who had gained victory in the south, Admiral Thomas C. Kinkaid, commander of the United States Seventh fleet — the transport and covering force for the Leyte Invasion — received word that a much larger Japanese force was heading toward Leyte Gulf from the northwest. Halsey's carrier force, now engaging Ozawa's force, was notified, but Halsey's Third Fleet was too far away to give immediate help. All Kinkaid could do was to use his destroyer and escort carriers to try to delay Kurita's attack. Kurita broke this thin American defensive screen and, again, turned to strike at the defenseless transports and supply ships in Leyte Gulf.

However, confused by intercepted communications between Kinkaid and Halsey, Kurita came to the conclusion that Halsey's carrier force was within striking distance of his main fleet. Therefore, he ordered his fleet northward and slipped away from his supposed American pursuers by sailing through the now unprotected San Bernardino Straits. To cover his retreat the Japanese Admiral resorted to the tactic of employing *Kamikaze* (Divine Wind) attacks. The object of these attacks was to destroy American ships by crashing explosive-filled piloted planes onto their decks. The use of suicide forces, such as the Kamikaze, proved less than effective at Leyte, but this tactic was extensively used during the remaining months of the war. The Kamikaze tactic was one of desperation. As a symbol it was so-named to evoke a period in Japanese history when the invader, the mongol ruler of China, was defeated by a great typhoon which sank the invasion fleet. In fact, the Kamikaze attack plan was promoted by its initiators as a rational use of air power. The argument was that, with American air superiority, conventional attacks were pointless. Therefore, the suicide pilot flying a bomb was an effective use of Japan's remaining air power. Though the Kamikaze's did destroy and damage some American ships they were hardly an effective weapon. Those young pilots who made the supreme sacrifice for the homeland, as often as not, did so in vain.

In all, the Battle of Leyte Gulf had been the biggest sea battle in history. American losses of a light carrier, two escort carriers, and three destroyers were very small compared to the Japanese loss of four carriers, three battleships, and 17 other ships of the line. This crushing defeat meant that Japanese sea power was no longer a viable threat to the Americans. Had America's military leaders appreciated the totality of this Japanese defeat, the timetable for the attack on Japan's inner ring of defenses might have been accelerated. However, planners continued to overestimate Japan's capacity to counter American sea power with the result that plans to attack this inner ring were delayed until the Philippines could be cleared or neutralized.

General Walter Krueger's Sixth Army was able to neutralize Japanese forces on Leyte by mid-December. On January 9, 1945 American forces invaded the main island of Luzon by executing a successful amphibious landing at Lyngayen Gulf. Yamashita's forces put up a stiff resistance, but the Americans continued to move forward. MacArthur also used airborne and seaborne forces to secure the Bataan Peninsula, and the fortress of Corregidor, though lightly held, was liberated by a daring and costly airborne assault. By February, American forces were converging on Manila. Though Yamashita had declared Manila an "open city," the local commander, Admiral Sanji Iwabachi, chose to make a fight of it. The city was cleared on March 4, 1945 after severe house to house fighting. Meanwhile, Yamashita's main force had retreated to the mountains of the north where they were to continue resistance for many months.

Continued Allied Gains

Iwo Jima and Okinawa constituted an inner-ring of defense, and both were considered important to the Americans as bases from which air attacks on the mainland could be carried out. The bases at Tinian and Saipan were distant from the mainland; therefore, it was considered necessary to secure Iwo Jima first as a base which could provide fighter cover for B-29 raids and serve as an emergency landing strip for disabled bombers. On February 19, 1945, American marines began the invasion. Three divisions were used in the taking of the island. Losses were heavy as, contrary to the Japanese general tactic of launching all-out destructive charges, this time the Japanese kept to their defensive positions. On March 26, 1945, the island was secured, but mopping-up operations were to continue for another two months. In all, the Iwo Jima campaign inflicted heavy casualties on the U.S. Marine divisions engaged in the campaign. Total American losses in killed, wounded, and missing exceeded 26,000 soldiers. The Japanese casualties included 25,000 soldiers killed in the battle and 1,000 captured. This fanatical resistance was to lead American planners to the dismal conclusion that in light of the Japanese tactic of remaining in their defensive strongholds, subsequent American invasions of Okinawa and the Japanese main islands would be even more costly.

As American forces moved toward the Japanese homeland, British, Chinese, and American forces struggled to clear Burma from Japanese control. The second half of 1944 brought significant change in the China-Burma-India (CBI) theater of operations. Stilwell was recalled, and General Wedemeyer replaced him as Chief-of-Staff to Chiang Kai Shek and the Chinese forces. Wedemeyer took a cooperative and conciliatory stance with his new chief and was to enjoy more success in dealing with Chiang than had his predecessor.

In October 1944, General Slim's 14th Army began an attack on the Central Front with the objective of crossing the Chindwin and advancing on Mandalay. Offensive operations were also begun in northern Burma and on the southern (Arakan) front. By February 1945 the Burma Road from India to China had been cleared. However, damage to this overland route was extensive, and its capture proved less of a boon to the Chinese than had been expected. By March 1945 the whole of southern Burma was in British hands. Mandalay was taken in April, and on May 3, Rangoon fell to the British. The conduct of the campaign in Burma was both costly and difficult. Yet those who fought there were embittered by the thought that theirs was a forgotten theater, forgotten by all save the Japanese. As noted before, the primary objective of the fight to clear Burma had been to secure land access to China. As the movement of the war in the Pacific gained momentum, the Burma theater of operations lost a great deal of its strategic significance.

In the Pacific theater the way was now clear for an attack on Okinawa. This island, the largest of the Ryukyu chain, occupies a strategic position in relation to Japan, China, and Formosa (Taiwan); therefore, it was an obvious objective for the American forces. As an air and naval base, the island was indispensable, and it would serve as an assembly point for the land forces needed for the invasion of the Japanese home islands. The Japanese recognized the importance of the island and were determined to hold it at all costs. In preparation for the invasion, American bombers pounded those Japanese air and naval bases which could give support to Okinawa in the event of an invasion. On April 1 the invasion of Okinawa began. American forces landing on the western coast of the island encountered no opposition. However, supporting naval vessels were subjected to repeated air attacks. On April 6 and 7, waves of Kamikazes succeeded in sinking or damaging thirteen American destroyers. Also on April 6, the super-battleship, *Yamato*, was sent into battle. American carrier planes attacked the battleship. On April 7, 1945, the *Yamato* was sent to the bottom. Thus, in the early part of the campaign the heaviest action occurred in the air and on the sea.

The land advance went surprisingly smoothly. By April 13 an advanced party of marines from the Sixth Division had reached the island's northern tip. Scattered resistance was to continue in the northern part of the island until May 6, but the more difficult fighting was to occur in the south. On April 19 three army divisions were thrown into an attack on the Japanese defensive positions on the southern part of the island. Gains were slight and losses high as the Japanese clung tenaciously to their defensive positions. By May army units reinforced with two marine divisions were hit by a costly Japanese counteroffensive. More than 5,000 Japanese died in this attack. On May 10, the American offensive moved forward. By mid-June the Japanese southern defenses had been broken, and the island was in American hands.

Throughout the campaign Kamikaze attacks had been used to destroy American shipping. As a result of these suicidal actions, 34 American ships were sunk and over 360 damaged. In all, the campaign had cost the Japanese over 110,000 casualties, but American losses had totaled 49,000 including more than 12,000 dead. Okinawa had been the bloodiest campaign of the Pacific War for the American forces. Such losses were, in the minds of those who were planning the invasion of the Japanese homeland, an indication of what might lie ahead. Projections, possibly exaggerated, suggested that an invasion of the home islands might cost the Americans one million casualties. This figure was considered unacceptable and was to have an important effect on the decision to use atomic bombs to force a Japanese surrender.

In fact, the Japanese had been contemplating surrender for some months. An attempt was made to use the good offices of the Soviets to establish some basis for negotiations with the Americans. The problem was not unconditional surrender, as such, but what would be the fate of the Emperor. To subject the Emperor, the symbol and center of Japanese cultural life, to trial for war crimes was unthinkable, and some members of the cabinet urged that Japan fight to the death rather than surrender. The Emperor, however, made it clear to the Japanese cabinet that peace must be made. From the benefit of hindsight it is now known that an early clarification of the future status of the Emperor would have ended the war. However, plans were already underway to demonstrate the formidable power of the United States by detonating a nuclear device on a Japanese target.

The debate as to the use of the bomb was acrimonious. Since the war, many of those close to the Manhattan Project, the cover name for the development of the atomic bomb, have revealed the nature and substance of these debates. Some demanded a demonstration of the bomb's power by a relatively harmless detonation over the ocean but near enough to Japan to be visible to the Japanese. Other schemes were presented, but for a variety of reasons, all such plans were discarded. Hiroshima was designated as a target, the population was warned of an impending bombing attack, and it was noted in the leaflets that this bombing attack would be of a new and terribly destructive nature. On August 6 a B-29 bomber, the *Enola Gay*, dropped an atomic bomb on Hiroshima. More than 80,000 Japanese were to die as a result of this attack. Three days later another nuclear device was detonated over Nagasaki. On August 10, 1945, the Japanese offered to surrender.

Though it has often been stated that the surrender was the direct result of the nuclear attacks on Hiroshima and Nagasaki, information now available indicates that clarification as to the status of the Emperor was a decisive factor. This is born out in part by studies made after the war on the effect of the bombing on Japanese decision making at the cabinet level. The man who made the final decision to drop the bomb, President Harry S. Truman, justified his decision as both necessary and vital to the rapid ending of the war. Others, utilizing information then either unavailable to the President or misconstrued by him and his advisers, present convincing arguments that the use of the atomic bomb was both unnecessary and unwise. Evidence then available indicated that conventional military powers had brought Japan to near collapse. Tightening of the blockade on the island would soon bring peace. It has been convincingly argued that the decision to drop the bomb had less to do with the saving of American lives than it did with political and economic considerations on both the international and national level. It is quite possible that a quick end to the war was sought to avoid the contingency of the Soviet Union's participation in the occupation of Japan. Secondly, a successful detonation of an atomic bomb was thought necessary to justify the enormous expense entailed by the United States in developing this new weapon. Whatever the motivation, this fateful decision, now much disputed, launched the world into the Atomic Age. Speculations based on hindsight will never be able to erase the sobering reality of that important fact.

Summary

In June 1943 the strategy of the Pacific War called for the isolation and capture of Rabaul. To do this, it was necessary to clear the Japanese from New Guinea and the Solomons. In the course of these offensive actions, it was found that more rapid progress could be made by isolating rather than reducing Japanese defensive positions in these areas. The American tactic then became that of cutting off Japanese supply lines and allowing garrisons to wither and die. Rabaul was isolated and rendered useless. Later, Truk was to suffer a similar fate. In action in the Central Pacific, Nimitz's forces began the process of island-hopping. To secure the Gilbert chain of islands an invasion was made on two of the Gilbert islands, Makin and Tarawa. The later action met with heavy resistance, and United States Marines took heavy casualties in securing this atoll. Lessons learned at Tarawa were, however, invaluable in subsequent amphibious operations. The object of this island-hopping strategy was to secure bases from which American planes, particularly the long-range B-29 bomber, could strike at the Japanese homeland.

As advances were made in the Central Pacific, and in the Southwest Pacific, U.S. Navy submarines were decimating the Japanese merchant fleet on the high seas and in Japanese waters. These losses led the Japanese to consider redrawing their defensive ring, tightening it to hold down losses. This decision meant that forces in the outer ring were more or less left to their own devices. Thus, the American strategy of isolation was aided by the Japanese decision to retrench its defensive perimeter. However, the Japanese made a desperate bid to hold the Marianas hoping to withhold Saipan and Tinian (within B-29 range of Japan) from the American advance. The battle for the Marianas, often termed the Battle of the Philippine Sea, was a debacle for the Japanese. Losses in carriers, planes, and ships seriously weakened the Japanese ability to counter American plans to secure the Philippines. Thus by June-July 1944 American forces in the Pacific were well on their way to attaining their objective of an advance on the Philippines.

In Burma the situation seemed less than bright for the hard-pressed British. The Allies, particularly the United States, hoped that northern Burma could be cleared and the land route opened linking China to India. If this could be accomplished, China, abundantly supplied via India, would serve as the springboard for an attack on Japan. However, the Japanese held fast to Burma. It was not until February 1944 that the British could launch an offensive. The Japanese met this attack by a counteroffensive which, though foiled, ruined any hopes for British control of northern Burma in 1944.

In the Pacific theater MacArthur's forces succeeded in clearing New Guinea and began preparation for the attack on the Japanese-held Philippine Islands. It had been decided in the spring of 1943 that a two-pronged attack by combined forces from the two American Pacific theaters of operations would converge on the Philippines. The drastic decline in Japanese sea and air power led some military planners to consider this strategy as obsolete, yet the original plan was carried out in October 1944 when American forces invaded the Philippine Island of Leyte. To counter the American attack, the Japanese devised a naval strategy to decoy Halsey's Third Fleet, with its carriers and warships, from screening the American landing force, the Seventh Fleet. To do this, a carrier force under Admiral Ozawa was dispatched as a decoy while a surface fleet, under Admiral Kurita, was sent to attack the invasion fleet in Leyte Gulf. The resulting action resulted in four separate battles. The decoy scheme worked in part, but Admiral Kurita missed his chance to destroy the relatively lightly armed invasion fleet and broke off the battle.

The so-called Battle of Leyte Gulf, October 23-25, 1944 was the largest naval battle ever fought. Japanese losses were enormous: 34 ships lost. American losses were light: six ships lost. This huge battle was unique in that, for the first time, the Japanese employed Kamikaze pilots to crash explosive-filled planes into American ships. The use of such suicide attacks was to continue until the end of the war. Leyte was secured. In January 1945 the main Philippine Island of Luzon was invaded. Fighting there was heavy, but by March 1945 Manila was in American hands. Yamashita's forces continued to resist in northern Luzon, but, in effect, the Philippine Islands were now under American control. The next step was to breach Japan's inner defenses.

In February 1945 an amphibious attack was made against Iwo Jima. The Japanese defenders kept to their prepared positions and inflicted heavy losses on the American attackers. The island was secured in March at a cost of 26,000 United States Marine casualties. More than 25,000 Japanese were killed in the battle of Iwo Jima, and 1,000 were taken prisoner.

In Burma, after command reorganization, the British launched an attack on the Japanese. By February 1945 British forces had command of the Burma Road. By April, Mandalay was under British control, and in May 1945 Rangoon fell to the British offensive. The reconquest of Burma had been accomplished, and Japanese power in Southeast Asia was broken.

In April 1945 American troops invaded the Japanese Island of Okinawa. Centrally located, this island was of great strategic importance, and the Japanese fought desperately to maintain control of Okinawa. The struggle for Okinawa continued for some three months, but by June 1945 American forces controlled the island. The attack had cost American forces more than 49,000 casualties, but the Japanese losses were an appalling 110,000. Kamikaze attacks accounted for the loss of 34 American ships and damage to more than 350 surface crafts. The heavy casualties sustained in conquering Okinawa led to the fear that the planned invasion of the Japanese homeland would result in an unacceptable casualty rate for the American attackers.

As plans for the invasion of Japan were being prepared, the Japanese were searching for avenues of communication to open peace negotiations. Their principal concern was clarification of unconditional surrender and the punishment of war criminals. More specifically, they wished clarification as to the fate of the Emperor if an unconditional surrender was accepted. While the Japanese were considering the possibility of surrender, American preparations were made for dropping an atomic bomb on a Japanese city. Hiroshima was chosen, the population warned, and on August 6, 1945 a B-29 bomber released the nuclear device over the city. Three days later a second bomb was dropped on Nagasaki. On August 10, 1945 the Japanese agreed to surrender. On September 2, 1945 surrender terms were signed aboard the *USS Missouri* by representatives of the Japanese government and the Allies.

At the time the decision to drop the bomb was being made, there were those who felt that conventional force had already accomplished the objective of bringing Japan to defeat. Therefore, the dropping of such a terrible weapon as an atomic bomb was seen as unjustified by military necessity. The rationale for the decision to use the atomic bomb has been seriously and thoughtfully questioned and continues to be a subject of controversy.

Suggested Reading

Gregg, Charles. *Tarawa*. New York, 1983. A detailed and very readable account of the battle termed ''the seedbed of victory in the Pacific.''

Manchester, William. *American Caesar, Douglas MacArthur*. New York, 1979. The best biography available of this famous and controversial military leader.

Morison, Samuel Eliot. *History of United States Naval Operations in World War II*. London, 1948-1962. This is a multi-volume official history, but the accounts of naval operations in the Pacific are authoritative.

Slim, William, First Viscount. *Unofficial History*. Westport, CT, 1959. An account of the Burma campaign from a commander who places more blame on himself for military mistakes than any other memoir writer of the World War II era.

Wheeler, Richard. *A Special Valor, The United States Marines and the Pacific War*. New York, 1983. An account of Marine Corps operation including the much neglected Peleliu campaign.

13

Observations

For the historian time is both a boon and a curse. As time passes, secret documents, memoirs, and other materials are made available to scholars. From these myriad, often conflicting sources of information, the historian attempts to reconstruct the past. Yet, such a task is all but impossible for what does emerge is but a consensus view of what the past (in this case the Second World War) was and what it has meant for those of us who either survived the war or live in the post-war world.

In popular terms the Second World War has come to be seen as a justifiable, even a moral struggle to free the world from tyranny. The Allied victory in Europe crushed the forces of nazism-fascism, yet the Europe that emerged from the ruin was not the free and happy place that was envisioned in that idealistic document, the Atlantic Charter. The vanquished, divided Germany, rose from the ruins to become prosperous. For the Japanese the curse of militarism brought about a pummeling of the home islands and a near destruction of its culture. From the ashes emerged a new Japan gaining by peace what it could not gain by war. Comfort has come to the defeated, responsibility and confusion to the victors.

Certainly, the post-World War II world is a much different place than that of the European-dominated world of pre-1939 days. Some few writers bemoaned the growth of Soviet hegemony and saw the domination of Eastern Europe as a product of American naivete. By naivete, they, of course, meant the failure of American leadership to consider carefully the political ramifications of military victory. The Americans, they argue, neglected the obvious in pursuit of a military decision. Careful scrutiny of political decisions made at the myriad conferences held during and shortly after the cessation of hostilities in Europe have been the subject of many books and articles. Some of these have been brilliant, many are but useful, and still others are best forgotten. In searching for the lessons to be gained from the war, in trying to determine how the course of the conflict helped shape the world we now live in, scholars of the period have labored mightily producing, unfortunately, more mice than mammoths.

This brief work on World War II has little pretensions of being but a relatively concise compilation of existing literature in the field. Like all students of the period, this writer would like to make some few modest conjectures as to the important consequences of that conflict known as World War II.

What the 1939-1945 conflict meant in terms of civilization and the consequent ethical and moral questions of humans and their culture are tempting subjects for those who paint with a broad brush. But put within a somewhat more constricted circle of light, the war does afford us some useful insights. It did accelerate the process of greater centralization of power of the nation-states. It allowed certain individuals to formulate policies and make life and death decisions with comparative impunity. In pursuit of victory, personnel and materials were sometimes wasted in testing theories which were found afterward to be either faulty or, at worse, quite wrong. An example of faulty if not wrong-headed theorizing is that of strategic bombing which sacrificed much for the attainment of relatively little. Another lesson which we might learn from this global conflict is that excessive secrecy may be used as an impenetrable shield to safeguard the incompetent or the patent malfeasant.

Propaganda, a word with pejorative connotations, was not solely the device of the ''enemy.'' The sometimes subtle process of shaping public opinion was perfected during this period. Doubtless, while it often served a useful purpose, it helped hide stupidity and even malevolence.

One should ask was it necessary for the warring powers to distort the image of the world in order to secure the complete loyalty of the populace? If so, can we who live in the world created in the aftermath of struggle allow ourselves the luxury of uncritical thinking? I doubt that Americans, for example, will ever again accept the inanities of commercial messages such as ''Lucky Strike Green has gone to war,'' a slogan which combines hucksterism and patriotism in a bewildering nonmessage. However, it should be noted that it was seen as neither bewildering nor inane by many who heard it and read it in the days after Pearl Harbor.

In the spate of materials produced since the war we have seen that many individuals who loom large on the canvas of history were as human and as flawed as mortal men. Psychohistorians now attempt to probe the psyche of such great figures and produce little more than tidbits of scandal and nastiness to enliven but not enlighten our view of history's greats.

Therefore, penetrating the mythology of the period becomes difficult. As our pool of information grows, our mental set toward the war becomes narrowed. It remains for future generations to place the 1939-1945 conflict in what may be a logical, historical context. But one can say that millions of people sacrificed everything for what they construed to be a moral and just cause. The heroism of individuals — on both sides of the conflict — was awesome indeed. Many died for ideals which their enemy saw as but sham and false teaching. The documents and other resources indicate that on the lowest level of decision making — in the squad, on the smallest of naval vessels, and within the narrow confines of aircraft — men fought not necessarily for the pervasive ideal but for each other. Once embarked upon a course of action the social mastic which holds people together is awesomely binding. Perhaps we should think of this aspect of human society — the mastic of the social world — as we debate the broader issues. For, in the end, life is singular and leadership is but a responsibility and not a mandate.

War is the ultimate test of the viability of social relationships. World War II tested that to the ultimate extreme. Immediately after the war some of those who led great armies in the field and attained victories and public acclaim were to note that such a war would not be fought again. The extreme sacrifices demanded would not be so readily accepted as had been the case during this "Great War." Certainly, subsequent developments have shown that the three elements which Clausewitz cited as necessary to wage a successful conflict — support of the government, the military and the people — have not been a constant or a given. Involvement of all segments of society was not apparent in the conflicts which, unfortunately, have occurred with frequency since 1945. Even the Soviet Union was to discover the ambivalence, even the hostility, of its people in the struggle in Afghanistan just as successive American presidents have found that support for their policies wore thin as casualties in Korea and Vietnam grew and objectives became less clear.

At this point in time the great coalitions which came about as a result of World War II are fragmenting. The world is no longer so neatly divided as that of the so-called "bipolar" world of the Cold War. Events of the last few years caught even our most sagacious political forecasters unprepared and dismayed. Perhaps we should take what we have learned from the events and aftermath of World War II to reflect on the impact of such a cataclysmic event on the history of our time. Future generations may well view the era of World War II as a major step for humankind toward the recognition of the value of the "small society" and away from the grandiose concept of the ideal and abstract "Great Society."

Index

Air power,
anticipated role in warfare, 15-16
calls for defense against, 15
demonstrated value of in Spanish
Civil War, 17
ensuring German success in Norway,
34-36
used by British in Middle East at the
expense of Asia, 68
See also Luftwaffe; Royal Air Force
Air warfare,
high-level bombers used by
Americans, 126
fighter support lacking for deep
penetration raids, 126
night raids increasing, 126
precision bombing developed, 126
production losses from bombing less
than expected, 126
strategic bombing, 15-16, 126, 192
urban targets bombed, 49, 126, 167
Aleutian Islands, 119, 125
Allied Powers. *See* Western allies
"America First" movement, 60
Anschluss, 5-6
Anzio landing, 151-52
Ardennes, 29, 40, 165-67
Arnhem, paratroop drop at, 165
Atlantic Charter, 59, 191
Austria, unified with Germany, 5
Axis Powers,
agreement with Japan, 58
aiding Franco in Spain, 6
axis formed, 6
freezing United States assets, 59
losses in North Africa, 106-07
surrendering in Tunisia, 107
See also Italy; Germany

Balkans, German victory in, 52
"Bataan Death March," 66-68
Battle of Bloody Ridge, 116
Battle of Britain, 46-50
Battle of Midway, 111-13
Battle of Santa Cruz Islands, 113
Battle of the Atlantic, 30, 90-92, 121
Battle of the Coral Sea, 125
Belgium,
capture of Antwerp, 165
France vulnerable through, 14-15, 28
German attack on, 39-43
German paratroops used successfully
in, 40-41
mining bridges to stop German attack,
40
not completing network of forts, 14
relying on neutrality, 14
surrender of, 43
Bessarabia, annexed by Soviet Union,
31
Black market, 124
Blitzkrieg, 17, 20, 25
Breakthrough strategy, used in World
War I, 12, 19
British Somaliland, Italian forces
invading, 51
Broz, Josip (Tito), supported by Allied
Powers, 123
Bukovina, annexed by Soviet Union, 31
Bulgaria, accepting Soviet demands to
declare war on Germany, 140
Burma,
American interest in, 118-19
captured by Japan, 70
importance of, as supply line for
China, 118, 179-80